THE ENGLISH COOKERY BOOK
HISTORICAL ESSAYS

Frontispiece. The frontispiece to The Housekeeper's Instructor or Universal Family Cook *by W.A. Henderson (sixth edition, ca. 1800).*

THE ENGLISH COOKERY BOOK

HISTORICAL ESSAYS

LEEDS SYMPOSIUM ON FOOD HISTORY
'FOOD AND SOCIETY' SERIES

edited by
EILEEN WHITE

PROSPECT BOOKS
2004

First published in 2004 by Prospect Books, Allaleigh House, Blackawton, Totnes, Devon TQ9 7DL.

Based on papers from the Sixteenth Leeds Symposium on Food History, March 2001, 'Books for Cooks, Housekeepers and Social Historians', with an additional paper. This is the twelfth volume in the series 'Food and Society'.

© 2004 as a collection, Prospect Books (but © 2004 in individual articles rests with the individual authors).

The authors assert their right to be identified as the authors of their several pieces in accordance with the Copyright, Designs & Patents Act 1988.

No part of this publication may be reproduced, stored in a retrieval system, or transmitted in any form or by any means, electronic, mechanical, photo-copying, or otherwise, without the prior permission of the copyright holder.

BRITISH LIBRARY CATALOGUING IN PUBLICATION DATA:
A catalogue entry for this book is available from the British Library.

ISBN 1 903018 36 6

Typeset by Tom Jaine.
Printed and bound by the Cromwell Press, Trowbridge, Wiltshire.

Contents

Acknowledgements — 6

Foreword — 7

List of Illustrations — 8

Notes on Contributors — 11

Preface
  Eileen White — 13

Chapter 1
  An Introduction to the Cookery Book Collection in the Brotherton Library, University of Leeds
  C. Anne Wilson — 19

Chapter 2
  The Language of Medieval Cookery
  Peter Meredith — 28

Chapter 3
  A Close Look at the Composition of Sir Hugh Plat's *Delightes for Ladies*
  Malcolm Thick — 55

Chapter 4
  Domestic English Cookery and Cookery Books, 1575–1675
  Eileen White — 72

Chapter 5
  From Murrell to Jarrin: Illustrations in British Cookery Books, 1621–1820
  Ivan Day — 98

Chapter 6
  William Alexis Jarrin and *The Italian Confectioner*
  Laura Mason — 151

Chapter 7
  Beyond Beeton: Some Nineteenth-Century Cookery and Household Books in the Brotherton Special Collections
  Valerie Mars — 175

Index — 199

Acknowledgements

To the staff, past and present, of Special Collections in the Brotherton Library, University of Leeds, are due thanks for their friendly service over many years of research by the contributors to this volume.

Unless otherwise stated in the captions, all illustrations are taken from books in the Brotherton collection, with the kind permission of Mr C. Sheppard, the Special Collections Librarian.

The page from Sloane MS 2189 (f.64a) is reproduced by permission of the British Library. Reproduction of the two manuscript plans for dinner at Hatfield House in Chapter 5 is by courtesy of the Marquess of Salisbury. Thanks also to Tom Jaine for bringing everything together.

C. Anne Wilson, a former member of the Brotherton Library staff, is a founder member of the Leeds Symposium on Food History. Her book *Food and Drink in Britain* (1973) has served as an important reference work in the growing study of food history and her fellow-contributors to this book are pleased to acknowledge her continuing interest and support.

Foreword

'Food and Society' Series
Publication of papers from the Leeds Symposium on Food History

The first six volumes were published by Edinburgh University Press and are now out of print; the following three by Sutton Publishing (two of them in association with The National Trust); the volumes from no. 10 have been published by Prospect Books.

The titles, with the series numbers, are:

1. *'Banquetting Stuffe': the Fare and Social Background of the Tudor and Stuart Banquet*, ed. C.A. Wilson (1986 Symposium), 1991.
2. *The Appetite and the Eye: Visual Aspects of Food and its Presentation within their Historic Context*, ed. C.A. Wilson (1987 Symposium), 1991.
3. *Traditional Food East and West of the Pennines*, ed. C.A. Wilson (1988 Symposium), 1991.
4. *Waste Not, Want Not: Food Preservation in Britain from Early Times to the Present Day*, ed. C.A. Wilson (1989 Symposium), 1991.
5. *Liquid Nourishment: Potable Foods and Stimulating Drinks*, ed. C.A. Wilson (1990 Symposium), 1993.
6. *Food for the Community: Special Diets for Special Groups*, ed. C.A. Wilson (1991 Symposium), 1993.
7. *Luncheon, Nuncheon and Other Meals*, ed. C.A. Wilson (1992 Symposium), 1994. Now republished in paperback as *Eating with the Victorians* (Sutton, 2004).
8. *The Country House Kitchen, 1650–1900: Skills and Equipment for Food Provisioning*, ed. P.A. Sambrook and P. Brears (double volume for 1993 and 1994 Symposia), 1996.
9. *The Country House Kitchen Garden, 1600–1950: How Produce was Grown and How it was Used*, ed. C.A. Wilson (1995 Symposium), 1998.
10. *Feeding a City: York*, ed. E. White (double volume for 1997 and 1998 Symposia), 2000.
11. *Food and the Rites of Passage*, ed. L. Mason (1999 Symposium), 2002.

List of Illustrations

Frontispiece. The frontispiece to The Housekeeper's Instructor or Universal Family Cook *by W.A. Henderson (sixth edition, ca. 1800).* 2
Figure 1. Title-page from The Accomplished Ladies Rich Closet of Rarities, *1715.* 12
Figure 2. Title-page of A Booke of Cookry *(1584).* 21
Figure 3. Bees in the hive, from The Feminin' Monarchi', or The Histori of Bee's *(1634).* 24
Figure 4. Root vegetables from the kitchen garden, illustrated in John Parkinson's Paradisus terrestris *of 1629.* 26
Figure 5. Making pasta, from Opera di M. Bartolomeo Scappi *(Venice, 1570).* 30
Figure 6. A field kitchen, from Scappi's Opera *(Venice, 1570).* 34
Figure 7. This illustration from Scappi's Opera *(Venice, 1570) also includes examples of smaller kitchen utensils.* 38
Figure 8. Pages from the 1609 edition of Delightes for Ladies, *showing the decorative borders.* 56
Figure 9. A page from British Library Sloane MS 2189 (f.64a), showing the respective hands of 'T.T.' and Hugh Plat.(Reproduction courtesy of the British Library.) 58
Figure 10. One of Hugh Plat's ingenious suggestions in The Jewell House of Art and Nature. 68
Figure 11. Frontispiece and title-page to Hannah Wolley's The Queen-like Closet. 72
Figure 12. Comparison of recipes for verjuice from Gervase Markham, The English House-wife *(1631 edition), and Robert May,* The Accomplist Cook *(1665 edition).* 78
Figure 13. Comparison of recipes for a 'Farsed Pudding' from Murrels Two Bookes of Cookerie and Carving (1638 edition), and Robert May, The Accomplist Cook *(1665 edition).* 80
Figure 14. The recipe for a Spanish olio from The Compleat Cook *(1655).* 82
Figures 15 & 16. Two portraits. Queen Henrietta Maria, the frontispiece to The Queens Closet Opened *(1655). Elizabeth Cromwell, as shown in the frontispiece to* The Court & Kitchin of Elizabeth, Commonly called Joan Cromwel, The Wife of the late Usurper *(1664).* 84
Figure 17. Frontispiece to The Country Housewife and Lady's Director, *by R. Bradley (1736).* 88
Figure 18. A set of manica (jelly bags) for straining the spices out of hippocras. Girolamo Ruscelli, The Secrets of Maister Alexis of Piedmont *(London: 1558).* 99
Figure 19. Illustration of a kitchen scene from the Koch und Kellermeisterey *(Frankfurt: 1547).* 100
Figure 20. Frontispiece of Hannah Wolley's The Ladies Delight *(London: 1672).* 102
Figure 21. A woodcut illustration from A Book of Fruits and Flowers *(London: 1653).* 102
Figure 22. Engraved frontispiece from Nathan Bailey's Dictionarium Domesticum, *published by Charles Hitch (London: 1736).* 104
Figure 23. Table plan to show how sweetmeats and fruit were to be arranged for the ultimo servitio of an Italian feast. From Matthias Giegher's Li tre trattati *(Padua: 1639).* 106
Figure 24. Two table-layout diagrams from John Murrel's A Delightful Daily Exercise for Ladies and Gentlewomen *(London: 1621).* 108
Figure 25. A rather debased woodcut copy of Giegher's banquet table (figure 23), printed in Giles Rose's A Perfect School of Instructions for the Officers of the Mouth *(London: 1682).* 108
Figure 26. Top, a detail of the King and Queen's table from an engraved plate by S. Moore in Francis Sandford's The History of the Coronation of James II *(London: 1687). Bottom, Sandford's table plan of the same table.* 109
Figure 27. (Top) A plan for a table from Giegher's Li tre trattati *(Padua: 1639). (Below left) A woodcut of an identical table plan from Rose (London: 1682). (Below right) A similar, though more complex table-layout from Patrick Lamb's* Royal Cookery *(London: 1710).* 110
Figure 28. Two table plans from Lamb (1710). 113
Figure 29. Two plates from Vincent La Chapelle's The Modern Cook *(London 1733).* 114

Figure 30. This plan shows how the terrines *and* pots d'ouille *were to be arranged on the table for the first course. It appeared in the first French edition of La Chapelle's book published in the Hague in 1735.* 115

Figure 31. A Royal Table of sixty covers with three surtouts de table. 116

Figure 32. A large folding engraved plate from Charles Carter's The Compleat City and Country Cook *(London 1732).* 118

Figure 33. A manuscript table plan for the first course of a dinner served to James Cecil, 4th Earl of Salisbury on Thursday January 20th? 1684 at Hatfield House. (Hatfield General 6/24 recto). Photograph courtesy of the Marquess of Salisbury. 120

Figure 34. The second course of the same Hatfield dinner. (Hatfield General 6/24 verso). Photograph courtesy of the Marquess of Salisbury. 120

Figure 35. A figure showing an Italian cook carving a joint in alto, *while his assistant uses a duck press to extract gravy. From Bartolomeo Scappi's* Opera *(Venice: 1570).* 121

Figure 36. Dissection plans for carving a roast pig in the Italian manner. The etching at the top of the page is from Giegher (1639). The woodcut below is from Rose (1682). 122

Figure 37. One of two plates from Giegher which show how to carve citrons in the form of animals. Below are two of Rose's much more primitive woodcuts, clearly showing the influence of Giegher's illustrations. 124

Figure 38. Designs for carving oranges from Giegher. (Bottom left) Three designs for carved apples from Rose. (Bottom right) A detail of Giegher's illustration showing the method to carve pears. 126

Figure 39. A dissection diagram showing how a roasted hare was to be carved in the native English style. Woodcut from John Trusler's The Honours of the Table *(London: 1788).* 127

Figure 40. Engraved carving plate from Collingwood and Woollams, The Universal Cook *(London 1792).* 127

Figure 41. Designs for bride pies (left) and mince pies (right), from Robert May's The Accomplisht Cook *(London 1660).* 129

Figure 42. School of Osias Beert. A detail from a still life showing a rabbit pie and other foods on a table. 130

Figure 43. Designs for rabbit and hare pies. 130

Figure 44. Custard designs from May (1660). 132

Figure 45. Designs for pies in the form of stag (top right) and an alpine chamois (bottom right). Conrad Hagger, Neues Saltzburgisches Koch-Buch *(Augsburg: 1719).* 134

Figure 46. Two woodcut pages of shaped pie designs from T.P., The Accomplisht Ladies Delight *(London: 1675).* 136

Figure 47. Engraved pie designs from Henry Howard, England's Newest Way *(London: 1703).* 136

Figure 48. Woodcut pie designs from T. Hall, The Queen's Royal Cookery *(London: 1709).* 136

Figure 49. Three designs for pies from Hagger (1719). 137

Figure 50. Designs for a lamb pasty and a venison pasty. From Edward Kidder's Receipts of Pastry and Cookery *(London: ca. 1720).* 138

Figure 51. Designs for set custards and egg pies. Kidder (ca.1720). 139

Figure 52. A late 17th-century trade card in the form of a dinner invitation to a cookery school. 140

Figure 53. A diagram to show how a hare was trussed. From The Whole Duty of a Woman *(London: 1737).* 141

Figure 54. A plate of trussing diagrams from Mrs Frazer, The Practice of Cookery, Pastry, Pickling, Preserving, &c. *(Edinburgh: 1791).* 141

Figure 55. Trussing designs from Bradley (1732). 141

Figure 56. A printed broadside showing the cuts of meat and their prices in the London markets on December 8th 1792. Printed by W. Simpkins of Clements Inn, London. 142

Figure 57. A wood engraving of a pièce montée *made by the Yorkshire confectioner Joseph Bell for the Prince of Wales. From Bell's* A Treatise of Confectionery *(Newcastle: 1817).* 144

Figure 58. Engraved table plan for a dessert setting with a plateau *consisting of three frames. From Frederick Nutt* The Complete Confectioner *(London: 1789).* 145

Figure 59. A sugar paste fountain from Bell (1817). 146

Figure 60. A detail from a folding plate of confectionery equipment from Jarrin's Italian Confectioner *(London 1820).* 146

Figure 61. A recently discovered mould signed by Jarrin. Boxwood ca. *1820s. (Private Collection).* 147

Figure 62. The four ages of William Jarrin: the portraits from successive editions of his work, dated 1820 (top left); 1827 (top right); 1829 (bottom left); 1844 (bottom right). 152

Figure 63. One of two folding plates (drawn by Jarrin himself) showing confectionery equipment, from the 1820 and subsequent editions of The Italian Confectioner. 154

Figure 64. Drawing of Jarrin's Patent Water Cooler, 1827. 157

Figure 65. Recreations of Jarrin's ices. Above: a composition of several pieces; below left and right: the pineapple and the melon in detail. (Photographs, Laura Mason.) 160

Figure 66. A selection of decorative desserts from Mrs Beeton's Book of Household Management *(1861), p. 695.* 176

Figure 67. Illustrations from Chapter IX, 'Boiling, Roasting, etc.', Modern Cookery for Private Families, *by Eliza Acton, first published in 1845.* 178

Figure 68. Two front plates from Mrs Rundell, A New System of Domestic Cookery 180

Figure 69. Chartreuse of Partridges from The Housekeeper's and Butler's Assistant. 183

Figure 70. Alexis Soyer's Hundred Guinea Dish. 188

Figure 71. Soyer's front plate for The Modern Housewife. 190

Notes on Contributors

IVAN DAY is a food historian with a special interest in re-creating the food of the past in period settings. His work has been exhibited at Fairfax House, York; the Bowes Museum; the Rothschild Collection, Waddeson Manor; the Museum of London; and the Paul Getty Research Institute. He is editor of *Eat, Drink and Be Merry: the British at table 1600–2000*.

VALERIE MARS' exploration of food in nineteenth-century social contexts is multi-disciplinary and derived from both library research and working with original techniques and technologies. Her most recent paper, with Gerald Mars, 'Fat in the Victorian Kitchen: a medium for cooking, control, deviance and crime', won an additional Sophie Coe prize in 2002.

LAURA MASON is a regular contributor to the Leeds Food Symposium. Her special interest in confectionery led to the investigation into William Jarrin presented here. *Sugar Plums and Sherbet*, published by Prospect Books, was the result of her confectionery research.

PETER MEREDITH is Emeritus Professor of Medieval Drama at the University of Leeds with the editing and performance of medieval plays as his major research activity. However, one of his main teaching interests throughout his career has been the history of the English language, especially semantic change and word borrowing, and one of his more recent publications was the section on 'English' in the *Encyclopedia of the Languages of Europe* (Blackwell, 1998).

MALCOLM THICK is a Fellow of the Royal Historical Society. He has written extensively on commercial gardening and vegetables in diet before 1801, including a book on early market gardening around London (Prospect, 1998) and a chapter on the supply of seeds, plants and trees in the Leeds Symposium volume *The Country House Kitchen Garden* (Sutton, 1998). An introduction to a facsimile edition of William Lawson's *A New Orchard and Garden* is published by Prospect (2003).

EILEEN WHITE began researching in the cookery collection at the

Brotherton Library after becoming interested in recreating old recipes for period suppers at Bolling Hall Museum in Bradford. She has contributed several papers to the 'Food and Society' series, and compiled the *Soup* volume for the Prospect series on the English kitchen.

C. ANNE WILSON is the overall editor for the 'Food and Society' series. She has recently been working on a study of the history of wine distilling and spirits.

Preface

Eileen White

The sixteenth Leeds Symposium on Food History celebrated the collection of cookery books in the Brotherton Library, University of Leeds, which had been the inspiration behind the setting-up of the Symposium in 1986. This collection is the focus of what has been described as the 'Leeds School' of food history, and has stimulated a range of publications and activities. The Symposium ranged from the medieval period to the nineteenth century, from the *Forme of Cury* to Mrs Beeton.

Cookery books are practical, but can be the starting-point of studies relating to topics far more diverse than merely food preparation. It may seem strange, initially, that cookery books, old and new, can form an important collection within a university library. Recipes are not generally perceived as a source of academic study: can they have the same intellectual, theological, historical or literary values of material in other collections? But everyone must eat, and the procurement, preparation and presentation of food, as it was done over the centuries and continues today, must be of interest to all and is part of the social and economic life of any society. Cookery books can therefore provide source material for a range of disciplines.

The Brotherton collection opens up a vista of life and attitudes covering many centuries. Recipes are not literature, but they can be used for literary and linguistic study. Their language is often blunt and straightforward, but contains the rhythm and directness of everyday speech rather than the self-conscious language of literary composition. They are not obvious historical sources, but reflect the expansion of international trade, reveal the essentials of everyday life, and embody attitudes and personalities. The papers presented here show how recipes can be the starting point for different kinds of investigation, not only into food or cooking practices. Like any text, they can be examined for sources, derivations and dissemination, and can inspire a search for the background of their authors. They can be used by people other than cooks.

Peter Meredith brings his expertise in philology and knowledge of medieval literature and drama to a preliminary study of the recipes in the late fourteenth-century collection, *The Forme of Cury*. These recipes can stand a scrutiny otherwise given to the writings of Chaucer and his fellows, and

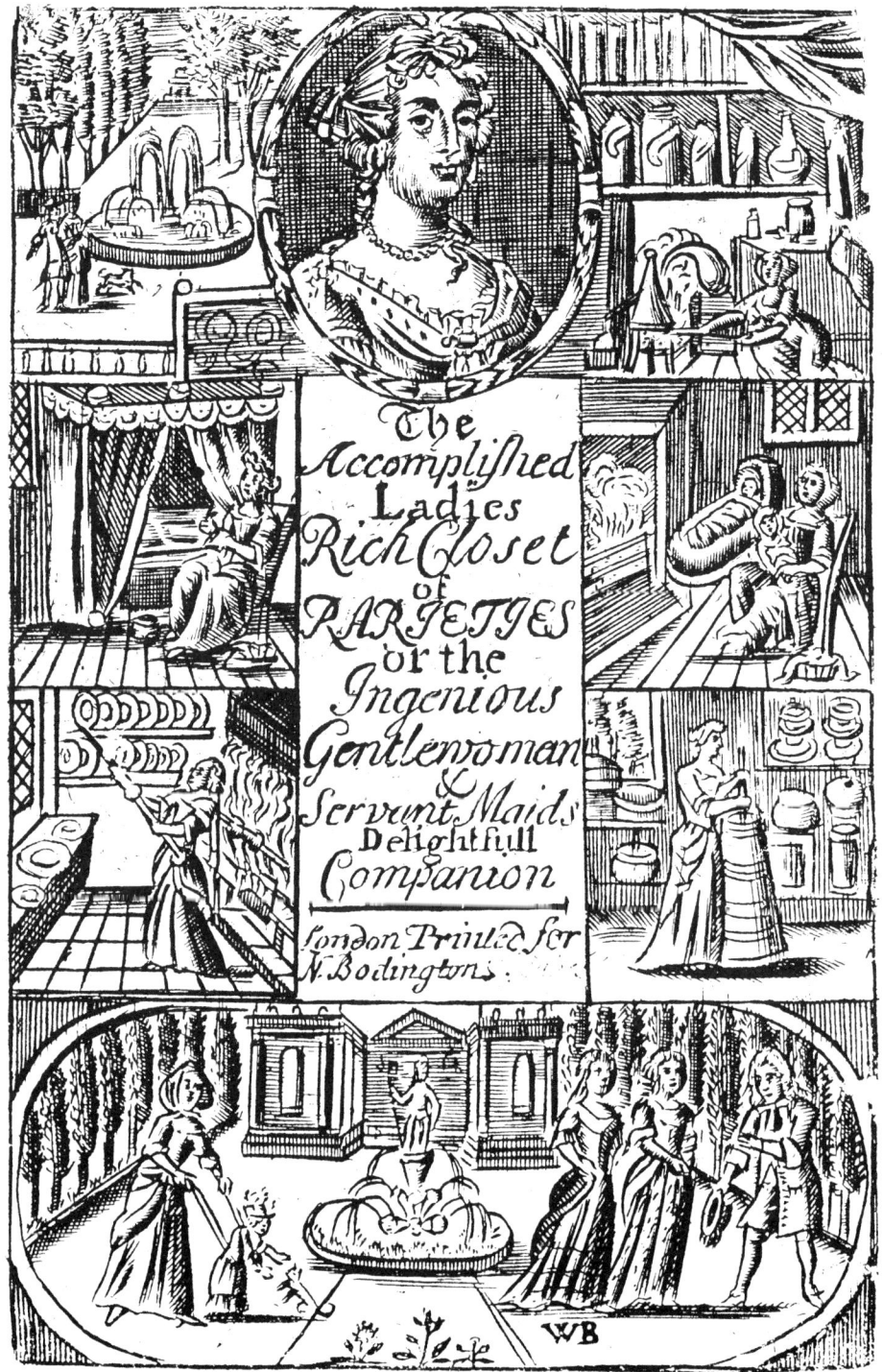

Figure 1. Title-page from The Accomplished Ladies Rich Closet of Rarities, *seventh edition, 1715.*

reveal something about linguistic forms as well as food preparation. Words such as 'bray' or 'seeth', that fell out of use in more literary forms or published books, survived in recipe manuscripts to indicate their continuing use in local dialects.

Writing down recipes suggests a literacy among cooks, but this cannot be assumed in the medieval period or even later. Professional cooks underwent a long apprenticeship, and domestic cooks would have learned from their mothers or other household members. They did not need instructions in the basic methods. *The Forme of Cury* and later fifteenth-century collections did not give instructions for roasting an ox, or even for making a boar's head, which featured regularly on bills of fare for great feasts. What was provided, however, were suggestions for spiced, ground meat that would be used for stuffing the boar's head, and for other specialities that would enliven a celebratory feast, and were not the everyday fare of the household. The medieval manuscripts may have been in the keeping of the literate clerk of the kitchen in a large household, who could advise the cook when necessary. A recipe collection does not necessarily reflect an everyday diet, but often records the dishes and ingredients provided for special occasions. Once printed books were established, such collections could be made more easily available for general use, cooks and compilers had a commercial market for their recipes, and new formats evolved.

The papers by Eileen White and Valerie Mars concentrate on two periods, the seventeenth and the nineteenth centuries, and reveal different aims and attitudes existing at the same time, male and female, professional and domestic, grandiose and practical. Cookery books reflected the conflict of the Civil War in England as much as other documents of the time, they record how trade made ingredients such as spices more readily available, and they take in new foods and dishes acquired as the British Empire expanded. Detailed examination of the books can reveal trends and developments in society as well as in food.

The recipes also remind us that until the era of industrialization and mass-production, providing food was long and laborious work. Food had to be preserved in the months of plenty, and bills of fare reflected seasonal availability. The modern town-dweller can easily become divorced from country activities, and may not even know what a cow is for. The seventeenth-century recipe, by contrast, would send the cook to milk the cow in order to make a syllabub. People are now more ready to eat out or heat up ready-prepared food than spend hours in the kitchen making broths or conserves, but shops stock more lavishly produced cookery books than ever before.

Sometimes it is possible to go beyond the printed book and study its origin, as Malcolm Thick has done with the manuscript sources of Hugh Plat's *Delightes for Ladies*. Anyone studying recipes very soon finds the same ones appearing in similar versions in several books, and it is tempting to chronicle this borrowing (plagiarism) by authors. But Hugh Plat's manuscript notes help to elucidate the use of sources, and although he may have acquired his ideas through many friends and acquaintances, like any good compiler he brings his own enthusiasms to the subject.

At other times, the book can be the starting point for investigations into the life or background of the author. Laura Mason describes 'the thrill of the chase' in following up the life of the confectioner William Jarrin: bankruptcy papers are not an obvious place to find out about sugar confectionery, but they preserved a fascinating insight into the business. She first presented her findings as part of the fifteenth Leeds Food Symposium in 2000, which took another look at the subject of the first Symposium, *Banquetting Stuffe*. It was not intended to publish the papers of this retrospective meeting, but the story of Jarrin's life, and the information in the several editions of *The Italian Confectioner*, have a place in the theme of the English cookery book, as well as representing the fifteenth Symposium.

Another element of cookery books is their illustrations, which range from crude woodcuts to the coloured plates in later editions of Mrs Beeton. Modern cookery books, especially those related to television programmes, present themselves through the quality of their colour photographs as much as their texts, but the earlier books can offer useful if less colourful portrayals of the cook, the kitchen and the environment. The etchings in Bartolomeo Scappi's 1570 *Opera* (of which the Brotherton Library has two editions, one with etchings and another with woodcuts) offer a glimpse of the working of a large Renaissance kitchen with its equipment conveniently labelled to provide a lesson in the Italian language. On a more modest scale, Eliza Acton gave illustrations of domestic equipment for an early Victorian kitchen in *Modern Cookery for Private Families* first published in 1845. Ivan Day looks at English illustrations in the wider context of Continental examples, providing many insights into the creations of cooks over the centuries.

The existence of the Leeds Symposium on Food History is due to the large and varied collection of cookery books in the Brotherton Library. These

Introduction

books are a rich resource, not only for cooks, and deserve to be celebrated. There is no better person to introduce them than Anne Wilson, who gives a personal view of their range, and explains how they came to be there. By her work in the Brotherton Library, she was inspired to write *Food and Drink in Britain*, which has become an essential reference book on the subject. It is hoped that the collection will continue to inspire researchers in the future.

The English Cookery Book

Four cookery book authors and their portraits. From the top left, clockwise: Robert May, 1661; Sir Kenelm Digby, 1674; Edward Kidder, ca. 1740; Elizabeth Raffald, 1784.

CHAPTER ONE

An Introduction to the Cookery Book Collections in the Brotherton Library, University of Leeds

C. Anne Wilson

The focus for the sixteenth meeting of the Leeds Symposium on Food History on 24 March 2001 was cookery books and manuscripts and their authors. And because the Symposium itself has always had strong links with the collections of early cookery books in the Brotherton Library we took the opportunity to remind the symposiasts that researchers are welcome to come and consult individual books in the Special Collections Reading Room at the Library.

One theme that recurred through the day was the question of how far the writers of cookery books were themselves the originators of the recipes, and how far they had taken them from existing texts, whether printed or manuscript. Medieval cookery manuscripts often incorporated groups of recipes to be found also in other manuscripts, and some of these can be proved to have descended from still earlier lost manuscripts. The tradition of copying and recopying recipes was thus well established in the Middle Ages, when English manuscript recipe collections were still produced anonymously (apart from *The Forme of Cury*, said to have been compiled by the mastercooks of King Richard II).

The tradition did not die out immediately once cookery books began to be printed. John Partridge borrowed from a friend a copy of a household book written for the private use of 'a gentlewoman in the country', and decided it was his duty to publish it in 1585 under the title, *The Widowes Treasure*. Queen Henrietta Maria, wife of King Charles I, collected recipes presented to her 'by the most experienced persons of our time', and when she was in exile in France 'her late servant W.M.' obtained copies of her receipt-books, and transcribed and published them as *The Queens Closet Opened* in 1655.

But other cookery book authors were already reproducing individual recipes gleaned from the manuscripts or printed books of earlier compilers;

and the practice went on through the centuries. The many cookery books in the Brotherton Library's collections allow food historians not merely to put their contents into the context of the food production and menus of their day, but also to trace some of the recipes to sources in a previous generation.

The Brotherton Library holds three named collections of historic cookery books, and contemporary books have been added up to the present day. There are, for instance, two shelves of cookery books and periodicals in Chinese, collected during the 1980s and 1990s. Books in English are chosen to illustrate and record particular trends in menus or cookery practices, such as nouvelle cuisine, deep-freezing and microwaving.

The Library's involvement with cookery books began in 1939 when Blanche Leigh presented her collection of over 1,500 items. She was a lady of some importance in Leeds; and she became Lady Mayoress when her husband Percy was Lord Mayor in 1935–6. She herself edited three cookery and household books, in 1905, 1918 and 1929, and through that period and beyond she collected cookery books and food-related books and records. The oldest item in her collection is a Babylonian clay tablet of about 2,500 BC inscribed with a list of foods in cuneiform; and the oldest European book is Platina's *De honesta voluptate* in an edition of 1487 printed in Venice. There is a good selection of French cookery books, and a smaller number in Italian, German, Latin and Greek. But the main section contains the English cookery books which date from 1590 to the time when she presented the books to the Library. They were catalogued after the Second World War, and thus made accessible for readers.

In 1954 the Times Bookshop in London held an exhibition entitled 'Cookery Books 1500–1954', and some books from the Blanche Leigh collection were on display there. Mr John F. Preston, a private collector who was exhibiting books of his own, became interested in the collection at Leeds and corresponded with Dr Page, then Librarian, with a view to bequeathing his books to the Library when he died. In the event, he and his wife moved into a smaller house in 1962, and he presented his collection to the Library at that time. I was a new member of the Library staff then, and involved in the cataloguing of the weekly through-put of academic and student books. But during the winter and spring of 1964 I was given the task of cataloguing the Preston gift. We were not supposed to spend any time reading the books we catalogued; but when the books were interesting ones, we could never resist reading a few paragraphs here and there. And my brief encounters with

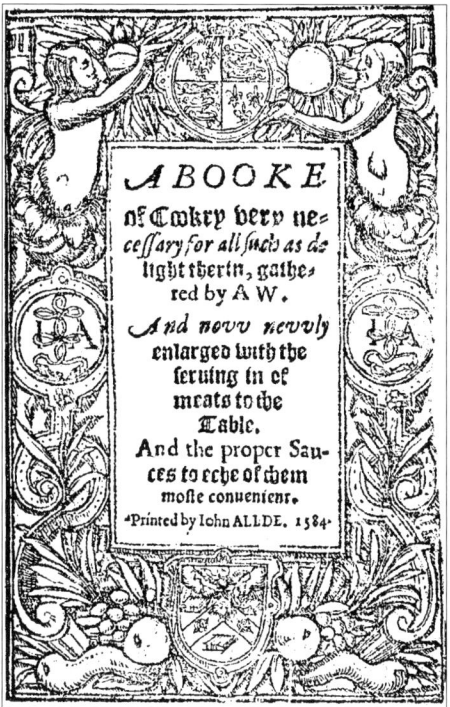

Figure 2. Title-page of A Booke of Cookry *(1584).*

John Preston's books inspired me with a lasting interest in food history.

The collection comprises over 600 English cookery books dating from 1584 to 1861 (the date of the first edition of Mrs Beeton's *Book of Household Management*), plus one or two later books. Eventually I met John Preston, and he twice came to Leeds and revisited his books, housed alongside the Library's other Special Collections. He was delighted to know that they were being used by researchers into food history and social history.

John Preston died at the age of 90 in the autumn of 1992. Had he stuck to his original plan, the books would not have reached the Library until perhaps early in 1993, when they would have been catalogued on computer by a member of the cataloguing team of that time. Had I not had the privilege of cataloguing them in 1964, I might never have become involved with food history, or have written *Food and Drink in Britain* – which contains much material drawn from the early cookery books during many subsequent hours of spare-time research. It was published in 1973.

Among other readers who consulted the books were Peter Brears, Lynette Hunter (series editor for the Prospect Books bibliographies of cookery and household books) and Jennifer Stead, all of whom I met in the context of discussions on food history and the books themselves. Had this not happened, we would never have got together to hold the day-school on the theme of 'Banquetting Stuffe' at the Department of Adult Education in 1986. That meeting became the first Leeds Symposium on Food History, launched for us by the late Alan Davidson who had instituted the Oxford Symposium on Food a few years earlier. The annual meetings of the Leeds Symposium have been held in March or April ever since.

Thus the arrival of the Preston books in Leeds led to the foundation of the Leeds Symposium. The earliest of those books is *A Booke of Cookry Very Necessary for All Such as Delight Therein, Gathered by A.W.*, 1584. (We have never discovered the identity of the Elizabethan A.W.) Another edition of 1587 is also in the collection: the contents are identical to those in the 1584 book, but at the end there is a handful of additional recipes for 'banquetting stuffe'. Other very early books to be found there are John Partridge's *The Widowes Treasure* of 1585, and a 1605 edition of Sir Hugh Plat's *Delightes for Ladies*.

There is inevitably some overlap with the Blanche Leigh books; for instance, both the Leigh and Preston collections have many editions of Hannah Glasse's *The Art of Cookery*, first published in 1747 as a quarto volume and reissued many times in octavo and smaller sizes. The latest Preston edition is dated 1803; and the Leigh collection includes an abridged version of 1842. There are seven editions of Eliza Smith's *The Compleat Housewife* of 1727 in the Leigh and eight in the Preston collection; again the holdings partly complement each other and partly overlap, the latest being the Leigh seventeenth edition of 1766. Both collections offer a very wide range of nineteenth-century books.

The Library's third named collection of cookery books came from a place rather than a person: the London borough of Camden. Hence it is called the Camden collection. After the war, the London borough libraries divided up the Dewey classification and each agreed to collect and house as many as possible of the new books published in Britain and classed within their section. Camden was allotted 635 onwards, which is agriculture, and 640 onwards, which is food and drink. In practice a large part of their allocation fell within 641: cookery books. By the late 1980s Camden Public Library had run out of space, and the cookery books were being kept in a Pickford's store at Swiss Cottage. The Camden librarian advertised in the *Library Association Record*, seeking a new home for them; and after many months of negotiation and a further wait for the books to be decommissioned from Camden's computer records, they came to Leeds to the Brotherton Library.

The collection includes a few late-Victorian books and many others published between 1900 and the late 1940s. These supplement the Leigh books which are not very numerous for the twentieth century. But the most notable feature of the Camden collection is its coverage of English cookery books published between 1949 and about 1975. They were most welcome, because our additions of twentieth-century cookery books have come by gift or by very modest purchases. So until the Library received the Camden collection, there were a great many gaps among the books for the period 1900–1975. It is Library policy to continue to add a few titles reflecting current developments in food fashions and cooking and preserving techniques. And one day, far in the future, we shall receive a bequest of the most significant books from the 1980s onwards from another food historian.

French influences on English cookery go back to Norman times, and were certainly in evidence from the 1660s onwards. The substantial French section of the Blanche Leigh collection makes it possible to pair up French works with the English translations made from them. In the Library are several French editions of La Varenne's *Le Cuisinier François* from 1669 onwards, and also the English translation, entitled *The French Cook*, in the third edition of 1673. Du Four's *De l'Usage du Caphé, du Thé et du Chocolat* of 1671 is there; as is *The Manner of Making of Coffee, Tea and Chocolate*, translated in an edition of 1685. Lémery's *Traité des Aliments*, second edition, Paris, 1705 had already been translated as *A Treatise of Foods in General* and published in London in 1704. The Library has both. And there are similar pairings for other significant French titles.

While the majority of books in English contain collections of cookery recipes, there are also some relating to food production. *The Feminin' Monarchi' or The Histori of Bee's* (in partially phonetic spelling) by Charles Butler, 1634, and John Hill's *The Virtues of Honey in Preventing many of the Worst Disorders*, the third edition, 1760, are two examples. There is good coverage for the growing of herbs and for their medicinal usage with Gerard's *Herball* of 1597 and Parkinson's *Paradisus terrestris* (*The Earthly Paradise*) of 1629, both large, handsome books with striking illustrations. A favourite of mine is *A Book of Fruits and Flowers, shewing the Nature and Use of Them either for Meat or Medicine*, 1653. It has both recipes and pictures, and several years ago I wrote an introduction for the Prospect Books facsimile reprint.

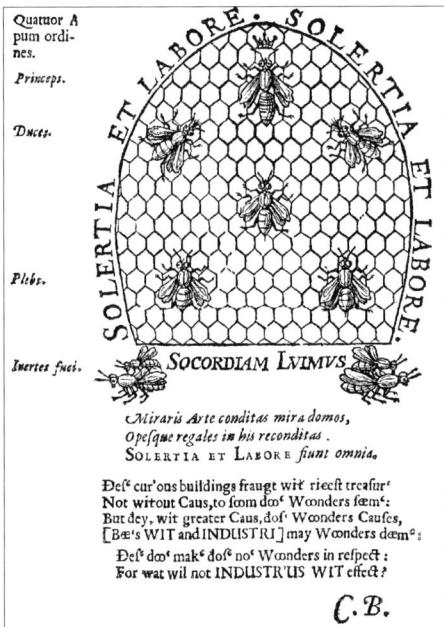

Figure 3. Bees in the hive, from The Feminin' Monarchi', or The Histori of Bee's *(1634). The page also shows the phonetic spelling employed by Charles Butler.*

Books that deal more directly with gardening methods include Thomas Tusser's *Five Hundreth Pointes of Good Husbandrie* of 1590, and an edition of William Lawson's *The Country Housewives Garden* issued with the eighth edition of Gervase Markham's *The Way to get Wealth* in 1653. These form part of Blanche Leigh's collection, as do books by several eighteenth-century writers on gardening, including John Laurence and Stephen Switzer; and Philip Miller's *The Gardeners Dictionary*, the second edition of 1733 and the eighth of 1768. French gardening is covered in the two volumes of de Combles, *L'ecole du jardin potager* in editions of 1752 and 1770.

For the cook and housekeeper, John Evelyn's *Acetaria* explains how to serve the salad plants available in 1699. For gardeners and cooks there is *Adam's Luxury and Eve's Cookery*, 1744: the first part tells how to grow vegetables and fruit and the second how to cook them, with a final section on the physical, or therapeutic, virtues of several garden herbs and roots.

Many of the cookery books include sections on preserving, dairying, brewing and distilling; and also a substantial number of medical recipes. They are thus household books in the fullest sense. The medical sections in such books as E. Smith, *The Compleat Housewife*, 1727 and later editions, and C. Cartwright, *The Lady's Best Companion…to which is added The Approved Family Physician*, 1789, remind us that until well into the nineteenth century the housewife had to produce the home-made remedies as well as the cooked dishes for mealtimes. A few books supply information on cookery for special groups of people. Examples are the chapter 'For captains of ships' in Hannah Glasse's *The Art of Cookery*, 1747 and many later editions; and the army meals recommended by A. Soyer in *Soyer's Culinary Campaign* (1857) based on his contribution to improving the diet of soldiers on active service in the Crimean War. Another group whose needs were considered from the late eighteenth century onwards were the very poor. *The Report of the Society for Bettering the Conditions of the Poor*, 1798, explains how some parishes tackled the problem of providing nutrition for the destitute. 'Charitable cookery' is included in M.E. Rundell, *A New System of Domestic Cookery*, 1806 and many later editions; and A. Cobbett, *The English Housekeeper,* third edition 1842 and sixth edition 1851, has a final chapter titled 'Cookery for the poor'. In most cases the principal food on offer was soup made with some cereal or vegetables, plus the trimmings from the meat eaten by the better-off families who provided this form of charity.

Other types of additional information to be found in the books include directions for marketing, and sample menus (in the eighteenth century the menus often take the form of diagrams depicting the arrangement of the dishes on the table). Glimpses of contemporary life appear in *Madam Johnson's Present*, 1755, which contains lessons on arithmetic, letter-writing and an English spelling-dictionary alongside the cookery sections. *A New System of Practical Domestic Economy*, third edition, 1823, has an appendix showing the system and amount of taxation payable on carriages with four wheels and on the horses to draw them; and another table listing the taxes payable on male servants, on a rising scale from £1 4s 0d for a single one to £3 16s 6d each for eleven or more servants in the same household. It is details like these that supply fodder for social historians.

Many of the mainstream Victorian writers and their cookery books are discussed by Valerie Mars in a separate chapter. A useful analysis of the progress of English cookery book publication in the nineteenth century was made by Lynette Hunter at the seventh Leeds Symposium on Food History, and was subsequently published by Sutton Publishing in the volume titled *Luncheon, Nuncheon and Other Meals*, edited by C. Anne Wilson, 1994. Copies of all the volumes of the papers of the Leeds Symposium have been deposited in the Library's cookery book collections.

More than twenty periodicals are also represented there. Among the titles

Figure 4. Root vegetables from the kitchen garden, illustrated in John Parkinson's Paradisus terrestris *of 1629. 1. Skirrit; 2. Parsnip; 3. Carrot; 4. Turnip; 5. Navew (wild turnip); 6. Black Radish; 7. Common Radish.*

are *The Country Magazine* for 1736; *The Englishwoman's Domestic Magazine*, 1852–59 and 1862–63; *The Dietetic Reformer*, 1872–86, and its successor, *The Vegetarian Messenger*, 1887–1935. Several bibliographies of cookery books are available for consultation; the older ones in the Blanche Leigh collection have been supplemented by others published more recently. And the Library holds over 60 manuscript cookery books, mostly falling within the period mid-seventeenth to early twentieth century. About half of them were collected by Blanche Leigh, and the rest have been added since through gift or purchase.

The Blanche Leigh and John Preston collections are catalogued on the Library's database, and can be checked out via author's name, title, and keyword. Anyone wishing to find out more may consult the Special Collections website: http://www.leeds.ac.uk/library/spcoll/spprint/21200.html which leads directly to information about the Library's cookery book collections, from where there is a link to the Library's catalogue. Information is also provided on how to gain access to the Special Collections.

CHAPTER TWO

THE LANGUAGE OF MEDIEVAL COOKERY

Peter Meredith

My earliest contact with medieval cookery was in the early 1960s when some students of mine in South Australia wanted to put on a medieval feast at one of their Honours camps. As it happened I had recently acquired the Early English Text Society's *Two Fifteenth-Century Cookery Books*, and I was able to offer some suggestions. In the course of hunting something out I read a number of the recipes and was struck by what seemed to me the personal violence of their language:

> **Gelyne endobat.** ¶ Take a hen, and roste hir al-moost ynogh, and chop hir small in faire peces, and caste hem into a potte…
> **Kede rosted.** ¶ Take a kydde, and slytte the skyn in þe throte, And seke the veyne, and kut him, and lete him blede to deth; and fle him.
>
> (pp. 80–81)

Some of the impression of personal violence is real, but some at least is a result of the nature of the language. The shedding of grammatical gender in the Old English and early Middle English periods had left a largely unregulated system behind as far as pronouns were concerned.[1] Choice of pronoun could be affected by vestiges which survived of the old grammatical gender, by natural gender, or by the second language of England, French, which retained (and retains) grammatical gender and was exerting a growing influence on English in the twelfth and thirteenth centuries. The French noun '*geline*' ('hen') is feminine, so though in **Gelyne endobat** the hen appears to be anthropomorphized by the use of 'hir', it is probably merely an example of grammatical gender. The pronoun situation is further complicated by the possessive and object cases of 'hit' ('it') in ME being 'his' and 'him' respectively and potentially adding a further sense of personal reference In the case of the 'kydde' in **Kede rosted**, the reference is depersonalized to some extent by the use of 'him' for the 'veyne' as well as for the kid itself. The violence may still be there but there is less sense of personal vindictiveness, and more of an appropriate agreement of pronoun and noun.

Apart from occasional forays into trying out a few recipes ('wardons in syrippe', 'payn purdeuz'), there the involvement rested; except that there remained a sense of unexplored language possibilities. The Leeds Food Symposium gave me the opportunity to look a little less emotionally and a little more formally at the language of the recipes – and I should perhaps make it clear that my subject is *English* recipes. What I have done here is use the first one hundred recipes from the *Forme of Cury* to investigate the form that they take, to see where the language of the recipes comes from, and whether there is a special language that might be said to be technical. A survey as brief as this can give only an impressionistic view of one small area at one period, and to balance this a little I have looked also at the language of recipes in one of the other collections contained in Hieatt and Butler's *Curye on Inglysch*, the early fourteenth-century 'Diuersa Cibaria'. This is particularly interesting in that it is partly a translation of a collection of Anglo-Norman recipes which still exists, and therefore allows comparison with a French source, and it is in the hand of a known author, William Herebert, a Franciscan friar from Hereford, so that its dialect and something of the man behind it is known. There is also occasional reference made to *Two Fifteenth-Century Cookery Books*.[2]

Most contemporary modern recipes are recognizable as such not just because of the subject matter but also because of the form that they take: title, list of ingredients with quantities, and the immediate move into an imperative mood for the verbs – 'prepare, bake, baste, use, cover'. Even something like Nigella Lawson's *How to be a Domestic Goddess* (London: Chatto and Windus, 2000) has the same basic format – with a little bit of preceding chat. Could the same be said of medieval English recipes? If one goes by the *Forme of Cury* then up to a point the answer is 'yes'; but the format is a little different. There is the same imperative mood but the list of ingredients is subsumed into the recipe itself and there are almost no quantities (no. 22 has 'ii pounde of sugur'). What is striking is that every recipe but one (there are two 'recipes' which are actually just notes) begins with the word 'Take' (97 out of 98). If one extends the survey to the rest of the *Cury* a similar picture emerges: out of 103 further recipes (there are in addition two more notes) 96 open with 'Take'. If one looks back to the earlier collection in Hieatt and Butler, the 'Diuersa Cibaria' simply lists ingredients, until no. 33 which begins 'Nim'. Thereafter 19 of the 30 recipes begin with 'Nim/Nym', which is the native English word for 'take'. Almost all the recipes in Austin begin

Figure 5. Making pasta, from Opera di M. Bartolomeo Scappi *(Venice, 1570). Scappi was the private cook of Pope Pius V, and his book illustrates the kitchen and equipment of a large medieval or Renaissance household.*

with 'Take'. Given that the word *'recipe'* means 'take' in Latin, this should not, I suppose, be much of a cause for surprise; but is it something which the English derive from French recipes? *'Prenez'* certainly features in Taillevent but not nearly so frequently as an opening word.[3] In the first of the two Anglo-Norman collections, 25 out of the 29 recipes begin with *'Pernez'*, 'take'. The second collection, of which the first part of 'Diuersa Cibaria' is a translation, contains only 32 recipes – in other words it contains only the recipes in 'Diuersa Cibaria' which are lists of ingredients and lack 'Take'. Even here, however, there is one use of *'Pernez'*.[4] Certainly the impression from this sample is that the predominance of 'Take/Nim' as an opening is an English feature.

Another feature of the recipes is their bluntness, their lack of frills. They mostly consist of imperative verbs and noun phrases; not that more is needed. 'Connynges in clere broth' is a typical example (NB since the relative numbers of French and English words in the recipes is a concern here, all French words in this recipe and those extracted later have been italicized):

> 67. *Connynges* in *clere* broth. Take *connynges* and smyte hem in *gobetes*, and waissh hem, and do hem in feyre water and wyne; & seeth hem and *skym* hem. And whan þey buth isode, pyke hem clene, and drawe the broth thurgh a *straynour*, and do the flessh þerwith in a *possynet* and *styue* it; and do þerto *vyneger* and *powdour* of *gynger* a grete *quantite*, and salt after the last *boillyng*, and *serue* it forth. (Hieatt and Butler, p. 113)
>
> [67. Rabbits in a clear broth. Take rabbits and cut them in pieces, and wash them, and put them in clean water and wine; and boil them and skim them. And when they are cooked, pick them clean, and strain the broth through a strainer, and put the flesh with it (the broth) in a pot and stew it; and add vinegar and a large quantity of powdered ginger, and salt after the last boiling, and serve it up.]

Occasionally, however, the abruptness is tempered with more precise instructions, greater picturesqueness, or the elaboration of a more complicated process:

> 1. ... lat it nauȝt *boyle* after þe eyren ben cast þerinne.
>   [don't let it boil after the eggs are put in.]
> 19. ... If it is to thynne, *alye* it vp with flour of *ryse*, oþer with oþere thyng.

[if it is too thin, mix it with rice flour or with something else.]

22. … lat it seeþ warly with a slowe fyre and not to thyk.

[let it boil (but watched) over a slow fire and not too thick.]

66. … *leshe* it in liknesse of a peskodde.

[slice it so that it looks like a pea-pod.]

68. … and *boile* it with *esy* fyre, and kepe it wel fro brennyng. And whan it hath *yboile*d a while, take a drope þerof wiþ þy fyngur and do it in a litel water, and loke if it hong togydre.

[and boil it over a gentle fire, and make sure it doesn't burn. And when it has boiled for a while, take a drop out with your finger and put it in some water, and see if it holds together.]

69. … make þerof *dyuerse colours*. If þou wolt haue ȝelow, do þerto *safroun* and no *persel*. If þou wolt haue it whyte … rede … *pownas* … blak … and set on the fyre in as many *vessels* as þou hast *colours* þerto, and seeþ it wel, and lay þise *colours* in a cloth, first oon, and sithen anoþer vppon hym, and sithen the þridde and the ferthe, and *presse* it harde til it be al out clene.

[make various colours from it. If you want yellow, add saffron and no parsley. If you want it white…red…'pownas'…black…and put it on the fire in as many pots as you have colours, and boil it well, and lay these colours on a cloth, first one and then another on top of it, and then the third and the fourth, and press it firmly till it is completely free (?of moisture).]

72. … *couere* hem þat no breth go out.

[cover them so that no air escapes]

73. … Take *chiches* and wrye hem in askes al nyȝt oþer al day, oþer lay hem in hoot aymers. At morowe waische hem in clene water.

[Take chickpeas and cover them in ashes all night or all day, or lay them in hot embers. In the morning wash them in clean water]

Besides demonstrating the nature of the language and the form of these recipes, these extracts also show the kind of relationship that exists here between French and English. The structural part of the text is almost entirely English, and one effect of word-borrowing is that the foreign word adapts to the native language by adopting the grammatical endings of that language. Consequently French verbs have endings which are English (eg **68**, '*yboile*d') In these extracts there is no sense of French as the dominant form.

The Language of Medieval Cookery

By the time of the *Forme of Cury* (late fourteenth century) French was no longer the dominant aristocratic language. Contact between French, in one form or another, and English had existed since before 1066. Edward the Confessor had been brought up in France and brought French courtiers with him when he became king. With William I's accession the upper levels of English society became French-speaking (Anglo-Norman). From 1204 onwards, however, owners of property in both England and France had to decide on which side of the Channel to hold their lands. For those who chose England, a greater identification with English was perhaps an inevitable development. At the same time the French of England became more and more sidelined as a less desirable dialect in comparison with the French of Paris and central France. A new influence on English, from this central French form of the language, came culturally rather than by conquest. French remained in use and remained an important influence but it was no longer the native aristocratic language of England. In 1362 English was established as the language of the law courts and in the same year Parliament was opened in English for the first time. The re-establishment of English as the language of the aristocracy and of adminstration no doubt encouraged the production of original works in English and of the large number of translations into English which appeared in the late fourteenth and early fifteenth centuries. Whether cookery books were amongst the former or the latter it is impossible to tell without clear examples of texts which have been translated, but the evidence from later periods would suggest that, as with dictionaries, copying and adaptation (and, in the case of recipes, translation) is far more likely than original composition.

Given the existence of an Anglo-Norman nobility in England for around two hundred years from 1066 speaking a variety of French,[5] and that cookery, at more than a mere subsistence level, is a product of the aristocratic life, it might be expected that the vocabulary of the recipes would be French-based. But the work of cooking would almost certainly have been done by English-speakers. To what extent does this intrude into the written record and to what extent do English or French provide a technical culinary language? A simple count of the different lexical words (nouns, verbs, adjectives and adverbs) as opposed to the grammatical words (prepositions, conjugations, pronouns, etc.) derived from French and those that existed in Anglo-Saxon England contained in this sample from the *Cury* (see Appendix A) shows that there are 218 that existed in Old English and

Figure 6. A field kitchen, from Scappi's Opera *(Venice, 1570), demonstrating roasting and boiling on a grand scale.*

162 from some form of French. So in simple terms of word-count the two sources are not greatly different.

It is worth noting that amongst the explicitly culinary words there are a number of pairs with similar meanings, derived from English and French respectively, which might be said to be in competition. Most obvious amongst them are 'boil' (OFr.) and 'seethe'(OE). There is now a clear distinction between the two words in meaning and in use. For most people 'seethe' is restricted in use to a human emotional state: 'seething with anger/rage'. In fact for many people it is clearly losing its function as a verb, since 'he seethed with anger' is less likely than 'he was seething', and 'I seethe' is most unlikely to occur; in other words its ability to act as a verb in forming tenses is disappearing. 'Boil' on the other hand is now the normal English word in a cooking context; interestingly it has moved very little outside culinary or connected areas. Like 'seethe', 'boil' can apply to the emotions, and the derived adjective, 'hard-boiled', to human character, but the two words are certainly no longer on an equal footing in the language. One of the factors that may have influenced the later development in the use of 'seethe' is that the forms of its past participle, 'isode/ysode, soden', are not obviously connected with the present tense 'seethe'. It is consequently easier for a new meaning to become attached to it ('cooked through' and especially 'stewed' becomes 'thoroughly soaked'), and for that meaning to oust the original meaning; certainly easier than it is in a clearly connected word like 'boiled'. Unlike the verb 'boil', 'seethe' then lacks a useable past participle and becomes a less flexible word.[6] In Middle English, however, 'boil' and 'seethe' were interchangeable, as is implied in recipe 67 quoted above: 'seethe' appears as an imperative 'seeth' (l.2) and as a past participle 'isode' (l.3); 'boil' as a verbal noun 'boillyng' (l.6). The interchangeability is even clearer in recipes 41, 46, 47 and 66, where the writer moves from one word to the other within the recipe, and it is apparent at an earlier date in one particular use of 'seethe' and 'boil' in the 'Diuersa Cibaria' (see Appendix D, recipe B) where the word **'boylys'**, the expected Anglo-Norman past participle, is translated *'ysoden'* (l.6), and **'boillé'**, a more unusual form of the past participle, is translated *'iboilled'* (l.8). In the *Forme of Cury* as a whole, not just the first 100 recipes, 'seethe' in all its forms predominates. It appears 160 times and 'boil' 69 times, or a proportion of 70 per cent to 30 per cent. This compares with 'seethe' 20 examples and 'boil' 21 examples in the earlier 'Diuersa Cibaria', an equality which might be accounted for by the work's being at least in part a translation from Anglo-Norman. Both words are primarily culinary terms and clearly, perhaps because they refer to such a basic activity, there is no question in their case of a technical language in which words of French origin predominate.

Turning to other pairs of apparent English and French synonyms, the situation is different and less clear-cut. In the case of 'boil' and 'seethe', there is no doubt about where they come from and that they refer to the same activity, but with pairs like 'alye/alay' and 'temper(e)' neither is certain. There is not much doubt that 'alye/alay' comes from Latin through French, but the exact source of the ME word is unsure. It has several different forms. It appears as 'alye, alay, lye' in the sample surveyed, and the *Middle English Dictionary* (*MED*) associates it with four different French words meaning respectively 'to ally', 'to alloy', 'to bind', 'to mix' (see *MED*, sv **allien, alaien, lien, leien**). 'Temper(e)' is Latin in origin and could come through either English or French. It certainly means 'mix', but with what precise connotations? Contexts sometimes help but at best they can only give a meaning that is likely in that instance, not the range of possible meanings. For example, in recipe 19 (quoted above) 'alye' certainly implies 'thicken': 'if the mixture is too thin, thicken it ['alye it vp'] with rice flour'. But 'mix' would work equally well here: 'if the mixture is too thin, mix it up with rice flour'. Is it 'alye vp' that means 'thicken', whereas 'alye' simply means 'mix'? Or vice-versa? In recipe 47 the mixture is 'tempered' with broth and 'alyed' with egg yolks, apparently a thinning and a thickening, and usually 'tempering' is achieved by adding a liquid; but in recipe 80 tempering is done with 'ayren, safroun and salt'. Perhaps all one can say is that both words meant 'alter the consistency of by adding' and the context determined the precise meaning. Neither has survived as a cooking term. Other possible pairs of words in opposition (in some cases both English) are: 'drawe/wryng, grynde/mynce (still differentiating English and American usage), lave/waisshe, pare/pill'. The investigation of pairs of words of this kind is important for the meaning of the recipes and is linguistically interesting in showing the effect that similarity of meaning has on words in the language, but it does not help with the larger question of the existence of a technical language of cookery in the period.

The commonness of a word in the recipes is no guide to its significance. By far the commonest word is 'take' – with 'do' running it close – both words from Old English: one Scandinavian, the other native English. But these are words in common use elsewhere at the time. Though 'Take' gives a format to the recipes, it is not in itself a culinary word. Of the words that are used in the first part of the *Cury*, many are of this kind. If it were possible to exclude these we would be left with a body of words commonly, primarily or only used in cookery. The only way of deciding whether a word is limited in its use in this way is through the *MED*. Like the *OED*, the *MED* provides a lists of quotations for each meaning of a word recorded in the language. Taking these quotations as a guide it should be possible to get some idea of the use of a word in its different meanings at a particular period. I have assumed that if a word only appears in a culinary text in the *MED*, then it is likely to have been restricted to cookery and therefore to rank as a technical word. That is the simple case. More often a word will appear in more than one context and then it is a question of deciding whether there is a preponderance of culinary uses or possibly whether the word has a specialized meaning which is culinary. In order to get some sense of what the culinary vocabulary consists of I have looked at the verbs, since in some respects it is not the ingredients but the method which is at the centre of a language of cookery. Amongst these, '*alye* [21], *blaunched* [15] / *unblaunched* [3], *bray* (to crush) [11], *frye* [15], *leshe* (to slice) [7], *messe* [29], *mynce* [19], *perboile* [20], *roost* [8], *tost* [4]' have only culinary uses or uses derived from the culinary one (especially the torturing of martyrs); '*boyle* [33], kerf (to carve) [6], *clarifie* [8], *dyce* [5], *grate* [7], *scald* [6], seethe [92], shrede [3]' are commonly used in culinary contexts or have specialized culinary uses, but do have other uses; 'drawe [33], grynde [34], *pare* [4], pill [3], salt [12], *stewe* [5], swyng (to beat) [5]' are general words with particular culinary uses. These might well be considered part of a technical vocabulary.

There then remains the question of origin. All of the first group are derived from French (words of French origin are italicized). Of the second group, 5 are French and 3 English. Of the third group, 2 are French and 5 English. Frequency of use is also important and I have indicated the number of uses in the sample surveyed in brackets after the word concerned. As a very rough guide to the frequency of words from the two languages, there are 216 French and 187 English verb usages. Without the large number of uses of 'seethe', however, the French words would not only predominate in number of separate words but also in frequency. These figures clearly need refinement, and the whole subject additional investigation. What significance, for example, did French words have in fourteenth-century England? Words

Figure 7. Brute strength was needed to work in a large kitchen. This illustration from Scappi's Opera *(Venice, 1570) also includes examples of smaller kitchen utensils.*

which were borrowed early from French are unlikely still to have 'felt' French; so the impression given by the recipes to a contemporary would not have been a foreign one, or probably even an aristocratic one, if all the words were early borrowings. On the other hand it may be that by this time the very fact that they were culinary words created a special tone. A further problem is that all the *MED* can provide is the earliest *recorded* use in English. It is reliant upon *written* texts (where they exist) and can take no account of the spoken language. There is also the necessity of adding other parts of speech to the investigation. These figures only represent numbers of verb forms. Though verbs are at the centre of culinary method, the nouns carry as great if not a greater force in giving a tone to the texts. Some indication of frequency of use of nouns is given in Appendix A. Though there is not the space here to deal with them in any detail, it is worth drawing attention to the nouns with the highest frequency: English: broth [59], salt [57], water [35], ayren ('eggs') [33], wyne [32], mylke [26], pot [19], 3olkes [18]; French: powdour [82], safroun [46], sugur [30], gynger [25], almand [30], flours [22], oynouns [21], ryse [16], grece [15], pork [15]. Despite the limitations of a survey of this kind, it is safe to say that there undoubtedly was a technical language of cookery and that the French element in the vocabulary was considerable, though not predominant, and it seems to me unlikely that the recipes would have sounded exotic. For exoticism one needs to turn to the names of the dishes, which remained largely unaltered for centuries, except by confusion and misunderstanding (see Appendix B). They represent the esoteric side of cookery; the side with which a cook dazzled his masters.

Chaucer when he characterized the activities of cooks in 'The Pardoner's Tale' spoke of:

> Thise cookes, how they stampe, and streyne, and grynde,
> And turnen substaunce into accident.
>
> (ll.538 9)[7]

The activities are immediately recognizable from the recipe books though only 'grynde' appears amongst the 'technical' words of my sample. To what extent was the language of cookery a language specialized enough and familiar enough to be useable by a writer to convey a particular tone or significance? In the first of the Wakefield Master's Shepherds' pageants in the Towneley plays, the shepherds sit down for their evening snack in the fields. But what they describe comes out of a cookery book rather than a shepherd's satchel:

2 Shepherd
   Sirs, let us crib first; for one thing or oder   <u>eat</u> <u>other</u>
   That these words be pursed, and let us go fodder   <u>shut away</u> <u>feed</u>
   Our mompins.   <u>teeth</u>
   Lay forth of our store;
   Lo, here brawn of a boar!
1 Shepherd
   Set mustard afore!
            Our meat now begins.   <u>food</u>

   Here a foot of a cow well sauced. I ween,   <u>think</u>
   The pestle of a sow that powdered has been;   <u>leg</u>
   Two bloodings, I trow, a levering between –   <u>blood-puddings</u>
                                                             <u>liver-sausage</u>
   Do gladly, sirs, now my brether, bedene!   <u>To it with a will</u>
                                                  <u>brothers</u> <u>straightaway</u>

           With more:
   Both beef and mutton
   (Of an ewe that was rotten),
   Good meat for a glutton -
           Eat of this store!
2 Shepherd
   I have here in my mail, sodden and roast: <u>bag</u> <u>boiled</u>
   Even of an ox-tail that would not be lost.
   Ha, ha, goderhail! I let for no cost.   <u>good health</u> <u>held back</u>
   A good pie ere we fail – this is good for the frost   <u>finish</u>
           In the morning!
   And two swine-grones,   <u>snouts</u>
   All a hare but the lones –   <u>loins</u>
   We mister no spoons   <u>need</u>
           Here at our manging.   <u>eating</u>
3 Shepherd
   Here is to record the leg of a goose,   <u>to be noted down</u>
   With chickens endord, pork, partridge to rose, <u>gilded</u> <u>worthy</u> <u>praise</u>
   A tart for a lord – how think ye this does?
   A calf-liver scored, with the verjose –   <u>cut up</u> <u>verjuice</u>
           Good sauce!

This is a restorité	restorative
To make a good appeté,	appetite
1 Shepherd	
Ye speak all by clergy,	learnedly
I hear by your clause.	conclusion
	(ll.208–50)

Everything that is mentioned (except perhaps the rotten ewe) could be paralleled in the *Cury* and quite clearly this is not an ordinary shepherds' meal. It is not only the content of the meal but the words that are being used to describe it that convey the comic inappropriateness of it: 'well-sauced, powdered, sodden, roast, endord, scored' (all French except the perhaps inevitable 'sodden'). Besides the comedy there is the underlying feeling of sufferers making the best of misfortune, and many have seen the episode also as a fore-shadowing of the abundance represented by Christ's coming that is about to be announced to the shepherds.

Also in the Towneley plays there is an episode that brings me back to my early memories of the cookery books. At the opening of the his pageant, Herod threatens the audience with his usual violence:

Stint, brodels, your din; yea, everichon!	Cease wretches everyone
I rede that ye hearken to I be gone;	advise till
For if I begin, I break ilka bone	every
And pull fro the skin the carcase anon,	from
Yea, pardee.	(ll.82–86)

It had not occurred to me before that Herod's threats are very much in line with cooking methods; and that this was perhaps in the writer's mind is suggested by the ending of the next stanza:

Stir not, but ye have leave,	
For if ye do, I cleave	
You small as flesh to pot.	(ll.97–99)[8]

Once again the words of cookery convey the tone. What Herod threatens the audience with is the kind of bloody feast that he is about to invite the Innocents to. Perhaps my initial impression of the recipes as being the repositories of personal violence was not simply modern squeamishness but a view shared by the Wakefield Master.

Notes

1. The Old English (OE) period dates from the late sixth to the late eleventh centuries. Grammatical gender was an original part of the structure of the language but was already disappearing from English during this period. Middle English (ME) covers the period from the late eleventh century to the late fifteenth. On grammatical gender see Barbara M.H. Strang, *A History of English* (London: Methuen, 1970), pp. 265–69 and 294–95, and Charles Barber, *The English Language: a historical introduction* (CUP: Cambridge, 1993), pp. 89–90 and 160.
2. *Curye on Inglysch*, ed. by Constance B. Hieatt and Sharon Butler, Early English Text Society SS 8 (London: OUP, 1985); *Two Fifteenth-Century Cookery Books*, ed. by Thomas Austin, EETS OS 91 (London: OUP, 1888). For William Herebert see the *Dictionary of National Biography* (under 'Herbert') and *Religious Lyrics of the XIVth Century*, ed. by Carleton Brown, 2nd ed. rev. by G.V. Smithers (Oxford: Clarendon Press, 1956), pp. xiii–xiv, and 15–27 (for his translations). He was *lector* of the Franciscan house at Oxford, died apparently in 1333, and was buried at Hereford which seems to have been his home. The language of British Library MS Additional 46919, which contains the recipes and his religious lyrics, has been analyzed in *A Linguistic Atlas of Late Medieval English*, ed. by Angus McIntosh, M.J. Samuels and Michael Benskin, 4 vols (Aberdeen: Aberdeen University Press, 1986). It is LP (Linguistic Profile) 7410.
3. *The* Viandier *of Taillevent*, ed. by Terence Scully (Ottawa: University of Ottawa Press, 1988).
4. Constance B. Hieatt and Robin F. Jones, 'Two Anglo-Norman Culinary Collections Edited from British Library Manuscripts Additional 32085 and Royal 12.C.xii', *Speculum* 61 (1986), 859–82.
5. Strang, pp. 215–18. For a brief discussion of the position of Anglo-Norman and Central French in England, see Barber, pp. 140–50. For a discussion and listing of French loan-words, see Mary S. Serjeantson, *A History of Foreign Words in English* (London: Routledge and Kegan Paul, 1935), which though old is still a useful source of information. Her results now need checking against the findings of the *MED*. Chapter 5 deals with the French element in English.
6. It could, of course, have developed a new past participle 'seethed', as was happening at the time in many words of French and English origin. But it appears never to have done so. As there was an already accepted word of French origin in place, with a newly-formed English-style past participle, 'boiled', there was no need.
7. *The Riverside Chaucer*, ed. by Larry D. Benson (Boston: Houghton Mifflin, 1987), p. 197.
8. All quotations are in modern spelling and taken from *The Towneley Cycle*, ed. by Peter Meredith, 2nd ed. (Leeds: School of English, University of Leeds, 1990), pp. 78–9 and 120–21. For the original see *The Wakefield Pageants in the Towneley Cycle*, ed. by A.C. Cawley (Manchester: Manchester University Press, 1958), pp. 34–35 and 66.

The Language of Medieval Cookery

Appendix A. Word list from *The Forme of Cury*, recipes 1–100

[Note: The use of 'u/v' has been modernized. Middle English 'y' (representing 'i') has been kept but given its modern position in the alphabet. The Middle English letters 'þ' ('th') and 'ȝ' (various 'g/y' sounds) have also been kept. Alphabetically, 'þ' has been treated as 'th', and 'ȝ' as if it were 'z'.

Abbreviations used are: Lat. for 'Latin'; OE for 'Old English'; OFr. for 'Old French'; ON for 'Old Norse'; (adj.), adjective; (adv.), adverb; (n.), noun; (v.), verb; and (pp), past participle. All nouns and adjectives, and some adverbs, have been included. All verb forms are given, with the exception of forms of 'be', 'do', 'have' and 'will'.

The numbers in square brackets indicate frequency of use. In the case of 'do' only the imperative 'do' and in the case of 'be' only 'buth' have been noted.]

Words present in Old English
abrode 'widely' [1]
anoon 'straightaway' [1]
apples (n.) [1]
arisith (v.) 'rises' [1]
askes (n.) ON 'ashes' [1]
aymers (n.) 'embers' [1]
ayren, eyren (n.) 'eggs' [28, 5]
benes (n.) 'beans' [3]
berst, breste (v.) 'burst' [1, 1]
best [1]
bete (v.) 'beat' [1]
betes (n.) 'beets' [from Lat.] [1]
bigynne (v.) 'begin' [1]
bladder (n.) [1]
blades (n.) 'stalks' [1]
blak (n.) 'the colour black' [1]
blode (n.) 'blood' [9]
boor (n.) 'boar' [1]
brayn (n.) 'brain' [1]
brede (n.) 'bread' [18]
breke (v.) 'break' [2]
breth (n.) 'air' [lit. 'breath'] [1]
briddes, bryddes, -ys (n.) 'birds' [2, 1, 1]
broth, broþ (n.) 'broth' [57, 2]
broun 'brown' [1]
buth (v.) 'are' [6]
butter, buttur (n.) 'butter' [from Lat.] [2, 4]
calf (n.) [1]
cast (v.) ON 'put, throw' [77]
cast (pp) ON 'put' [2]
chese (n.) 'cheese' [from Lat.] [7]
chykens, chikens (n.) 'chickens' [3, 1]
cleeve (v.) 'cut' [1]
clene 'clean'; (adv.) 'fully' [16]
cloth (n.) [4]
colde 'cold' [5]
cole (v.) 'cool' [6]
cool (n.) 'kale' [from Lat.] [1]
cowe (n.) 'cow' [5]
-cressis (n.) 'cresses' [1]
day, -es (n.) 'day(s)' [5, 2]
deer (n.) 'animal, deer' [1]

disshes, dysshes (n.) 'dishes' [from Lat.] [8, 3]
do (v.) 'put' [116]
doust (n.) 'dust, powder' [2]
dowe, dowh, dowȝ (n.) 'dough' [1, 1, 1]
drawe (v.) 'push, squeeze' [31]
drope (n.) 'drop' [1]
dry(e) (v.) 'dry' [1, 1]
erthe (n.) 'earth' [2]
erthen 'earthen' [3]
ete (v.) 'eat' [1]
faire, feyre 'good quality' [3, 1]
fallith (v.) 'falls' [2]
fast 'firmly, quickly' [3]
fat [1]
fenkel, fenel (n.) 'fennel' [from Lat.] [2, 1]
ferthe 'fourth' [1]
feþer (n.) 'feather' [1]
fire, fyre (n.) 'fire' [8, 9]
fle (v.) 'flay' [1]
flessh(e), fleissh, fleyssh (n.) 'flesh' [7, 1, 3, 1]
fowle (n.) 'bird' [1]
fresch 'fresh' [1]
ful 'full, fully' [1]
fylle (v.) 'fill' [1]
fyngur (n.) 'finger' [1]
fysshe, fisshe, fysche (n.) 'fish' [3, 1, 1]
gadre (v.) 'gather' [1]
garlec, garlek (n.) 'garlick' [5, 2]
gees (n.) 'geese' [4]
good, god(e) 'good quality' [3, 1, 42]
go(o)n (v.) 'go' [1, 1]
greke 'Greek' [from Lat.] [1]
grene 'green' [3]
grete 'large, long' [6]

grete (adv.) 'well, coarsely' [2]
groundon, -en (pp) 'ground, minced' [1, 1]
grynd(e), grinde (v.) 'grind, mince' [1, 27, 1]
gryndyng 'grinding' [1]
gyngever, gyngyver (n.) 'ginger' [or OFr.; from Lat.] [1, 1]
hakke (v.) 'chop' [1]
half [12]
harde 'hard' [5]
hares (n.) [2]
hatte (n.) 'scum, froth' [lit. 'hat'] [1]
hawthorn (n.) [1]
hede (n.) 'head' [1]
helde (v.) 'pour' [1]
hennes (n.) 'hens' [5]
heppes (n.) 'rose-hips' [2]
hewe (v.) 'cut, chop' [14]
hippe bone (n.) 'hip-bone' [1]
hole (n.) [1]
honde (n.) 'hand' [1]
hong (v.) 'hang' [1]
hony (n.) 'honey' [9]
hole, hool(e) 'whole' [4, 4, 2]
hote, hoot 'hot' [1, 4]
hulle (v.) 'remove husk, shell' [1]
hulles, hulkes, holes, -us (n.) 'hull(s)' [1, 1, 1, 1]
ihewe (pp) 'cut up' [1]
imelte (pp) 'melted' [1]
isode, y- (pp) 'boiled' [3, 6]
kele (v.) 'cool' [2]
kepe (v.) 'keep' [3]
kerf, kerue (v.) 'carve, cut' [2, 4]
kidde(s) (n.) ON 'kid(s)' [2]
knyf (n.) ON 'knife' [1]

kyn(e) (n.) 'cows, kine' [2]
lat (v.) 'let' [20]
lave (v.) 'wash' [or OFr. or Lat.] [1]
lay (v.) 'put, place' [20]
leke(s), -ys, leek (n.) 'leek(s)' [2, 3, 1, 1]
Lent (n.) [1]
leyve (n.) 'leaf,' (cf. *foile*) [1]
loke, look (v.) 'make sure' [7, 1]
lombe (n.) 'lamb' [1]
lyre, lire (n.) 'flesh' [1. 2]
lytel(l), lytle, litell (adj.; n.) 'little' [5, 1, 1, 1]
lyvour (n.) 'liver' [1]
make (v.) [23]
mede (n.) 'mead' [1]
meltede (pp) 'melted' [2]
mete (n.) 'food' [1]
morowe (n.) 'morrow, following day' [1]
morter (n.) 'mortar' [from Lat.] [8]
mylk(e) (n.) 'milk' [2, 24]
myng (v.) 'mix' [2]
myntes (n.) 'mints' [from Lat.] [1]
nede 'need' [1]
nost (n.) 'oast, kiln' [1]
ny3t (n.) 'night' [1]
nym (v.) 'take' [2]
offall (n.) 'offal' [1]
ootmeel (n.) 'oatmeal' [1]
opere, ooper 'other' [6, 5]
ovene (n.) 'oven' [1]
panne (n.) 'pan' [from Lat.] [3]
peeres (n.) 'pears' [from Lat.] [1]
peper (n.) 'pepper' [from Lat.] [8]
peskodde (n.) 'peascod' [1]
pesoun (n.) 'peas' [from Lat.] [3]
pigges (n.) 'pigs' [1]

pill, pulle (v.) 'peel' [2, 1]
pluk (v.) 'pluck' [1]
poke (n.) 'stomach' [lit. 'bag'] [1]
pot (n.) [from Lat.] [19]
pounde (n.) 'pound' [from Lat.] [1]
pryk (v.) ' prick' [1]
pulle (v.) 'pull' [1]
put (v.) [3]
pyke, pike (v.) 'pick (clean)' [or OFr., ON] [4, 3]
rawe 'raw' [11]
rede (n.) 'the colour red' [1]
rede 'red' [8]
rennyng 'liquid, runny' [2]
reþer (n.) 'ox' [1]
right 'really' [2]
roo (n.) 'roe-deer' [1]
rosis (n.) 'roses' [from Lat.] [1]
salt (n.) [57]
salt (v.) [12]
same [3]
self 'same, self' [10]
set (v.) [11]
seeþ, seþe, sethe, seeth (v.) 'boil' [68, 4, 3, 3,]
sew(e) (n.) 'sauce, broth, liquid' [or OFr.] [1, 12]
shepe (n.) 'sheep' [1]
shrede (v.) 'shread' [3]
skyn (n.) ON 'skin' [2]
slowe 'slow [1]
slyt(te) (v.) 'slit' [?OE/ON] [1, 1]
small, smale 'small' [12, 19]
smyte (v.) 'chop, break' [13]
sode, sodyn, -en (pp) 'boiled' [2, 1, 2]
sowe (v.) 'sew' [1]
spryng (v.) 'sprinkle' [1]

stede, in ... of 'in place of' [1]
stere (v.) 'stir' [1]
stondyng 'thick [of a sauce], set' [9]
stones (n.) [2]
stoppe (v.) 'stuff' [1]
strawe (v.) 'strew, sprinkle' [1]
strong [cf. (*powdour*) *fort*] [1]
sum 'some' [1]
sumdel 'fairly' [1]
sumwhat 'fairly' [1]
swete 'sweet' [3]
swyne (n.) 'swine' [3]
swyng (v.) 'beat' [5]
synewes (n.) 'sinews' [1]
table (n.) 'board, table' [or OFr.; from Lat.] [1]
tak(e) (v.) ON [4, 197]
take (pp) ON 'taken' [1]
teere (v.) 'tear' [1]
temper(e) (v.) 'mix' [or OFr.] [10, 1]
tese (v.) 'pull apart' [1]
teysed (pp) 'pulled apart' [1]
thik (v.) 'thicken' [1]
thridde, þridde 'third' [1, 2]
thriddendele (n.) 'third part' [1]
thryse 'thrice, three times' [1]
togedre, togydre, -er 'together' [1, 11, 8]
toun- (n.) 'town-' [1]
twyse 'twice' [1]
thyk(ke), thicke, thik 'thick' [4, 1, 1, 1]
thyng(es) (n.) 'thing(s)' [1, 1]
thynne, þin 'thin' [3, 1]
unwaisshed 'unwashed' [1]
wais(s)he, waische (v.) 'wash' [2, 10, 3]
warly 'with care' [1]
water (n.) [35]
wel(e), well 'well' [20, 5, 1]

wete 'wet' [2]
whete (n.) 'wheat' [1]
while (n.) [2]
whyte (n.) 'the colour white' [1]
whyte, white, wyte (n.) 'white (of egg, of leeks)' [4, 2, 1]
whyt(e), white (adj.) 'white' [1, 6, 12]
wise (n.) 'way' [2]
won (n.) 'quantity' [1]
wrye (v.) 'cover' [1]
wryng (v.) 'press' [2]
wyndewe (v.) 'winnow' [1]
wyne (n.) 'wine' [from Lat.] [32]
ybroke (pp) 'broken apart, in pieces' [1]
ycorve (pp) 'carved, cut' [1]
ydrawe (pp) 'strained, separated' [2]
yfere, in fere 'together' [3, 1]
yground(e) (pp) 'ground, minced' [1, 1]
yhewe (pp) 'chopped' [2]
yholed (pp) 'covered' [1]
ynowh(ȝ) 'sufficiently, enough' [6, 2]
yong 'young' [1]
ypylled (pp) 'peeled' [1]
yslyt (pp) 'sliced' [1]
yteysed (pp) 'pulled apart' [1]
ysope (n.) 'hyssop' [from Lat.] [2]
ȝelow (n.) 'the colour yellow' [1]
ȝolkes, ȝelkys (n.) 'yolks' [17, 1]

Words probably OE

codlyng (n.) 'codling' [1]
haddok (n.) 'haddock' [1]
hake (n.) [1]

Words from French

almand, almaund, -e(s), -us (n.) 'almond(s)' [1, 3, 3, 22, 1]

46

alye, alay (v.) 'mix, thicken' [12, 5]
amydoun (n.) 'wheat starch' [2]
aneys (n.) 'anise' [5]
aray (v.) 'prepare, do' [1]
avance (n.) 'avens' [1]
bacoun (n.) 'bacon' [1]
blaunched (pp) 'blanched, skinned' [13]
boile, boyle (v.) 'boil' [22, 4]
boiled, boyled (pp) [1, 1]
bolas (n.) 'bullace plum' [1]
borage (n.) [2]
boyl(l)yng (adj., n.) 'boiling' [2, 1]
brawn (n.) [4]
bray(e) (v.) 'crush, grind, break up' [7, 1]
brayed (pp) 'ground' [2]
braying 'grinding' [1]
caboches (n.) 'cabbages' [2]
canel(l) (n.) 'cinnamon' [7, 3]
capouns (n.) 'capons' [or OE] [9]
caraway (n.) [or Lat.] [1]
cawdel (n.) 'caudle' [1]
charlet (n.) [a dish name] [2]
chawf (v.) 'heat' [1]
chibolles (n.) 'chibols, spring onions' [1]
chiches (n.) 'chick-peas' [1]
chiryse, chelberyes (n.) 'cherries' [1, 1]
clarifie, clarify, claryfye (v.) 'clarify' [1, 1, 1]
clarified, claryfied (pp) 'clarified' [4, 1]
close (v.) 'enclose' [2]
clowes (n.) 'cloves' [4]
coliaundre, coly- (n.) 'coriander' [or OE] [1, 1]
colour(e) (v.) [20, 1]
colours (n.) [3]
comyn (n.) 'cumin' [1]
confyt (n.) 'comfit, sugar-coating' [3]
connynges, connes (n.) 'conies, rabbits' [8, 1]
-coraunce, corauns 'of Corinth, currants' [5, 1]
covere (v.) 'cover' [3]
cowche (v.) 'lay, place' [1]
crem (n.) 'cream' [1]
curlewes (n.) 'curlews' [1]
-cypre 'of Cyprus' [1]
dates (n.) [4]
defaute (n.) 'lack' [1]
douce, dowce (adj.) 'sweet (powder)' [21, 2]
dresse (v.) 'prepare, serve' [4]
dyce (n.) 'dice, cubes' [2]
dyce (v.) 'cut in cubes' [4]
dyverse 'various, diverse' [1]
erbes, -is, herbes (n.) 'herbs' [7, 2, 1]
esy 'easy' [1]
esely 'easily' [1]
fars (n.) 'stuffing' [1]
fesauntes (n.) 'pheasants' [2]
florissh (v.) 'garnish' [10]
flour (v.) 'garnish' [6]
flour(s) (n.) 'flour, the best part; flower(s)' [21, 1]
foile, foyle(s) (n.) 'leaf/leaves, foil(s)' [2, 1, 1]
force (v.) 'season' [1]
found (v.) 'mix' [1]
fort (adj.) 'strong (powder)' [19]
fry(e) (v.) 'fry' [5, 4]
fryed (pp) 'fried' [4]
furmente (n.) 'frumenty' [1]
fyges (n.) 'figs' [2]
fylet(t)es (n.) 'fillets' [1, 2]

galantyne (n.) 'galantine' [2]
gleyre (n.) 'egg white' [1]
gobet(t)es (n.) 'gobbets, lumps' [2, 6]
gowrdes (n.) 'gourds' [1]
grapes (n.) [2]
grate (v.) [2]
grated(e) (pp) 'grated, minced' [1, 1]
grece, grees (n.) 'fat' [14, 1]
grewel (n.) 'gruel' [2]
gylofre (n.) 'gillyflower' [2]
gynger, ginger (n.) 'ginger' [or OE] [24, 1]
iblaunched(e) (pp) 'blanched, skinned' [1, 1]
iboiled (pp) 'boiled' [1]
ifounded (pp) 'mixed' [1]
iowtes (n.) 'pot herbs, [dish made from them]' [1]
langdebef (n.) 'lang-de-boeuf' [1]
lard (n.) '(pork) fat' [1]
lesh(e) (v.) 'slice' [2. 4]
licour (n.) 'liquid' [1]
los(e)yns (n.) 'losenges' [2, 1]
loyne(s) (n.) 'loin(s)' [1, 1]
lye (v.) 'mix, thicken' [4]
lyre, lyour, layour (n.) 'thickening' [2, 2, 3]
macys (n.) 'mace' [1]
manere (n.) 'manner' [2]
medle (v.) 'mix' [5]
messe (v.) 'serve, arrange, garnish' [29]
morcels (n.) 'morsels' [1]
motoun (n.) 'mutton' [2]
mynce (v.) 'mince, cut small, grate' [7]
mynced (pp) 'minced, cut small, grated' [5]
noumbles (n.) 'entrails' [6]

obleys (n.) 'round wafers' [1]
oile, oyle (n.) 'oil' [8, 6]
orage (n.) [1]
oynouns (n.) 'onions' [21]
paper (n.) [or OE] [1]
pare (v.) 'peel, trim, prepare' [3]
part, pertye (n.) 'part' [2, 2]
past (n.) 'dough' [or Lat.] [1]
payndemayn (n.) 'good quality white bread' [3]
pecys (n.) 'pieces' [or Lat.] [11]
peions (n.) 'pigeons' [1]
pellydore (n.) 'the herb, pellitory' [1]
perboile, -boyle (v.) 'partially/ thoroughly boil' [15, 5]
perr(e)y (n.) 'vegetable purée' [2, 1]
persel (n.) 'parsley' [or OE] [9]
pertruches (n.) 'partridges' [1]
pestels (n.) 'pestles, legs' [1]
plauntede (pp) 'stuck, decorated' [1]
pomme garnat (n.) 'pomegranate' [1]
porcioun (n.) 'portion' [3]
pork(e) (n.) 'pork' [14, 1]
porrettes (n.) 'leeks' [1]
porpays, -eys (n.) 'porpoise' [1, 1]
possynet (n.) 'posnet, pot' [4]
potell (n.) 'pottle' [1]
powdour(s), -or, pouder, -ur (n.) 'powder' [76, 3, 1, 1, 1]
powdur (v.) 'sprinkle, dust' [2]
pownas (n.) '?a purple colour' [1]
presse (v.) 'press, squeeze' [2]
purslarye (n.) 'purslane' [1]
pynes (n.) 'pine nuts' [6]
quantite (n.) 'quantity' [10]
quarter 'cut in quarters' [1]
quarter (v.) [3]

quybibes (n.) 'cubebs' [or Lat.] [1]
quinces (n.) [1]
raisouns, rays- (n.) 'raisins' [5, 5]
ravioles (n.) 'ravioli' [1]
rew (n.) 'rue' [1]
roller (n.) 'rolling-pin' [1]
rosee (n.) 'rosé, [a dish name]' [1]
roost (n.) 'roast' [1]
ro(o)st (v.) 'roast' [4, 2]
rosted (pp) 'roasted' [1]
rostyng 'roasting' [1]
ruayn 'of the late hay harvest' [1]
rys(e) (n.) 'rice' [14, 2]
safroun, saffron, saff(e)roun (n.) 'saffron' [42, 2, 1, 1]
saveray (n.) 'savory' [3]
saundres (n.) 'sandalwood' [6]
sawge (n.) 'sage' [6]
sawse (n.) 'sauce' [2]
scald, skalde (v.) 'scald' [2, 1]
scaldyng 'scalding' [1]
serve (v.) [44]
siryppe (n.) 'syrop' [1]
sklyse, sclyse (n.) 'slice' [1, 1]
skym (v.) 'skim' [2]
skyrwittes (n.) 'a root vegetable' [1]
spices (n.) [2]
stewe (v.) 'stew' [2]
straynour, -owr (n.) 'strainer' [11, 1]
sugur (n.) 'sugar' [or Lat.] [30]
tartletes, turteletes (n.) 'tartlets' [2, 1]
tendre 'tender' [2]
tost (v.) 'toast' [2]
turnesole (n.) 'turnsole' [1]
unblaunched 'unskinned' [3]
veel (n.) 'veal' [2]
venesoun (n.) 'venison' [1]

verious (n.) 'verjuice' [5]
vessel(s) (n.) 'container(s)' [2, 1]
violet (n.) 'the plant violet' [1]
vyneger, -ur, -re (n.) 'vinegar' [11, 1, 1]
wafrouns (n.) 'wafers' [1]
yboiled (pp) 'boiled' [1]
ydyced (pp) 'cut into cubes' [1]
yfarsyd (pp) 'stuffed' [2]
yforced (pp) 'seasoned' [2]
yfoundred (pp) 'mixed, steeped' [1]
yfryed (pp) 'fried' [2]
ygrated(e) (pp) 'grated' [2, 1]
yleeshed (pp) 'sliced' [1]
ymynced (pp) 'minced, cut small' [7]
ypared (pp) 'peeled' [1]
yrosted (pp) 'roasted' [1]
yskaldid (pp) 'scalded' [2]
ystyued, ystewed (pp) 'stewed' [2, 1]
ytosted, i- (pp) 'toasted' [1, 1]

Words from Latin
alkenet (n.) 'alkanet' [4]
elena campana (n.) 'elecampane' [1]
funges (n.pl.) 'fungus' [1]
lopins (n.) 'lupins' [1]
pasturnakes (n.) 'parsnips' [1]
rapes (n.) 'turnips' [or OFr.] [1]
rosemarye (n.) 'rosemary' [1]

APPENDIX B. TITLES OF THE FIRST ONE HUNDRED DISHES FROM *FORME OF CURY.*

The French elements are in italic.

1. *frumente*
2. *blaunche porre*
3. *grounden* benes
4. *drawen* benes
5. grewel *forc*ed
6. *Caboches* in *potage*
7. *Rapes* in *potage*
8. *Iowtes* of Flessh
9. *Chebolace*
10. *Gourdes* in *potage*
11. *Ryse* of flessh
12. *Funges*
13. *Bruce*
14. *Corat*
15. *Noumbles*
16. *Roo* broth
17. *Tredure*
18. *Mounchelet*
19. *Bukkenade*
20. *Connat*
21. *Drepe*
22. *Mawmenee*
23. *Egurdouce*
24. *Capouns* in *councy*
25. Hares in *talbotes*
26. Hares in *papdele*
27. *Connynges* in *cyuee*
28. *Connynges* in *grauey*
29. Chykens in *grauey*
30. *Fylettes* in *galyntyne*
31. Pygges in *sawse sawge*
32. *Sawse madame*
33. Gees in hoggepot
34. *Caruel* of *pork*
35. Chykens in *cawdel*
36. Chykens in *hocchee*
37. For to *boile* …
38. *Blank maunger*
39. *Blank dessorre*
40. *Morree*
41. *Charlet*
42. *Charlet* y*forc*ed
43. *Cawdel ferry*
44. *Iusshell*
45. *Iusshell* en*forc*ed
46. *Mortrews*
47. *Mortrews blank*
48. *Brewet* of *Almayne*
49. *Peiouns* y*stew*ed
50. *Losyns*
51. *Tartlettes*
52. *Pynnonade*
53. *Rosee*
54. *Cormarye*
55. Newe *noumbles* of deer
56 & 57. Nota
58. *Spynee*
59. *Chyryse*
60. *Paynfoundew*
61. *Crytayne*
62. *Vinegrate*
63. *Founet*
64. *Douce iame*
65. *Connynges* in *cyrip*
66. *Lumbard Leche*
67. *Connynges* in *clere* broth

68. *Payn ragoun*
69. *Lete lardes*
70. *Furmente* with *porpays*
71. *Perrey* of pesoun
72. Pesoun of *Almayne*
73. *Chyches*
74. *Lopins*
75. *Frenche iowtes*
76. *Makke* (?)
77. *Aquapatys*
78. *Salat*
79. Fenkel in *soppes*
80. *Elat*
81. *Appulmoy*
82. Slyt *soppes*
83. *Letelorye*
84. *Sowpes dorry*
85. *Rapey*
86. *Sawse Sarzyne*
87. *Creme* of *almaundes*
88. *Grewel* of *almaundes*
89. *Iowtes* of *almaund* mylke
90. *Cawdel* of *almaund* mylk
91. *Fygey*
92. *Pochee*
93. *Brewet* of ayren
94. *Rauioles*
95. *Makerouns*
96. *Tostee*
97. *Gynggaudy*
98. *Erbowle*
99. *Rysmole*
100. *Vyaunde Cypre.*

APPENDIX C. A SPECIMEN OF THE *FORME OF CURY* AS IT EXISTS IN BRITISH LIBRARY, MS HARLEY 1605 PT.3, FOL.107V. (SEE THE FRONTISPIECE TO HIEATT AND BUTLER, *CURYE ON INGLYSCH*.)

Mortrewes of fiche
Take colde lynge . haddok oþer hake &
þe lyueres wᵗ þo rownes . & sethe hit welle .
in watur . pyke owte þe bones . & grynde
smal þo fiche . drawe a lyoure of almaun
des . & bred wᵗ þo self broþ . & do þer to þi fiche
igrownden . & sethe hyt . do þer to powdur
fort . salt & saffron . & make hit stondyng
Blaunche almaundes . & grynde hem .
and drawe hem up wᵗ watur . wesche
þi ryse clene . & do þer to sugur roche . and
salt . let hyt be stondyng . frye almaundes
browne & floriche hyt þer wᵗ . or wᵗ sugur.

This represents recipes 128 and 129 in Hieatt and Butler. Underlinings and superscript letters represent abbreviations in the manuscript. Punctuation is given as it is in the manuscript. 'colde lynge' in l.2 is an error for 'codlynge'. The second recipe begins with 'Blaunche almaundes' and is headed in Hieatt and Butler 'Ryse of fische daye'.

Appendix D. A linguistic comparison of two recipes: a Middle English translation of an Anglo-Norman original

The recipes contained in British Library, MS Additional 46919 are translated from an Anglo-Norman original represented by British Library, MS Royal 12.C.xii. In the two recipes that follow, the first lines are a translation of the Anglo-Norman, the second the AN text itself (in **bold**), the third the Middle English text (in *italic*), and the fourth a translation of the ME. Modern punctuation has been introduced into the translations.

A.	Milk of almonds, flour of rice, flesh of capon,	1
Blanc desiree.	**Let de alemaundes flur de rys braoun de chapoun**	
Blanc desire.	*Milke of alemaundes flour of ris braun of chapoun*	
	Milk of almonds, flour of rice, flesh of capon,	

ginger choice, sugar white, wine white; each of these ingredients should be boiled   2
gyngyvre triee sucre blank vyn blanc chescun des parties deyvent estre boillez
gyngere itried sucre hwit wyn uchon of þoes schulen boillen
ginger choice, sugar white wine; each one of these should boil

in a clean pot and then put in the container in which it will be made,   3
en un net possenet and pus mys en le vessel en quei il serront fet
in a clene possenet & soppen idon in þe vessel waryn hit schal beon imad
in a clean pot and then [be] put in the container in which it is to be made,

in a place without dust; pomegranate placed on top   4
en un lu saunz poudre poumme gernette paunté desus
in a stude wyþouten vulþe & poume gernet to strey3en aboven
in a place without dirt, and pomegranate to scatter on top

The Language of Medieval Cookery

B.   Grape from the vine, hock of sheep; when these sweet things are well   5
Hauseleamye.   **Grape de vigne garette de motun quant ces deus choses seient bien**
Hauceleamye.   *Grape of vine garette of moutoun qwen þeos swete þinges beoþ wel*
                          Grape from the vine, hock of sheep; when these sweet things are well

boiled together in a little of the broth with verjuice, then it should be well strained   6
boylys ensemble en poi de breo ou vertjus donqe doit estre bien colee
ysoden togedre a lute broþ in þe vergus
boiled together [in] a little broth in the verjuice,

and thoroughly; then take a spring chicken and cut it up and put it in that boiling   7
e nettement donqe pernez poule de mars e le coupez e metez en cel boiller
              nim poule de mars & hew am & do am to þilke boillyng
              take spring chicken and chop them and put them in that boiling

and when it is well boiled put a large amount of powder of ginger   8
e quant il soit bien boille metez grant plente de poudre de gyngyvre
& qwen abeoþ wel iboilled do god plente of poudre of gynger
and when they are well boiled put a large amount of powder of ginger

to remove the bitterness of the grapes. Colour should be green   9
pur oster le amerete des grapes colour ert vert.
vorte don awy þe bitternesse of þe grapes þe colour grene.
to get rid of the bitterness of the grapes; the colour, green

French words used in the ME version of the two recipes quoted above are, nouns: *alemaundes, braun, chapoun, colour, flour, garette, gyngere, grapes, moutoun, plenté, possenet, poudre, poume gernet, poule de mars, ris, sucre, vergus, vessel*; verbs: *boillen, iboilled, itried*. French words not used are: nouns/adjectives – **amereté**/*bitternesse*, **blank**/*hwit*, **breo**/*broþ*, **choses**/*þinges*, **deus**/*swete*, **grant**/*god*, **let**/*milke*, **lu**/*stude*, **net**/*clene*, **plaunté**/*streyȝen*, **poudre**/*vulþe*, **vert**/*grene*; verbs – **boylys**/*ysoden*, **coupez**/*hew*, **fet**/*imad*, **mys**/*idon*, **oster**/*don awy*, **pernez**/*nim*.

Evidence of this kind is difficult to interpret. By the early fourteenth century (the date of the manuscript) English had a long history of contact with French in one form or another. By that date many French words were so common in English that they had taken over entirely from any earlier

English or Norse words, and were no doubt simply thought of as English. At the same time, some French words alternated in use with English words with the same meaning (doublets), some were still being introduced into English (briefly or permanently), and some remained purely French in use. The translator may have used an AN word because it was the appropriate culinary term or he may have used it because he didn't know what the word meant, and therefore couldn't translate it. If the translator of these recipes is indeed William Herebert, then we might expect him as a learned man to know what **garrette** or **poule de mars** mean. But, on the other hand, his learning simply may not have extended into such areas

Many of these words never entered into normal English usage (**amereté, choses, let**). Some entered the language (often only for a limited period) with a specialized meaning or use (**blank, deus, net, possenet**), or only momentarily (**garette**). Some words used here retain French spellings (for example, *sucre*); and French word order is sometimes kept (for example, *gyngere itried*) – very possibly the effects of translating. On the other hand, it is worth noting that the stems of some French words are given English prefixes or suffixes (for example: i-*tri*-ed, *boill*-en, *boill*-yng, i-*boill*-ed); a clear sign that the words are naturalized. It is, by and large, the ingredient words which are French, the words descriptive of the method that are English, but in translation there is always the temptation to use the word, if one exists, that is like the one in the original language (in these two recipes, 'boil' [4 appearances] as opposed to 'seethe' [1 appearance]).

The importance of the existence of these comparative texts is that they show the effects of translating from Anglo-Norman, demonstrating up to a point the extent to which the vocabulary is influenced by the language translated from. What this present comparison reveals, it seems to me, is the difficulty of deciding whether a specialized culinary language existed at this date, and if it did to what extent it was distinguished by its French-based vocabulary or grammar. A Franciscan *lector* at Oxford may or may not be the best guide to normal culinary usage. Too little is known about William Herebert to tell.

CHAPTER THREE

A CLOSE LOOK AT THE COMPOSITION OF SIR HUGH PLAT'S *DELIGHTES FOR LADIES*.

Malcolm Thick

Sir Hugh Plat's father was a Hertfordshire man who became a successful London brewer. Hugh was left property and land in London and elsewhere. He lived as a gentleman, first in London and then in the suburban village of Bethnal Green, having been suitably educated at Cambridge and Lincoln's Inn. He was a 'virtuoso', a gentleman with time on his hands who engaged in the study of a wide range of subjects including agriculture, gardening, metallurgy, distilling, wines and beers, alchemy, colours and dyeing, medicine, food and drink. Such a list understates his breadth of research for he applied his knowledge to a number of practical problems, such as the need to feed London in the dearth years of the 1590s, the preservation of food and water for long sea voyages, new types of fertilizer and a range of miscellaneous mechanical inventions. He was a practising, albeit unlicensed, doctor. Although a gentleman, a status confirmed by a knighthood in 1605, he was interested in ways of making money from his inventions and ideas.

He wrote a number of books and pamphlets, including *Delightes for Ladies* which is the main concern of this paper. The British Library has some of his manuscripts, including many relating to the subject matter of *Delightes for Ladies* and these notes, although not complete, allow us to examine the preparation of the book as we can of few others of this age. I hope to show how Plat produced the book from his notes, what his sources were, why some recipes and ideas appear in the book, and to use some of the material in the book as an introduction to his ideas and personal ambitions.

Delightes for Ladies was, to judge from its publishing history, very successful. Entered into the Stationers' Company records in October 1599, it may have first appeared in 1600. There certainly was an edition on 1602, four more by 1610, and at least a further 16 editions by 1656.[1]

It undoubtedly is a very pleasing book to handle. The pages of early editions are small with the text on each page surrounded by an ornate border.

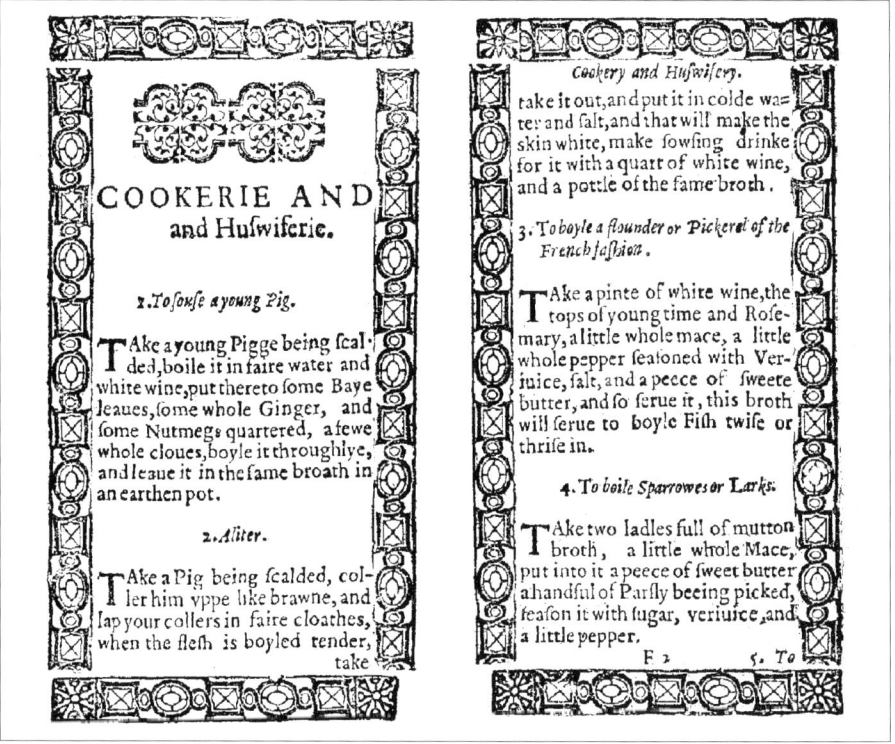

Figure 8. Pages from the 1609 edition of Delightes for Ladies, *showing the decorative borders.*

An introductory poem by Plat, much better than most doggerel found at the beginning of popular books of the time, summarizes the contents and also Plat's publications to date. Indeed, the poem serves as an excellent, and elegant, abstract of the work. (Maybe learned journals today should require abstracts in verse.) A decent index leads one into the text, arranged in small numbered chapters in four sections: 'The Art of Preserving, Conserving, Candying &c.'; 'Secrets in Distillation'; 'Cookery and Huswifery'; and 'Sweet Powders, oyntments, beauties, &c.' By no means the first book published in England to tackle these subjects, it is better arranged than most of its predecessors, with less evidence of recipes culled uncritically from the 'books of secrets' popular at the time. Pleasing to the eye and easy to use, the book's success can be readily understood.

As we are considering food in this volume, I will say little of the last section on cosmetics etc., bar telling you there are 37 recipes here, some for perfumed soap and washing water, and many for improving the appearance: such as to colour hair, remove facial blemishes or clean teeth, a fair representation of the preoccupations of the time, especially in the competitive world of the Court which Plat knew well. Some gentlewomen (and men) were tempted to go to extreme lengths to improve their looks: Plat warns gentlewomen to be careful when barbers clean their teeth with aqua fortis (nitric acid), 'for unlesse the same be well allayed, and carefully applied, shee may bee forced to borrow a ranke of teeth to eat her dinner, unlesse her gummes do help her the better.'[2]

On reading the text, it is clear that the cookery and household management section is the weakest part of the book. Only 35 pages long, it consists of several chapters[3] on preserving, some interesting and detailed passages on flavoured butters, a few miscellaneous chapters on such topics as candle-making, table-salt, flavoured vinegars, bottling beer and oddities like how to keep flies from oil paintings. The recipes do not provide even a basic guide to the main cooking techniques – sousing and boiling only are included. Many of the recipes themselves are poor, missing out vital stages of the cooking process. Take the recipe (illustrated opposite):

> To boil Sparrows or Larks.
> Take two ladles full of Mutton broth, a little whole mace: put into it a peece of sweet butter, a handfull of Parsly being picked: season it with sugar, veriuice, and a little pepper.

This one-sentence recipe does not specify a cooking vessel, gives no instructions for cooking or serving the birds – in fact, no birds are mentioned at all![4]

Why, when most of his recipes and instructions are detailed and comprehensive, are the cookery ones relatively poor? Part of the answer is that Plat did not have an interest in cookery as such – there are no cookery recipes in his own hand in the pages of manuscripts on food which have survived.

The cookery recipes in *Delightes for Ladies* were not, in fact, written by Plat. In a notebook in the British Library, now Sloane MS 2189, we find the origin of the bulk of them. These manuscript notes, headed 'Divers receipts of cookery', are not in Plat's hand or usual spelling – they are not his work. He simply placed them in the cookery section, with all faults, to form the backbone of this part of the book.

Plat's borrowing from this source did not end with cookery recipes. Twenty-seven out of the seventy-three chapters in the preserving section (the largest section of the book) are from this source. And these are not minor recipes used to fill out the text: one is an eleven-page treatise, 'The art of

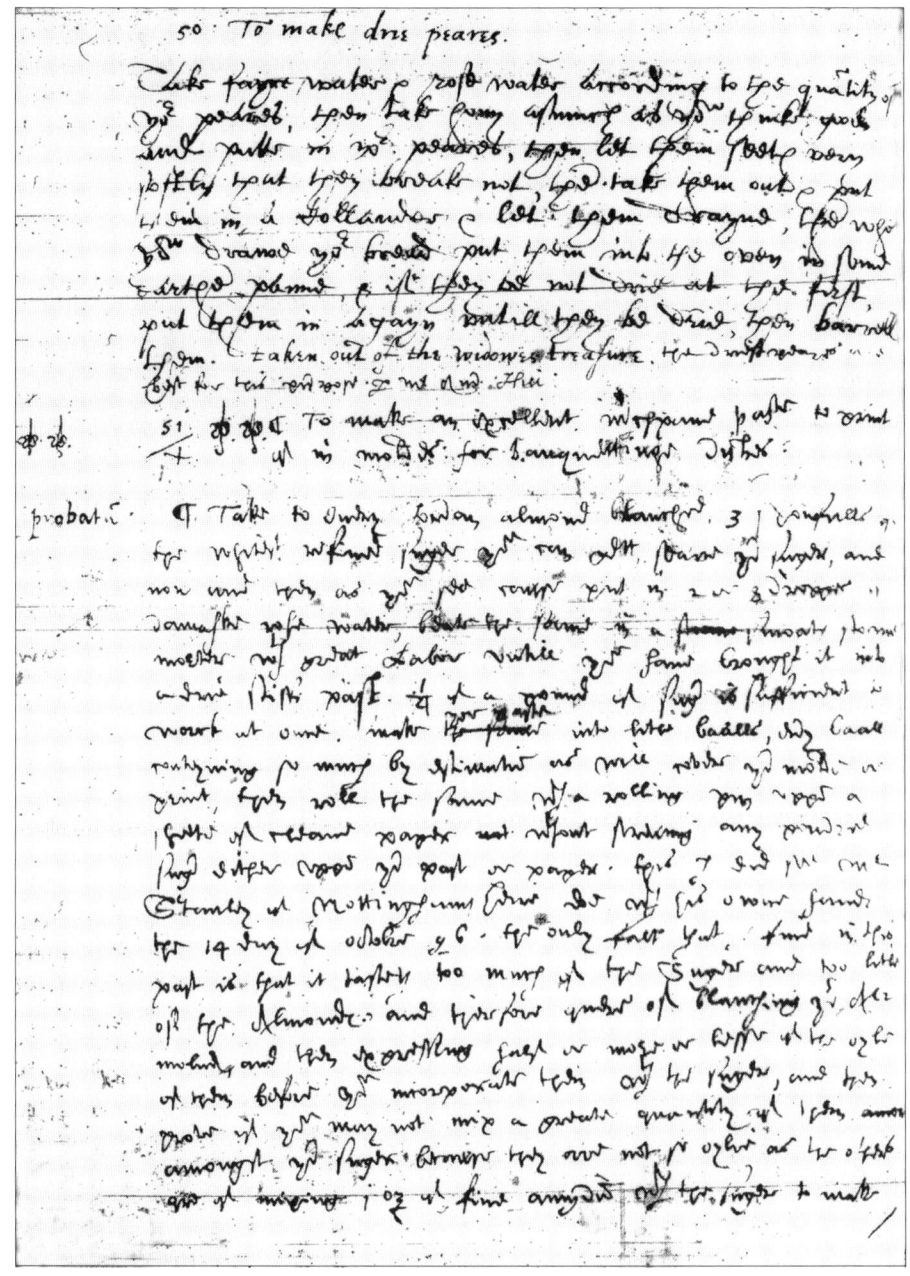

Figure 9. A page from British Library Sloane MS 2189 (f.64a), showing the respective hands of 'T.T.' and Hugh Plat. (Reproduction, the British Library.)

comfet-making, teaching how to cover all kinds of seeds, fruits or spices with suger.'[5] This detailed and practical chapter takes one through the whole process of manufacturing comfits, beginning with a list of the utensils required, then moving from basic comfit-making to variations of flavour, shape and colour. The other 'borrowed' preserving recipes cover the making of sugar plate, jumbolls, marchpane, ginger breads and bisket-breads, puff pastry, jellies, quince pastes, marmalades, preserving citrus fruits, and candying with hard-rock candy. The recipe 'To make sucket of Lettuce stalks' which has been commented upon as one of Plat's more unusual ideas, comes from the borrowed source, as does that for gingerbread 'used at the Court, and in all Gentlemens houses at festivall times' and that for 'Quidini of Quinces'. In short, many recipes which have been quoted by historians over the years from *Delightes for Ladies* as the work of Plat, are by someone else.[6]

Who was the author to whom Plat was indebted? The Sloane manuscript 2189 is composed of two notebooks bound together. The original first leaf of the larger one was written by our unknown author: instructions to make putty.[7] The putty recipe concludes, 'The first that ever I made proved T.T.' Numerous other recipes 'proved' by 'T.T.' in the manuscript provide us with the initials of the author.

A gap of a page after the putty recipe is followed by two-and-a-half pages of bread-making advice in the unknown hand, followed by recipes written by Plat. This pattern of recipes by T.T. with additions by Plat is repeated throughout the notebook, with sections on preserving and cookery, bread, beer, gardening, candle-making, dyeing, leather, ink, paints, and organ pipes. T.T. thus wrote his notes before Plat and Sir Hugh used them as a template around which he entered his own observations, a conjecture confirmed by the older spellings used by T.T. and a couple of dates in his manuscript: a candle wax recipe dated 1559 and a small comfit recipe of 1561. Two recipes out of *The Widowes Treasure* of 1585 were, I think, added by another hand, so Plat probably acquired the papers after that date but before 1588, the earliest dated recipe in Plat's hand in the manuscript.

In *Floreas Paradise*, his book on gardening, Plat reproduced many of the notes T.T. wrote on gardening, attributing one to '*T.T.* a Parson'.[8] T.T.'s observations on the repair of organ pipes and his detailed notes on candle-making support this profession: in particular, a recipe for a Candlemas candle 'for a trendell on Candlemas day'. A *trental* was a set of 30 successive masses for the dead, a Catholic rite. I believe that T.T. may have been a priest in Mary's reign and much of his manuscript may date from as early as the 1550s. He mentioned frequently the urban occupations of apothecaries and brewers, making it probable that he was a Londoner. His cookery recipes are not good but he had a close acquaintance with comfit-making and banqueting stuff, as evidenced by the detail of some of the recipes Plat published.[9]

Only two men can I find who might fit the few facts known of T.T. Thomas Thurland, who was appointed master of the Savoy Hospital, probably in 1557, and died in 1574, and Thomas Tymme, Rector of St Anthony in Budge Row, who was appointed in 1566. Thurland, a priest but also a mining entrepreneur, foreign traveller and an embezzler described as 'a papist of scandalous life' was an intelligent man who might well have made the sort of notes produced by T.T. Unfortunately his handwriting is not the same as T.T.'s. Thomas Tymme was also an unusual clergyman, who turned from writing devotional works to books on alchemy, a subject of great interest to Plat. Given this shared interest, Tymme might also have been T.T.[10]

I believe that the manuscript by T.T. was the starting point of *Delightes for Ladies*. As noted above, there is a dated recipe by Plat from 1588, the next is from 1595 and a scattering of dates occur between then and 1599 (the year the book was entered in the Stationers' Company records). The position of these later dated recipes in the manuscript indicate that Plat added many recipes in the few years before *Delightes for Ladies* was published, building up around T.T.'s notes a corpus of ideas from which he could write his new book. He also drew some recipes from another notebook written-up in the 1590s[11] and took material from his earlier book of 1594, *The Jewell House of Art and Nature*. These sources account for most of the recipes in the food sections of *Delightes for Ladies*.

Plat used about a dozen recipes copied exactly or paraphrased from *The Jewell House of Art and Nature* but he was not merely filling up *Delightes for Ladies* with old material.[12] Some have been copied without passages later considered irrelevant – he removed a long criticism of vintners for adulteration from the wormwood wine chapter and recipes for drying rose leaves and extracting spirit of roses are cut down.[13]

The chapter 'To keep the iuyce of Orenges and Lemmons all the yeare for sauce…' is a good example of a rambling entry in *The Jewell House* which Plat edited and revised, adding for his London lady-readers a useful tip to save money:

And because that profit and skill united do grace each other, if (curious Ladies) you will lend eares, and follow my direction, I will heer furnish a great number of you (I would I could furnish you all) with the iuyce of the best Civill Orenges at an easy price. About Allhollantide, or soone after, you may buy the inward palp of Civill Orenges, wherein the iuyce resteth, of the comfit-makers for a small matter, who doe onely or principally respect their rindes; to preserve and make Orenge doles withall, this iuyce you may prepare and reserve as before.[14]

There is a chapter on purifying salad oil in both books, but they are entirely different, and although both *The Jewell House* and *Delightes for Ladies* have instructions for keeping oysters, he rethinks his earlier reliance on sea water or brine as a preservative, adding wine vinegar to produce a more reliable liquor. In the case of flavoured butter, Plat provides a cross-reference to the earlier book, as he does in the detailed chapter on moulding and casting animals in sugar-paste, where he speculates that the wax moulds described in *The Jewell House* might be used for these elaborate banqueting conceits.[15]

The only other published book acknowledged by Plat as source for material in *Delightes for Ladies* is the treatise on cookery by Bartolomeo Scappi, published in Venice in 1570. Plat mentions this book by 'the maister cooke of Pope Pius Quintus, his privie kitchen', both in *The Jewell House* and in *Delightes for Ladies* and he was clearly impressed by it, as indeed he was by many aspects of Italian cuisine.[16]

Plat gathered a number of the recipes in *Delightes for Ladies* from friends and acquaintances, although specific attributions in the text are few. Eleanour Sinclair Rohde praised Plat's revelation of his sources in his gardening book *Floreas Paradise*, which 'is full of information gleaned in all parts of England and in every case he mentions the name of his informant'.[17] But *Floreas Paradise* is the only book where sources are liberally quoted. It appeared in 1608, soon before his death, and Plat, as he wrote in the introduction '…not knowing the length of my dayes, nay, assuredly knowing that they are drawing to their periode', simply had not time to tidy his manuscript by removing the attributions, queries and notes which litter the pages. He was probably too ill to supervise the printing.[18]

Although few names of informants are printed in *Delightes for Ladies*, we can augment our knowledge of Plat's sources by going back to his manuscripts and also looking for allusions in the text. In particular, he includes many references to London tradesmen involved in supplying food, drink, and medicine. He suggests using lead-lined earthenware pots 'such as the Gold finers call their hookers, and serve to receive their Aqua fortis' for storage of rose-water and dried rose leaves. London traders supply him with materials – the orange pulp from comfit-makers mentioned already and wine lees to preserve quinces from taverners or wine merchants.[19]

Sometimes he claims that he has improved on the traders' own practices: so his wormwood wine was 'a more neat and wholesome wine for your body, than that which is sold at the Stillyard', (presumably imported from Germany); by following the recipe for syrup of violets 'you may gain one quarter of syrup, more than diverse Apothecaries doe'; he promised bottled ale 'that should farre exceede all the Ale that mother Bunch made in her lifetime'.[20] He was afraid that his method of preserving lobsters and other crustaceans would hurt fishmongers' businesses 'who, onely in respect of their speedy decay, doe now and then afford a penny worth in them'. But, if they took note of his way of preserving salmon, 'Vintners and Cookes may make profit thereof when it is scarce in the markets and salmon, thus prepared, may be profitably brought out of Ireland, and sold in London or elswhere'. He was scathing about ready-made mustard sold in London: 'I thought it very necessary to publish this manner of making your sawce, because our mustard which we buy from the chandlers at this day, is many times made up with vile and filthy vinegar, such as our stomacks would abhorre, if we should see it before the mixing therof with the seeds.'[21]

From apothecaries he got both recipes and ideas: he was on good terms with the regular suppliers of materials and medicines he used in his medical practice.[22] One Crosley provided a number of recipes, mostly medicinal, including one interesting preparation of fine powdered steel for the bloody flux, a powerful chemical and metallic medicine such as those advocated by Paracelsus, the German doctor and alchemist whose books caused controversy amongst the medical professions in Plat's time. Plat was strongly influenced by Paracelsus and patronized apothecaries who supplied medicines based on his precepts, such as 'Maister Kemmish' a well-known apothecary of the day who provided Plat with his recipe for Doctor Stephen's Aqua Composita and to whom Plat recommended readers wanting oils distilled from herbs. They might 'repair to Maister Kemish, that auncient and expert Chimist dwelling neere the glashouse, at whose hands they may buy any of the aforsaid oiles in a most reasonable manner'.[23]

A third apothecary, Mr Parsons, was commended as an 'honest and painefull Practicer in his profession'. He provided Plat with two of the preserving recipes in *Delightes for Ladies* and also told him much about commercial rabbit production. Parsons was more to Plat than a supplier of chemicals, being referred to as 'my Cosin' and 'scholefellow'.[24]

Another acquaintance whose profession was germane to the contents of Plat's book was a Mr Webber who told Plat how to make 'A most delicate and stiff suger past, wherof to cast Rabbets, pigeons, or any other little byrd or beast, either from the lief, or carved in moldes'. With this paste one could mould fowls and other animals, cover them 'with crums of bread, cinnamon and suger boiled together: and so they will seem as if they were rosted and breaded. …By this meanes, a banquet may bee presented in the forme of a supper, being a very rare and strange device.'[25]

Webber was skilled at moulding for he also told Plat how to make *papier maché* into 'frontages, antiques, or other beastes to abide the weather' which 'the Italians garnishe the owtsides sides of theyre howses wth'. He was probably a leading expert on banqueting conceits being, when Plat met him in December 1595, 'one of her Ma[jes]ties Privie Kichin'.[26]

Outside the food, drink and medical suppliers, Plat had a wide circle of friends and acquaintances, including his tenants, fellow private medical practitioners, alchemists, lawyers from the Inns of Court, courtiers and civil servants, leading citizens of London, neighbours and family. Some of those who provided him with many recipes and ideas – Master Rich of Lee (probably Lee in Essex), 'Nepper the Scot', and Thomas Gascoine, who had an old parchment book from which Plat took recipes, are as yet unidentified, although further research may reveal their backgrounds. Auditor Hill, who provided recipes for Aqua Rubea and drying rose leaves and whose name crops up frequently in Plat's manuscripts, was a senior civil servant, an auditor working in the Exchequer.[27]

Some of Plat's informants were foreigners who brought with them experience of strange lands. One such was a Spaniard identified only as 'Sr Romero', an intriguing figure who was the source of just one recipe in *Delightes for Ladies* ('Chestnuts kept all the yeere') but, from the evidence of Plat's manuscripts, provided him with many ideas on food, wine, medicine, military technology, as well as general knowledge, such as the principles of the diving bell and how to engrave on glass. Who he was – diplomat, merchant, or religious exile – I have not established, but he knew a great deal about Naples, then under Spanish rule, and probably lived there prior to his arrival in England. On Christmas Eve 1590 he met Plat and told him about macaroni in Naples: how it was eaten, how it was made in mechanical presses, then 'honge upp, uppon foddes to drie presently after they are made like candells', and that it was sold 'by the l. in Naples, where (as Sr Romero assureth mee uppon his creditt) that more then 100 persons doo live very richly by making of them.' Naples was the area of Italy most associated with macaroni and spaghetti, where the first presses for its production were made and where, in the sixteenth century, one was most likely to encounter pasta dried and sold in shops, rather than freshly produced at home.[28]

Some of the ideas for *Delightes for Ladies* came not from abroad but from Plat's own household, more specifically, his wife. A recipe not included in *Delightes for Ladies* but found in manuscript, for 'sallets of flowers all ye yeere', involving reconstituted dried flowers, was 'my wiffes invention'. In the book she is associated with dairy produce, traditionally a housewife's domain.[29]

Plat was very taken with recipes to flavour and colour both butter and cheese. Many are to be found in his manuscripts and they appear in print in *The Jewell House of Art and Nature*, to be developed further in *Delightes for Ladies*. In the earlier publication, after explaining his method of extracting oils from herbs and spices, he describes 'how to make sundry sorts of dainty butter with the saide oils,' providing us with a glimpse of his family's breakfast table at Bishop's Hall, Bethnal Green: 'In the moneth of may it is usual with us to eat some of the smallest, and youngest, sage leaves with butter in a morning.' He suggests using oils with butter instead for 'far more lively and penetrative taste then can be presently had out of the greene herbe.' He continues, 'This last sommer I did entertaine divers of my friends with this kinde of butter amongst other country dishes, as also with cinnamon, mace, and clove butter…and I knew not whether I did please them with this new found dish, or offend them by denying the secret unto them.' Despite his expertise with butter, he confesses himself no countryman, for he 'never kept but twoe kine, in any one summer.'[30]

In *The Jewell House* Plat suggests a flavoured cheese made by mixing vegetable and spice oils with the curds and continues to describe 'a tricke in the making of a cheese' subjecting it to a gentle pressing only, thereby expelling only a thin whey, 'and so your cheese wil bee much bigger, and better than otherwise it would be.' Not going into details, he explains, 'I would be loath to offend a Gentlewoman that presumeth of a great secret herein…But I think I have given light sufficient to a good dairie Woman to find out al the circumstances therof in time.' [31]

In *Delightes for Ladies* Plat is much more expansive about this new type of cheese, giving details of precise quantities of ingredients, the design of a press, and the exact handling of the cheese. The object, it appears, is to produce a close-textured but full-cream cheese, 'your ordinarie Cheeses are more spongious and full of eyes by reason of the violent pressing of them; whereas these cheeses setling gently and by degrees, doe cut as close and as firme as Marmalade.' [32] The gentle pressing yields, he estimates, about 25 per cent more cheese than by ordinary pressing. Displaying a knowledge of Continental cheeses, Plat speculates, 'I suppose that Angelores[33] in France may bee made in this manner in small baskets, and so likewise of the Parmeesan.'

The anonymous gentlewoman of 1594 whose secret he guarded is now revealed as his wife: 'I have robbed my wives Dairy of this secret, who hath hitherto refused all recompences that have beene offered her by gentlewomen for the same: and had I loved a Cheese myself so well as I like the receipt, I thinke I should not so easily have imparted the same at this time.' To impress his readers with the sacrifice he has made (albeit of his wife's secret), he adds: 'And yet I must needs confesse, that for the better gracing of the Title wherewith I have fronted this pamphlet, I have been willing to publish this with some other secrets of worth, for the which I have many times refused good store both of crowns and angels. And therefore let no Gentlewoman think this Booke too deare, at what price soever it shall be valued upon the sale therof: neither can I esteem the work to be of lesse than twenty yeeres gathering.' [34]

From what I have said so far, you must be wondering if Plat had any ideas of his own. He did include recipes which were clearly derived from his own experience and from considering these we can learn something of his main interests in food and medicine. Plat often tells us that a recipe is his own, or at least he has used it regularly, with such phrases as, 'This way I have often proved excellent'; 'accept [this] as a new conclusion'; 'I know by mine own experience'; 'This an approved Secret, easie and cheap'. Talking of preserving artichokes, he digresses into another glimpse of his household: 'In a milde and warm winter, about a moneth or three weeks before Christmas, I caused great store of Artichokes to bee gathered with their stalkes in their full length as they grew: and, making first a good thicke Lay of Artichoke-leaves in the bottome of a great and large vessell, I placed my Artichokes, one upon another, as close as I could couch them, covering them over, of a pretty thicknesse with Artichoke-leaves: these Artichokes were served-in at my Table all the Lent after, the apples being red and sound, onely the tops of the leaves a little vaded, which I did cut away.'[35]

Whether or not recipes were originally his, he put considerable effort into perfecting them. In the preserving section is a very small chapter of one sentence giving directions for sweet cakes made from pounded dried parsnips and flour. Plat's original manuscript note of this recipe is beset with inserts and marginal notes: 'qre of stammpinge these rootes, iff so they will bee made into a paste to mak cakes of'; 'qre iff they will not grinde'; 'qre of dried pompions./ qre of dried chestnutts./ skirret rootes, & the cakes of almonds after the oyle is expressed will mak excellent bread…'; 'qre what the seedes of pompions wolde doo in any victuall'. So, this simple recipe has generated several ideas and variations in his mind. Many recipes in Plat's manuscripts are festooned with queries, insertions, and addenda of this kind. He concludes the manuscript of this recipe by confirming that 'this I did both Invente and prove in Cakes'. The cakes first appeared in his pamphlet on famine relief published in 1596 and, despite their origin as a desperate measure to eke out flour in hard times, Plat took a liking to them, eating them 'diverse times in my own house.'[36]

A project Plat worked on for many years was the improvement of victuals for the navy and the army in Ireland. He devoted much effort to this project, bringing together ideas for keeping drinking water fresh at sea, new and refreshing drinks for sailors, preserving lemon juice as a preventative against scurvy, preserving meat at sea without oversalting it, and new types of food for use in the navy and army.[37] In *Delightes for Ladies* are hints of this project such as: 'Trosses for the Sea' (cough sweets); 'How to keepe rosted Beefe a long time sweet and wholesome' (a recipe involving wine vinegar which was tried on Drake's Cadiz expedition); and the detailed 'Conceipt of the Authors, how Beefe may be carried at Sea, without any strong & violent impression of salt, which is usually purchased by long and extreame powdering.' This last recipe, by which beef was to be preserved in a box full of holes dragged behind a ship using the flow of sea water as preservative, is uneasily inserted into the text with an apology to his 'courteous Gentlewomen' readers for his sudden launching 'a little from the shoare'. Plat clearly wants to take the opportunity of a new publication to publicize further his ideas for naval victuals, promising to follow up with a new way of storing food at sea and another way of keeping roast meat of all kinds at sea for up to six months. 'And this I hold to be a most singular and necessary Secret for all our English Navie; which at all times, upon reasonable terms, I will bee ready to disclose for the good of my countrey.'[38]

The last sentence, linking a hope of gain with the good of the country, is a hint of another major concern of Plat's, making money and gaining honour and recognition. His efforts to promote naval and army victuals included selling barrels of home-made pasta for both commercial and military voyages, advertising for sale food, preservatives and medicines for sea voyages, and lobbying government officials to provide food for the army in Ireland. More generally, his surviving manuscripts and publications contain details of many attempts to make money from his inventions, both food and non-food. Pamphlets were issued hinting at new inventions which he would disclose for a fee; he sold pills against the plague; negotiated with another medical practitioner to sell recipes of some of his medicines; attempted to sell both distilling recipes and alchemical secrets to Moritz, Landgrave of Hesse, a Continental ruler deeply interested in alchemy; and made frequent lists both of inventions and secrets which he considered saleable, and of individuals and organizations who he hoped would help him promote his ideas. Some of the advertisements are surprisingly bold: towards the end of the preface to *Floreas Paradise*, he launches into a four-and-a-half-page 'publique offer of a spagiricall Antidote', which he claimed would cure agues and fevers, the 'trembling passion of the heart' and 'that most fearefull, and infectious disease of all the rest, which wee tearm the plague.…I dare commend it, and will wage for it to any reasonable summe, against any animall, or vegetable medicine whatsoever.' He went further, claiming 'till it please God to blesse me with the true Oleum Solis, that hath passed all his philosophical Rotations in Caelo Philosophicum, I will hazard and set my rest upon it.' He warned his readers that the ingredients for this medicine were 'exceeding scarce and hard to come by, & the preparation long and tedious' but if he had none available, he could supply another preparation immediately to relieve agues. The whole advertisement, a mixture of reassurance that the medicine was safe, palatable, and effective but in worryingly short supply and urgently needed should the plague reoccur, is a fine example of early advertising copy.[39]

Despite all his efforts, he lamented in the introductory poem to *Delightes for Ladies* the lack of public appreciation of his work and, in 1607, he was sorrowful of his failure to make a significant amount of money from naval victualling but consoled himself with the recent knighthood bestowed upon

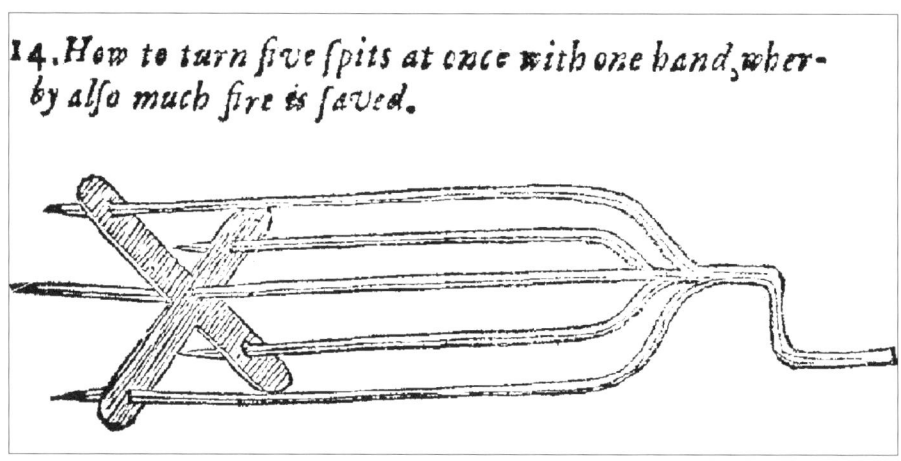

Figure 10. One of Hugh Plat's ingenious suggestions in The Jewell House of Art and Nature, *which he confessed he borrowed from Scappi's* Opera.

him, 'purposing to content my spirits, with my place and dignitie, and in likelyhood proove also more profitable in the ende, then if I had thankelesly devoted my selfe to Bonum Publicum. In which course, happy men are sometimes rewarded with good words: but few or none, in these dayes, with any reall recompense.' [40]

What conclusions can we draw from this scrutiny of the background to *Delightes for Ladies*? The substantial manuscript of 'T.T.' which forms a backbone to *Delightes for Ladies*, plus the many recipes and ideas from friends, relatives, and acquaintances acknowledged by Plat, may leave us disappointed that so much of what the book has to say on food and drink did not originate with him. Cookery, however, is rarely truly original, recipes and methods are variations on themes suggested by others, indeed subtle changes may transform a recipe into a dish far superior to the original. Cooks throughout the ages have kept notes and some have turned these into books with or without revealing the origins of recipes copied from others. Close examination of the origins of material in Gervase Markham's *The English House-wife*, published in 1615 only a few years after *Delightes for Ladies* first appeared, reveals parallels between the two works (and indeed between the writers). Markham, like Plat, spent time on the fringes of the Court and, after early flirtations with poetry, applied himself to writing on many topics but mainly agriculture, horticulture, and household management. Like Plat, he was a gentleman who was keen to find ways of making money. And *The English House-wife* was based on the work of others: the printer of the first edition announced, 'this is no collection of his whose name is prefixed to this work, but an approved manuscript which he hath happily light on, belonging sometime to an honourable personage of this kingdom.' A recent editor has established that Markham in fact based the work on several manuscripts. Markham also took recipes for *The English House-wife* from published books, including one from *Delightes for Ladies*. Sir Hugh Plat was, therefore, not exceptional in his reliance on others for his material, only in leaving so many manuscripts from which we may discern how he arrived at his published text.[41]

And, let us not belittle Plat's achievement, both with this book and others on agriculture and gardening. Consider *Delightes for Ladies* not as an early cookery book, but as a contribution to the advancement of knowledge. This is no book of secrets, rehashing untried recipes from other printed sources, nor is it a work based largely on classical authors. Plat's ideas came, in the main, from contemporary experience: his own, his friends' and those of tradespeople whose living depended on the success of the secrets they divulged to him. He was a contemporary of Francis Bacon, and some of the more experimental approach advocated by him can be detected in Plat's writing. The idea for a 'history of trades' which runs through the seventeenth century from Bacon, through Samuel Hartlib to Evelyn and the Royal Society, can be seen at work in Plat's questioning of apothecaries, comfit-makers, and professional cooks.[42] In short, the praise heaped on Plat's gardening book, *Floreas Paradise*, for its freshness and originality, could equally be applied to *Delightes for Ladies*, and the frequent reissue of both books in the seventeenth century shows that they were well regarded for a considerable time. Plat summed up his research in the final stanzas of the introductory poem to *Delightes for Ladies*:

> No idle thoughts, or vain surmised skils,
> By fancy fram'd within a theorick brain,
> My Muse presents unto your sacred eares;
> To win your favours safely, I distain.
> From painfull practice, from expereince,
> I sound, though costly, mysteries derive.
> With fiery flame, in scorching Vulcan's Forge,
> To teach and fine each Secret, I do strive.

Notes

1. Bent Juel-Jensen, 'Some Uncollected Authors XIX, Sir Hugh Plat ?1552–?1611', *Book Collector*, 1959, pp. 64–66; Sir Hugh Plat, *Delightes for Ladies*, intr. G.E. & K.R. Fussell, 1948, p. vi.
2. Sir Hugh Plat, *Delightes for Ladies*, 1628, d.26. Unless otherwise specified, I refer throughout to the 1628 edition. There is no pagination. I have followed the index to this edition, which allocates a letter to the four sections of the book: a. *The Art of Preserving, Conserving, Candying, &c.*; b. *Secrets in Distillation*; c. *Cookery and Huswifery*; d. *Sweet Powders, oyntments, beauties, &c.* Chapters are numbered within each section.
3. I refer to the numbered recipes as 'chapters' and the parts of the book dealing with preserving, cookery etc., as the 'sections'.
4. Contrast this recipe with 'To Stue Sparrowes or larkes' in *A book of Cookrye*: 'Take the best of Mutton broth, and put it in a Pipkin, and put to it a little whole Mace, whole Pepper, Claret wine, Marigolde leaves, Barberies, Rosewater Vergious, Suger, and Marrowe, or els sweet Butter. Perboile the Larkes before and then boyle them in the same broth and lay them uppon Sops.' *A Book of Cookery*, 1591, p. 11.
5. Plat, *Delightes for Ladies*, a.54 (which in some editions is mis-printed as a.24).
6. Plat, *Delightes for Ladies*, a.22, a.28, a.32; Laura Mason, *Sugar-Plums and Sherbet*, 1998, p. 229.
7. British Library, SL 2189, f.55.
8. Sir Hugh Plat, *Floreas Paradise*, 1608, p. 17.
9. Plat, *Delightes for Ladies*, a.54.
10. Robert Somerville, *The Savoy*, 1960, p. 42; M.B. Donald, *Elizabethan Copper*, 1955, pp. 15–35; G.L. Hennessy, *Novum repertorium ecclesiasticum parochiale Londinense*, 1898, pp. 295, 302; Public Record Office, State Papers, 12/36; Bruce Janacek, 'Thomas Thymme and Natural Philosophy', *Sixteenth Century Journal*, XXX, 4, 1999.
11. BL, SL 2216.
12. The Fussells exaggerated when they wrote, 'Many…recipes were later included in *Delightes for Ladies*', G.E. & K.R. Fussell, *Delightes for Ladies*, 1948, introduction, p. xvi.
13. Sir Hugh Plat, *The Jewell House of Art and Nature*, 1594, i, 15, iii, pp. 34, 42; Plat, *Delightes for Ladies*, a.36, b.17, c.33.
14. Plat, *The Jewell House of Art and Nature*, iii, pp. 36; Plat, *Delightes for Ladies*, c.35.
15. Plat, *Delightes for Ladies*, a.10, c.21.
16. *Opera Di M. Bartolomeo Scappi*, Venice, 1570.
17. Eleanour Sinclair Rohde, *The Old English Gardening Books*, 1972, p. 32.
18. For instance, the printer mistook 'Aud Hill' (short for Auditor Hill) as Andrew Hill, and printed the name Andr. or Andrew throughout the book.
19. Plat, *Delightes for Ladies*, a.3, a.67, c.35.
20. Plat, *Delightes for Ladies*, a.4, c.30, c.33; 'Mother Bunch' was a generic name for London alewives.
21. Plat, *Delightes for Ladies*, c.16, c.25, c.29.
22. Notes of his medical practice are to be found in BL, SL 2209. As well as a general practice in London, he actively promoted a range of medicines for seamen.
23. Plat, *Delightes for Ladies*, a.53; BL, SL 2189, ff. 155–156a; SL 2203, f. 213a; SL 2189, f. 156a. George Baker, who edited a translation of a work by Conrad Gesner concerned with the new chemical medicines, published as *The Newe Jewell of Health* in 1576, in the preface listed those who sold such preparations in London, including 'one mayster Kemech an Englishe man dwelling in Lothburie'. Quoted in Paul H. Kocher, 'Paracelsan medicine in England', *Journal of History of Medicine*, Autumn 1947, p. 460. Plat was also a friend of Master Jacob, who ran the glasshouse, and they talked of ways to use waste heat from glassmaking to keep

plants warm indoors, see Sir Hugh Plat, *Floreas Paradise*, 1608, pp. 38–9.
24. Plat, *Delightes for Ladies*, a.69, a.70; BL, SL 2209 f. 2; SL 2216 ff. 50a–52.
25. Plat, *Delightes for Ladies*, a.10.
26. BL, SL 2189, f. 71a.
27. These men occur in *Delightes for Ladies* as follows:
    Rich: Plat, *Delightes for Ladies*, a.2, a.3; BL, SL 2189, f. 71.
    Nepper: Plat, *Delightes for Ladies*, b.21; BL, SL 2189, f. 151a.
    Gascoine: Plat, *Delightes for Ladies*, a.45, a.46; BL, SL 2216, ff. 230–231.
    Hill: Plat, *Delightes for Ladies*, b.7; BL, SL 2189, f. 155a; CSPDomestic, 1595–7, pp. 68, 157, 167.
28. BL, SL 2210, ff. 87, 131a, 134–134a.
29. BL, SL 2189, f. 38a.
30. Plat, *The Jewell House of Art and Nature*, pt. 3, pp. 10–12.
31. Plat, *The Jewell House of Art and Nature*, pt. 3, p. 13.
32. Plat, *Delightes for Ladies*, c.22.
33. According to an application for EC listing as a regional speciality for Livarot cheese, 'Livarot is one of Normandy's oldest cheeses; like Pont-l'Evêque, it claims to be the descendant of the Angelot cheese referred to in the *Roman de la Rose*, written by Guillaume de Lorris in 1260. Thomas Corneille, in his *Dictionnaire Universel Géographique et Historique* of 1708, recites its praises. In the 19th century it was consumed in greater quantities than any other cheese by the people of Normandy. In April 1970, the producers of Livarot formed an association and applied for the Appellation d'Origine, which they obtained in December 1975 (Regulation of 17 December). 'Method of production: The curds, after being cut into large cubes, are left to stand then cut again, pressed, allowed to settle and put into moulds. After being turned several times and drained in a drying area, the cheese is salted with cooking salt or in brine. During its time in the cellar, it is turned over and washed at least three times with water, to which annatto is added for the final wash. It can be eaten after a ripening period of at least three weeks.' *Council Regulation (EEC) No. 2081/92 Application for registration.*

    John Evelyn made 'Angelots' by breaking up 2- or 3-week-old 'winter' cheese, mixing it with clotted cream, then pressing the mixture well. *John Evelyn, Cook*, ed. Christopher Driver, 1997, p. 87.
34. Plat, *Delightes for Ladies*, c.22.
35. Plat, *Delightes for Ladies*, a.69, b.11, b.23, c.24, c.29.
36. Sir Hugh Plat, *Sundrie new and Artificiall remedies against Famine*, 1596; BL, SL 2210, f. 31.
37. A forthcoming book will examine Plat's ideas on military food in detail.
38. Plat, *Delightes for Ladies*, a.39, c.18, c.20.
39. Plat, *Floreas Paradise*, preface. His money-making plans are scattered throughout his manuscripts in the British Library. A forthcoming book will fully explore this aspect of Plat.
40. Plat, *Certaine philosophical preparations of foode and beverage for sea-men, etc.* [ca. 1607].
41. Gervase Markham, *The English Housewife*, ed. Michael R. Best, Kingston, Canada, 1986, pp. xii–xiv, xvi–xxii, lvi–lviii.
42. Michael Hunter, 'John Evelyn in the 1650s: A Virtuoso in Quest of a Role', pp. 86–91, in *John Evelyn's "Elysium Britannicum" and European Gardening*, Washington DC, 1998.

Figure 11. Frontispiece and title-page to Hannah Wolley's The Queen-like Closet *(third edition, 1675). It illustrates boiling, roasting, cooking over a chafing-dish and baking in the oven in the kitchen, whilst the lady of the house works in the still-room.*

CHAPTER FOUR

DOMESTIC ENGLISH COOKERY AND COOKERY BOOKS, 1575–1675

Eileen White

By the end of the sixteenth century, printed books were being produced on a range of subjects, not just religious, academic or literary.[1] These included recipe books and volumes on domestic management, and the number increased throughout the following century. Their popularity can be judged by the repeated editions of certain titles: Gervase Markham's *The English House-wife*, for example, ran to thirteen between 1615 and 1683.[2] This study is based on books to be found in the Brotherton Library at Leeds University, but there are several modern editions and facsimiles available so it is possible to bring the recipes into the modern kitchen.

The printed cookery books were aimed at a variety of people. First there was the housewife, with her range of domestic activity: not just cookery, but the making of soaps, perfumes and medicines. All levels of society were considered, Gervase Markham declaring 'our House-wife is intended to be generall, one that can as well feed the poore as the rich'.[3] Many were intended for ladies and gentlewomen, who were able to pay servants to work in the kitchen and prepare everyday dinners, but who were responsible for providing medicines, and who could have helped to make conserves, preserves and sweetmeats. Even Queen Henrietta Maria was known to have 'honoured with her own practice, when she pleased to descend to these more private Recreations', many of the recipes presented in *The Queens Closet Opened*, published in 1655.[4] The books would also have been of use to professional cooks, in domestic service or commercial establishments.

The titles of printed cookery books of the last quarter of the sixteenth century often reveal that they were aimed at the housewife. *A Proper newe Booke of Cokerye* appeared about 1557–8, and A.W. brought out *A Booke of Cookry* in 1584. *The Widowes Treasure* of 1585 interspersed cookery recipes amongst 'secretes in phisick, and chirugery', and Thomas Dawson added medicinal recipes to his collection of 'conceites in Cookery' in *The good huswifes Iewell* of 1596 and 1597.[5]

By the seventeenth century, the authors – or, more properly, compilers – had distinct personalities, and can be examined under several headings. The Gentlemen Compilers opened private rooms (or closets) to reveal secrets and delights. Sir Hugh Plat published *The Jewell House of Art and Nature* in 1594, and the 1611 edition of his *Delightes for Ladies* included *A Closet for Ladies and Gentlewomen*.[6] Such books were directed, as the titles suggest, at ladies and gentlewomen, or to those who would aspire to such status. The recipes that circulated in aristocratic circles and the Court itself were also made available. In 1655, during the Commonwealth, a former servant of Queen Henrietta Maria, identified only as W.M., produced *The Queens Closet Opened*. This starts with a section of medicinal recipes, *The Pearl of Practise*, followed by *A Queens Delight*, with recipes for preserving, conserving, candying, making perfumes and distilling sweet waters. *The Compleat Cook*, a more general cookery book, completed the volume.[7] The Queen is more likely to have descended to practising from the first two collections rather than the third, which was probably a separate compilation, having new pagination. Unlike the prececeding two sections, its title-page makes no reference to the Queen, nor does it proclaim like the others that it was 'never before published'. Perhaps the publisher, Nathaniel Brook, combined it with the first two in order to benefit from the selling point of an association with the exiled Queen. Such compilations were not necessarily made with the intention of publication. *The Closet of the Eminently Learned Sir Kenelme Digby, Kt., Opened* was published in 1669, four years after the compiler's death, with the consent of his son, and it illustrates the gastronomic interests of the Court circles in the period before the Civil War.[8]

The Professional Compilers had publication in mind, and either made their own compilations or admitted to making use of existing manuscripts. Gervase Markham confessed in his dedicatory letter at the beginning of *The English House-wife* (1631 edition) 'that much of it was a Manuscript which many yeeres agon belonged to an Honourable Countesse'. This was first published in 1615, as the second part of *Countrey Contentments*, a companion to the slightly earlier *The English Husbandman*, so Markham covered the whole business of the production, processing and cooking of food. He also augmented a translation by Richard Surflet of a French original from 1570, *Maison Rustique, or, The countrey farme*, in 1616.[9] Another compiler, John Murrell, produced *A Daily Exercise for Ladies and Gentlewomen* in 1617, and *A New Book of Cookerie* about 1630. This had several editions along with *The*

Second Book of Cookerie, under the general title *Murrels Two Bookes of Cookerie and Carving*. The 'Carving' and 'Sewing' are a reprint by Murrell of directions first published by Wynkyn de Worde in 1508, and so reveals an interest in medieval practice that continued through the seventeenth century.[10]

The Professional Cooks revealed the secrets of their art and 'mystery' or craft, and carried an air of authority which was backed up by brief summaries of their professional careers in the introductions to their volumes. Robert May's *The Accomplisht Cook, or the Art and Mystery of Cookery* was published in 1660, at the end of a long career; his portrait, showing him at the age of 71, fronts the book, a rare honour for a cook at this time, and his credentials were provided in an accompanying biography by W.W.[11] William Rabisha provided his own autobiography in the epistle 'To the Reader' when he brought out *The Whole Body of Cookery Dissected* the following year. He, too, repeated the instructions for carving and sewing published by Murrell, adding an account of the famous feast for the installation of Archbishop Nevill at York from the fifteenth century.[12]

Hannah Wolley, credited as the first female professional cookery writer, could not claim that her book came out of courtly circles, but nevertheless allied herself to that group of compilers when she called it *The Queen-like Closet*; this publication ran to several editions from 1670.[13] However, women had already contributed to published works. For example, Sir Hugh Plat revealed at the end of a recipe, 'How to make a large and daintier cheese' in *Delightes for Ladies*, 'I haue robbed my wifes Dairy of this secret';[14] and Gervase Markham admitted to using a manuscript that had belonged to an unnamed Countess.

Several household manuscripts survive: they give a direct connection with seventeenth-century housewives, being their personal compilations.[15] From the cookery manuscripts in Leeds University Library two have been taken as examples. MS 621 is described as 'Dame Mary Lister's Household Book', although there are several contributors to the volume. Internal dates range from 1625 to 1635, but entries begin before these dates and continue afterwards. Mary was the wife of Sir William Lister of Thornton-in-Craven in Yorkshire, and her hand can be identified from an inventory at the back of the book, 'Mary Lister, A noat of all my Bookes'.[16] MS 506 has a relatively modern pencil note at the beginning to say it has many Manchester and Yorkshire recipes. There are cookery recipes in an early seventeenth-century hand and more with an internal date of 1674.[17] Another manuscript is only known from a printed facsimile published in 1890 and edited by George Weddell: *Arcana Fairfaxiana Manuscripta*.[18] It has references to the well-known Yorkshire family of Fairfax, and again reveals a mixture of hands from the earlier part of the seventeenth century to the eighteenth century.

The manuscripts show the concerns of the compilers. There are relatively few directions for everyday dishes, which were learned by example and remembered through repetition. A large proportion are for conserves, preserves and sugar-work, which could be prepared by the lady of the house who was, presumably, compiling the manuscript. Recipes for household items, such as soaps and perfumes, are included. Above all, there are medicinal recipes, for the ointments, plasters, pills and syrups that would be administered by the housewife for a range of complaints. Although this study concentrates on the cookery recipes, it should not be forgotten that the preparation of medicines was an important duty, and successful recipes were passed between households. It is also being assumed here that these manuscripts were the woman's personal collection, but one major hand in the *Arcana* manuscript was identified by the editor as that of the Reverend Henry Fairfax, uncle of the Civil War general Thomas Fairfax, and he contributed both medicinal and cookery recipes to the collection.

Often the recipes in the manuscripts served only as reminders to the writer, who knew the method. Henry's wife Mary Fairfax has been identified as one of the contributors to the *Arcana*, and she was very brief in recording one recipe:

> To seson a flourintine with the
>   kidnay of veel
> Take yor kidnay shred it smal; 2 Aples shred tham smal; 2 eges; Little rosewater; sinamon Nottmoge some suger; a Little cream, & som candid oringepils cutt smal, curans, & rasons, a date or tow, if yo^w pleas/
> [p. 121]

The manuscripts are irregular collections: a few recipes were added at a time, in several hands and over several generations. These do not appear chronologically, and later hands filled in blank pages or odd spaces. At times it is obvious that at least two people were adding new items at the same period. The process can easily be detected in the original, through the different hands or changes of ink or pen size. If, however, the manuscript had been taken to a printer and published as it stood, the result would be a jumble of recipes with no apparent order or theme, and there would be no way of detecting how it had been gradually compiled. This explains the setting out of several printed cookery books, such as *The Compleat Cook*, and emphasizes the different approach found in the publications of those people described here as 'professional' compilers or cooks. Gervase Markham has clearly delineated chapters in *The English House-wife*, and the chapter on cookery is further subdivided. He may have used a manuscript belonging to a Countess, but it has been ordered and presented to follow his theme in a way not normally seen in the manuscript collections. John Murrell separated *A New Booke of Cookerie* into boiled meats, baked meats, fritters, salads and puddings; a section on English cookery is similarly ordered. The more ambitious compilations of Robert May and William Rabisha were divided into chapters for specific methods or ingredients. Rabisha explained in the foreword 'To the Reader' that he presented his 'small Tract in a methodical form'. He further pointed out that 'Rare Receipts in Cookery' (pp. 191–267) 'was intended to be placed in the first part, in order and form, every sort by it self, as the first part is composed; but the Author being absent in the Country, that and many things more intended were neglected,' and he asked 'the Reader to correct it in his own thoughts, and enlarge it by what is done, until the Author gets further opportunity to add thereto.' It is also notable that the professional cooks did not include recipes for medicines as such, although they included diets for the sick. Gervase Markham did include medicines, in his first chapter of *The English House-wife*, but he was dealing with the whole duty of the housewife, which included care of the sick.

The printed cookery books that mix medicinal and cookery recipes in no consistent order seem to be the result of a printer reproducing a personal collection of recipes – probably made by a woman or several women – that had been taken to him. The first part of Hannah Wolley's *The Queen-like Closet* is very typical of the manuscript collections. She may be claimed as the first female professional cookery writer, but her book is an example of a housewife's miscellaneous collection of medicines, conserves and sugar-work, rather than the organized material of a professional cook or compiler. The second part has everyday cookery, but it still gives the impression of a collection over a period of time, and not material organized for publication. It may represent her own family recipe manuscript, but there is no way of

> **To make ver-**
> **juyce.**
>
> To make Verjuyce, you shall gather your Crabbs as soone as the kernels turne blacke, and hauing layd them a while in a heape to sweate together, take them and picke them from stalkes, blackes and rottennesse: then in long troughs with beetles for the purpose, crush and breake them all to mash: then make a bagge of courſe haire cloth as square as the preſſe, and fill it with the cruſht Crabs; then put it into the preſſe, and preſſe it while any moyſture will drop forth, hauing a cleane veſſell vnderneath to receiue the liquor: this done, tun it vp into ſweet Hogſheads, and to euery Hogſhead put halfe a dozen handfuls of Damaske Roſe leaues, and then bung it vp, and ſpend it as you ſhall haue occaſion.
>
>
> *To make Verjuyce.*
>
> Take crabs as ſoon as the kernels turn black, and lay them in a heap to ſweat, then pick them from ſtalks and rottenneſs; and then in a long trough with ſtamping beetles ſtamp them to maſh, and make a bag of courſe hair cloth as ſquare as the preſs; fill it with ſtamped crabs, and being well preſſed, put it up in a clean barrel or hogshead.

Figure 12. Comparison of recipes for verjuice from Gervase Markham, The English House-wife *(1631 edition), p. 152 [above], and Robert May,* The Accomplisht Cook *(1665 edition), p. 156 [below].*

detecting its method of compilation from the printed book. One modification the London-based printers did make was to standardize the eccentric spelling of the manuscripts, and to remove the variations of local pronunciation that make the manuscripts a delight to read.

Several of the published books reveal a court circle where personal recipes were passed around. Sir Kenelm Digby acknowledged the source of many in his collection, which included My Lord of Carlisle's Sack Posset, and the Queen's Barley Cream. Then as now, celebrity could add an extra spice. There are examples in *The Compleat Cook* too, starting with 'To make a Posset, the Earl of Arundel's way', and including 'Mrs. Shellyes Cake' and the Countess of Rutland's Banbury Cake amongst others (pp. 3, 38 and 109).

It can be very beguiling to track recipes through the printed books. Many, of course, describe the same procedures but use different wording; others can be compared more directly.[19] A few examples can be cited. *The Compleat Cook* version (1655, p. 6) of a Steak Pie with a French Pudding is very similar to that in Murrell's book of 1638 (p. 31). Robert May also echoes closely a recipe for verjuice (p. 156) found in *The English House-wife* (1631 edition, p. 152), and one for a Farsed Pudding in Murrell (Murrell, p. 42 and May, pp. 184–185). It is interesting to note, however, how May has abbreviated the earlier published versions. Did all the compilers work from the same source, and did May, when making his notes, not need to go into as much detail because as a professional cook he understood the method? It should be remembered that although his book was published in 1660, he was then 71, and his working life had begun as a boy alongside his father. He could have begun compiling his personal collection at the time Markham and Murrell were active. May also has recipes that can be found in *A Queens Delight* and *The Compleat Cook*. This could indicate that the collections were being made within the same court and aristocratic circles immediately before the Civil War, and not that one writer was plagiarizing an earlier published work. Another book, *The Court & Kitchin of Elizabeth, Commonly called Joan Cromwel* (1664), has a number of recipes exactly as found in May; this compilation will be discussed later. William Rabisha's *The Whole Body of Cookery Dissected* (first published in 1661) has recipes also found in Murrell and in *The Court & Kitchin*. Hannah Wolley, publishing in the early 1670s, included detailed instructions for comfit-making that repeated almost exactly Sir Hugh Plat's recipe in *Delightes for Ladies* which in turn had been derived from the manuscript of T.T.[20]

It is interesting to see later writers repeating the traditions and styles of a generation or more earlier, and a detailed study of apparent plagiarism could show not so much theft as the inter-connecting circles of court and professional, commercial and private cookery, especially if the origins of the printed books can be seen in the on-going compilations of personal manuscripts.

This dissemination of recipes does not preclude a personal voice. It is tempting to generalize, and say that if a recipe rolls up its sleeves and gets on with the task, it was written by a woman, and if it shows how clever and opinioniated it is, it was written by a man. Most recipes are in fact practical and objective, but occasionally there are direct communications from the writer to the reader so it becomes possible to sense Thomas Dawson or Hugh

A fierced Pudding.

Mince a Legge of Mutton with sweet Hearbs: searce grated Bread through a Collinder, mince Dates, Currans, Raisins of the Sunne being stoned, a little Orengado cut finely, or a preserued Lemmon, a little Coriander-seedes, Nutmeg, Ginger, and pepper: mingle all together with milke and Egges raw, wrought together like Paste: wrap the meat in a cawle of Mutton or of Veale, & so you may either boyle or bake them. If you bake them, beat the yolke of an Egge with Rose-water, Sugar, and Sinamon. And when it is almost bakt, draw it out, and stick it with Sinamon & Rosemary.

To make a farced Pudding.

Mince a leg of mutton with sweet herbs, grated bread, minced dates, currans, raisins of the sun, a little orangado or preserved lemon sliced thin, a few coriander-seeds, nutmeg, pepper, and ginger, mingle all together with some cream and raw eggs, and work it together like a pasty, then wrap the meat in a caul of mutton or veal, and so you may either boil or bake them. If you bake them, indorse them with yolks of eggs, rose-water, and sugar, and stick them with little sprigs of rosemary and cinamon.

Figure 13. Comparison of recipes for a 'Farsed Pudding' from Murrels Two Bookes of Cookerie and Carving *(1638 edition), p. 42 [above], and Robert May,* The Accomplisht Cook *(1665 edition), pp. 184-5 [below].*

Plat, Gervase Markham, Robert May, Kenelm Digby, William Rabisha or Hannah Wolley reaching across the centuries with their advice and comments. This is not only when each writer strives to point out what makes their book worth buying, which is usually to be found in the preface. Even the anonymous compilers of household manuscripts can be heard as they add their observations to an existing recipe.

Examples can be taken from *The Compleat Cook*. Although part of *The Queens Closet Opened* publication, there is a consistency of style in this section that makes it more than the gathering of disparate recipes presented to Queen Henrietta Maria over the years. It is probably, as noted above, a separate manuscript added to the others by the publisher. There appears to be someone who has gone over the collection in manuscript and added comments or expanded recipes. At the end of 'To make Metheglin' (a honey and herb drink) is the comment:

> sometime I make a Bag, and put in good store of Ginger sliced, some Cloves and Cinnamon, and boyl it in, and other times I put it into the Barrel and never boyle it, it is both good, but Nutmeg and Mace do not well to my Tast.
>
> [pp. 94–95]

The recipe 'To make scalding Cheese towards the latter end of May' gives instructions to lay it in hay which are immediately followed by a disagreement:

> I seldome lay in Hay, I turne and rub them with a rotten cloth especially when they are old once a week least they rot.
>
> [pp. 122–123]

Had we access to the original manuscript, no doubt the hand of this commentator would be apparent. A further example of this personal voice can be seen in the recipe for a Spanish olio, which also illustrates the more extravagant side of seventeenth-century cooking (pp. 92–93).

Small details of habit or style can also be the starting-point to detecting an individual at work amongst the compilations. For example, in Hannah Wolley's *The Queen-like Closet* many of the recipes ask simply for 'spice' rather than specifying any in particular, a much greater use of the general term than is found elsewhere. These personal touches can be set against the evidence of apparent plagiarism.

> 92 *The Compleat Cook.*
>
> *A Spanish Olio.*
>
> Take a peece of Bacon not very fat, but sweet and safe from being resty, a peice of fresh beef, a couple of hoggs Ears and four feet if they can be had, and if not, some quantity of sheeps feet, (Calves feet are not proper) a joynt of Mutton, the Leg, Rack, or Loyne, a Hen, half a dozen pigeons, a bundle of parsly, Leeks, and Mint, a clove of Garlick when you will, a small quantity of pepper, cloves, and saffron, so mingled that not one of them overrule, the pepper and cloves must be beaten as fine as possible may be, and the saffron must be first dryed, and then crumble in powder and dissolved apart in two or three spoonfulls of broth, but both the spices and the Saffron may be kept apart till immediatly before they be used, which must not be, till within a quarter of an hour before the Olio be taken off from the fire; a pottle of hard dry pease, when they have first sleept in water some dayes, a pint of boyld Chesnuts: particular care must be had that the pot wherin the Olio is made, be very sweet, Earthen I think is the best, and judgement
>
> *The Compleat Cook.* 93
>
> is to be had carefully both in the size of the Pot, and in the quantity of the Water at the first, that so the Broth may grow afterwards to be neither too much nor too little, nor too gross, nor too thin, thy meat must be long in boyling, but the fire not too feirce, the Bacon, the Beef, the Pease, the Chesnuts, the Hogs Eares may be put in at the first I am utterly against those confused Olios into which men put almost all kinds of meates and Roots, and especially against putting of Oyl for it corrupts the Broth, in stead of adding goodness to it. To do well, the Broth is rather to be drunk out of a Porringer then to be eaten with a Spoon, though you add some small slices of Bread to it, you will like it the worse. The Sauce for the meat must be as much fine Sugar beaten small to powder with as little Mustard as can be made to drink the Sugar up, and you will find it to be excellent, but if you make it not faithfully and justly according to this prescript, but shall either put Mace, or Rosemary, or Tyme to the Herbs as the manner is of some, it will prove very much the worse.
>
> *To*

Figure 14. The recipe for a Spanish olio from The Compleat Cook *(1655), showing the individual voice of the cook.*

All the authors present insights not only into culinary matters but also into the social and political life of the period. The divisive event of the seventeenth century was the Civil War, when some of the medicinal recipes would have been needed. MS 621 includes 'A water for wounds by ye lady fairfax' (f. 48), 'A Medicine for Scaldinge burninge or hurt of an hand Gunne' (f. 56), 'To take away a heate or burninge wth gunpowder' (f. 66) and 'An Oyle of St Johns Grasse wch will heale any wound in 24 howers' (f. 72v). The same page has another recipe using St John's Wort, 'An excellent balsom for any wounde'. The Lister house at Thornton-in-Craven was attacked in 1643, and was later burned down, so this collection of recipes proved necessary.[21] MS 506 has a recipe 'ffor one that is burnt in the face wth gunpowder' (f. 16v). In these circumstances, it is not surprising to find Robert May giving instructions 'To make Mustard divers wayes … grinde it in a mustard quern, or a bowl with a cannon bullet', and 'Fritters in the Italian Fashion …make the balls as big as a nutmeg or musket bullet'.[22] More playful times looked for other analogies, and the *Arcana* recipe for 'Paste of Jenua' instructs, 'make it in some Beades to the bignes of a Tennis ball' (p. 107).

Robert May's career had been affected by the austerities of the Commonwealth. In 'A short Narrative of some passages of the Authors Life' included in the introductory material to *The Accomplisht Cook*, his biographer W.W. describes how he first worked with his father in the establishment of Lady Dormer, who employed four other cooks,

> such noble Houses were then kept, the glory of that, and shame of this present age; then were those golden dayes wherein were practised *the Triumphs and Trophies of Cookery*; then was Hospitality esteemed, Neighbourhood preserved, the Poor cherished, and God honoured; then was Religion less talkt on, and more practised; then was Atheism and Schism less in fashion; and then did men strive to be good rather then to seem so.

The War caused May to move from household to household, and having served lords he found himself working for the gentry in Essex, Kent and Yorkshire. By the time his book was published at the Restoration, when he was 71, he was back in more noble circles, working for Lady Englefield.[23]

The Commonwealth found many people out of their former service, and no doubt looking for remuneration as well as striving to keep the memory of their former employers alive. W.M., who had worked for the Queen, helped to compile the collection that became *The Queens Closet Opened*, 'there being few or none, of these receipts presented to her Majesty, which were not transcribed into her book by my selfe, the Originall papers being most of them preserved in my own hands, which I kept as so many Reliques' (Epistle, p. [ii]). He was persuaded to publish the collection because unauthorized copies had been circulating:

> otherwise I should not have thought it less than Sacrileg, had not the lock been first pickt, to have opened the Closet of my distressed Soveraigne Mistresse, without her Royall assent; but since that unfortunate miscarriage, I thought this publication to stand upon no

Figures 15 & 16. Two portraits. The one on the left is of Queen Henrietta Maria, the frontispiece to The Queens Closet Opened *(1655). That on the right is of Elizabeth Cromwell, as shown in the frontispiece to* The Court & Kitchin of Elizabeth, Commonly called Joan Cromwel, The Wife of the late Usurper *(1664). A verse beneath the portrait reads: 'From feigned glory and Vsurped Throne / And all the Greatnesse to me falsly shown / And from the Arts of Government set free / See how Protrectresse & a Drudge agree'.*

ordinary tearmes of honour, as it might continue my Soveraigne Ladies remembrance in the breasts and loves of those persons of honour and quality, that presented most of these rare receipts to her.
Epistle to *The Queens Closet Opened* [pp. iii–iv]

This was published in 1655, six years after the execution of Charles I, and the publisher did not seem to expect any suppression by the authorities for such sentiments; they may indeed have helped to boost sales. An engraved frontispiece of 'Henrietta Maria Regina' was provided.

The reaction against the puritan regime after the Restoration is best seen in *The Court & Kitchin of Elizabeth, Commonly called Joan Cromwel, The Wife of the late Usurper*, published by Randal Taylor in 1664,[24] which purports to be the cookery book of Mrs Cromwell. The main reason for its publication is the introduction, a diatribe against Mrs Cromwell as representative of the regime of the Commonwealth, providing, as was confessed towards the end of the section 'To the Reader', 'a little transitory mirth for twenty years duration of sorrow'. She could have done nothing to please the author. If her court and household showed any state, she was vilified for acting above her station, but her homely housekeeping activities were sneered at, such as allegedly keeping two or three cows in St James Park, and creating a dairy in Whitehall (p. 32). The recipes are said to be 'the most usual Meat and Diet observed at her Table, most of them ordinary and vulgar, except some few Rarities' (p. 46). The postscript says that they were given in no order, but in the form they were received 'from a near servant of hers' (p. 130), but this would not be unusual for a genuine manuscript collection. However, as already noted, some recipes can be found word for word in Robert May's book of four years earlier. Either Mrs Cromwell had access to the same private sources as May, or (more likely) the compiler made a choice of recipes from available sources as a vehicle for his diatribe. He only had to add the occasional comment to link the recipes in common circulation to his theme: 'How to make Scotch collops of Veal. (this was almost Her constant Dish)' (p. 49), or 'How to make Marrow Puddings, (which she usually had to her Breakfast)' (p. 56).

There must have been many household servants like W.M. and the near servant of Mrs Cromwell cast adrift by the vicissitudes of the Civil War who helped to disseminate the recipes of families at different levels of society.

Apart from giving a new viewpont on historical events, the recipes combine to give hints and information about the process of cooking, the household, its kitchen equipment and ingredients. Often the manuscripts can provide details not found in the printed collections. MS 621, in a recipe for preserving cherries, instructs 'yo^w must vse a silver sponne about them … yo^w must take no ladle nor knife that hath bene occupied about flesh for that will make mytes to breed in them' (f. 3v). The earlier hand in MS 506 directed that in grinding almonds to make marchpane, 'as you beate them wett the pestle in rosewater' (f. 46). Most recipes simply advise using rosewater to prevent the almonds oiling as they are beaten; this indicates how it could be done. The same writer also suggested working the paste for sugar rosecakes with cool dry hands, otherwise it would melt (f. 46v), and later described how to prepare jelly moulds when making jelly of apples: first boil them in water, then put them into cold water, then let them be 'somwhat dry' before the jelly is poured in (ff. 73v–74). *The Compleat Cook* (1655) often reveals a personal touch. Before roasting a pike, it is larded with pickled herring, but 'you must have a sharp Bodkin to make the holes, no Larding Pins will go thorow' (pp. 102–103). Shrewsbury Cakes, before baking, should be pricked 'with a pen made of wood, or if you have a comb that hath not been used, that will do them quickly, and is best to that purpose' (pp. 119–120). The instructions to make Spanish cream are very graphic:

> Put hot water in a Bucket and go with it to the Milking, then poure out the Water, and instantly milke into it, and presently strain it into milk Pans of an ordinary fulnes, but not after an ordinary way; for you must set your Pan on the ground and stand on a stool, and poure it forth that it may rise in bubbles with the fall, this on the morrow will be a very tough Cream, which you must take off with your Skimmer, and lay it in the dish, laying upon laying; and if you please strew some sugar between them.
>
> *The Compleat Cook* (1655) [p. 30]

Many writers assumed flexibility in interpreting the recipes. Cooks were told when to be guided by their own taste, or that of the master of the house. Gervase Markham expected the English Housewife to make her own adjustments:

> Thus I haue from these few presidents shewed you the true Art and making of all sorts of boild meates, and broths; and though men may coine strange names, and faine strange Art, yet be assured she that can doe these, may make any other whatsoeuer; altering the taste by the alteration of the compounds as shee shall see occasion: And when a broth is too sweet, to sharpen it with veriuyce, when too tart, to sweeten it with sugar: when flat and wallowish, to quicken it with Orenges and Lemmons; and when too bitter, to make it pleasant with hearbes and spices.
>
> *The English House-wife* (1631) [pp. 84–85]

Gervase Markham, through his several publications, typified the extended household at which the recipes were directed, with the husbandman who was concerned with the work of the farm, pastoral and arable, and the housewife in charge of the kitchen, bakehouse, brewhouse, dairy, still-room and garden. He described the equally important roles of the man and woman in sustaining the home and the family, and demonstrated the sheer amount of work needed to produce and prepare food, and conserve the produce at the time it was gathered or harvested.

In the kitchen, work began with the basics:

'After you have stuck the Pig, let him bleed wel …'
'Take a living Carp and knock him on the head …'
'Take a good Carpe and cutt his throte …'[25]

Water had to be fetched and some recipes specify, for example, conduit water or spring water. Sugar loaves had to be cut up, and the sugar beaten and searced until fine enough for the purpose. Currants would have to be washed and picked before use. Some processes could take days. Oranges for preserving would be in soak four or five days, with the water being changed twice a day; apricots would stand in syrup five or six days, being constantly turned and given a boil every day; a cock might have been stewing gently for twenty-four hours in a sealed pipkin placed in a brass pot of water, with the simmering water topped up as necessary. Sausages would be hung up in the chimney a month or two, and cheeses had to be pressed and wrapped, then rubbed, and turned every day. The lady or gentlewoman in a more affluent family would be contributing to the running of the household by taking on time-consuming if not arduous tasks, such as distilling or preserving, whilst servants prepared the daily meals.

The methods of cooking are all familiar, if relying on open fires or charcoal in chaffing dishes: roasting, boiling, grilling, frying or baking. All the recipe books assume an oven is available, but baking must have been an art and based on long experience. Kenelme Digby, in a recipe for making a White-Pot (an egg pudding with bread and raisins), advised steaming it in a covered dish set in a pot of water:

> You may bake it in an oven if you will; but it is hard to regulate it so, that it will be not too much or too little: whereas the boiling water is certain.[26]

Books and manuscripts combine to give some idea of the process.[27] The brick-lined oven was heated by lighting a fire inside; then the ashes were swept out, the oven floor swabbed clean, and the bread, pies or cakes laid in, sometimes on paper or trays, and left until done. Experience would teach what was too much or too little a heat, described occasionally as 'soft' or 'slack' for fine biscuits, or 'being no whotter then you may abide your hand in the bottome'.[28] The oven could be made cooler by leaving the door off, or reheated by putting a little fire or chaffing-dish of charcoal at the mouth. The benchmark

Figure 17. The labours of the countryside provided for the labours of the kitchen and dairy: frontispiece to The Country Housewife and Lady's Director, *by R. Bradley (1736).*

for heat seems to have been 'as hot as for manchet' (fine bread or rolls) or 'after the bread has been taken out': larger, coarse-grained household bread would need a hotter oven than the manchets. The final, dying heat of the oven was good for drying conserves and fruit pastes.

An oven was not always necessary if you had a baking-pan. MS 506 describes the process in the recipe 'To make a Marchpaine':

> ...set it on a board and couer it wth a bakeing pann and laie fire on it, when it is a little hardned, take of your pan and yse your march payne ... laie it [the icing] on the marchpaine wth [a] knife or a feather, then set on the pan and let it stand till the sugar be of an Ice, take it off and sett the bottome of the pann while the pann is hott to harden the bottome of the Marchpaine
>
> MS 506, f. 46

Fruit pastes, preserves and comfits could be dried in a stove or a drying cupboard, 'the heat of it [to] be renewed three times a day with a temperate drying heate.'[29]

The other methods of cooking are clearly set out by Gervase Markham in the second book of *The English House-wife*, 'Skill in Cookery'. He gives sections on fricassees, which could be made over chaffing dishes of charcoal as well as in a frying-pan on the fire; grilling or broiling; stewing, which could also be done gently over a chaffing dish; boiling in a kettle or cauldron suspended over the fire, or in a pot on a trivet set in the hot ashes; and spit roasting. Markham himself preferred to grill on a plate-iron with hooks on which the meat was hung, and which was set in front of the fire. He explained that drops of fat falling from the meat laid on a grid-iron over the flames caused the fire to smoke and the meat was blackened. Another implement was the wafering iron: the round flat irons at the end were heated in the fire, batter was poured on one of them and the other closed down to cook the wafers.

The most common word for cooking was 'boil'. The older term 'seethe', equally used with 'boil' in recipes at the end of the fourteenth century, gradually disappeared, and in the later sixteenth century the cookery books consulted here used 'boil' three times as often. By the seventeenth century, 'seethe' was rarely used, but it may have continued longer as an alternative word in more provincial locations. MS 506, located in the Lancashire-Yorkshire area, uses the older term about half the number of times it uses 'boil'. The early seventeenth-century compiler gave another term in a medicinal recipe to make a powder for the stone: it was taken in a posset that had boiled 'a wallop or two' (f. 63). Choice of word was probably not related to the intensity of the boiling process, which would be understood and regulated by the cook based on experience. However, a new term, 'simmer' or 'simper' emerged in the sixteenth century which does seem to indicate a low boil. This is illustrated by the recipe for 'Orenges, citrons, and all other fruites in syrup' in the second part of *The good huswifes Iewell* of 1597, which instructs 'heat it a little with a smal fire, for it must not seeth, but let it simper a litle' (p. 44). Two uses in *The Compleat Cook* of 1655 enforce this definition: a 'Posset the Earl of Arundels way' should be left 'to simper over the fire an hour or more' (pp. 3–4), and a 'Pudding after the French Fashion' was put in a pot and hung 'over a very soft & gentle fire, there to continue six hours in a simpering boile' (pp. 106–107). 'Stew' had been used as a cooking verb since medieval times, and was a common term in the seventeenth century, as part of the recipe title if not in the recipe itself. Its use as a noun, to represent the dish itself, came later.

The recipes also indicate what equipment would be needed in an ideal kitchen, and provide a comparison with the items listed in inventories of the period.[30] Working surfaces were provided by tables, boards and dressers. There were troughs and presses for cheese-making. Large containers included barrels, vats and tubs, with boxes and glasses for sweetmeats and conserves. At the fire were spits or broaches of different sizes, trivets, gridirons and broiling irons. The chaffing dish, holding charcoal, could take pans or dishes with ingredients that needed gentle simmering or constant stirring like custards. Cauldrons or kettles were suspended over the fire, and there were frying-pans, saucepans, skillets, pipkins and posnets. It is not necessary to be pedantic over the precise definition of these pans: in *A Queens Delight* a recipe 'To make jelly of raspis the best manner' uses 'Posset' (1655 edition) or 'Posnet' (1671) and 'skillet' for the same vessel.[31] Pots were of stone or earthenware, silver or brass. Pans similarly could be defined as earthenware or brass, or by their use for stewing, preserving or for puddings. Gallypots, or small glazed pots, were used for cooking or storage of liquids. Mortars and pestles were essential; occasionally recipes specify a wooden pestle in a marble mortar, or the mortar was of alabaster, stone, wood or brass. Graters were used, or implied by the instructions. There were cullenders, strainers and sieves, with hippocras and jelly bags; the bags could be of coarse hair or woollen cloth. Cloths were variously used for bolting flour, wrapping puddings, or straining; they were coarse, or made of cushion-canvas, fine canvas, linen or lawn, tiffany, cambric or wool. Food was prepared in basins or bowls, and served on dishes, chargers, plates, platters or trenchers. Sauce was served in a 'saucer' (sauce boat). Also available were porringers, cups, flagons, jugs and pitchers. Cutlery included ladles, cleavers, knives and spoons, but no forks were specified. It was also useful to have a coring iron, and a jag or spur 'such as the Pastry Cooks do use'[32] for cutting out pastry. Rolling pins were used, with one example of 'battle-dores' for the same purpose.[33] A straw, rush or reed was needed to test if fruit had been sufficiently cooked-through for a preserve. Scales and weights were mentioned or implied.

Measurements were becoming more precise, especially in the seventeenth century, although terms such as handful, ladleful, spoonful, dishful, gobletful or thimbleful were retained. Amounts used were bushel, peck, pound, quarter and ounce, with liquid measurements of a gallon, quart, gill, pint, pottle and dram. Sometimes there was further definition, such as wine pint.

The words of recipes for the domestic kitchen show none of the violence of the large, male-dominated medieval kitchen where they brayed, ground, smote, hacked, hewed and cleaved. Like their predecessors, the cooks of the sixteenth and seventeenth centuries stamped, cut, chopped, minced and pared, but preferred to beat or pound rather than bray, and slice rather than hew. Just occasionally in the northern and provincial MS 506 is 'bray' retained. Whatever words were used, however, preparation in the kitchen was hard work. Initially, this included washing, scouring, scraping and plucking; steeping, scalding and straining; shredding, coring and grating; bolting, sifting and searsing. Where earlier the ingredients had been tempered, meddled, drawn, alayed or done together, by this time they were more often mixed, mingled, worked or strained together. Mixing of the ingredients could take time, especially when bisket-bread, a kind of sponge cake or biscuit, was being made. At the very least the mixture needed an hour's beating, but the version in the *Arcana* (p. 70) took over three hours.

The process of cookery continued to evolve gradually, and new ingredients were being assimilated. John Gerard had included suggestions for cooking the potato in his *Herball* of 1597, 'either rosted in the embers, or boiled and eaten with oile, vineger and pepper, or dressed any other way by the hand of some cunning in cookerie'. William Rabisha had a recipe for Potato Pie in *The Whole Body of Cookery Dissected*, using nutmeg, cinnamon, ginger, sugar, the marrow from three marrow-bones, raisins, dates, candied orange and citron peel, eringo roots and butter, with a sauce of vinegar, sack, sugar, egg yolk and butter added at the last moment. Sir Kenelm Digby had collected a recipe for tea with eggs, and Hannah Wolley had one using chocolate but, along with coffee, these drinks did not generally appear in recipe books until the end of the century.[34]

Oranges and lemons were popular, both as ingredients in savoury and sweet dishes, and as a garnish. Supply of these could be adversely affected if relations with Spain deteriorated, as Oliver Cromwell discovered when he asked for his favourite orange sauce to accompany a loin of veal. He 'was answered by his Wife, that Oranges were Oranges now, that Crab Oranges would cost a Groat, and for her part, she never intended to give it; and it was presently whispered, that sure her Highness was never the adviser of the *Spanish* War, and that his Highness should have done well to have consulted his Digestion, before his hasty and inordinate appetite of Dominion and Riches in the *West Indies*.'[35]

Vegetables are always a hidden item outside stews and salads, which included boiled vegetables. This emphasizes the importance of Gerard's *Herball*, which shows the range of vegetables and herbs that were being cultivated, including new introductions. However, recipes call for cabbage and colewort, spinage, samphire, endive and lettuce, beans and peas, cauliflowers, onions, shallots, scallions, garlic, leeks, carrots, skirrets, potatoes, cucumber for pickling and radish in salads. Artichokes and asparagus became more usual in the seventeenth century, but celery was not evident until the later years. Perhaps vegetables could not have a separate identity in the menu until the habit of eating with a knife and fork was established, and the meat-with-two-vegetables format evolved. The recipes in the books under review here, up to the mid-1670s, do not indicate any changes in the centuries-old method of eating that used knife, spoon and fingers, and it was not until the end of the seventeenth century that knife-and-fork sets for the table were produced, indicating that change happened slowly.[36]

The most often-used herbs in the recipes were parsley, thyme, rosemary, sage, marjoram and savory. Saffron was still popular to colour food, but it was not in evidence as much as it had been in medieval times. Herbs used for medicinal purposes were far more varied.

The number of references to a particular ingredient does not necessarily mean that it was actually used in such quantities, or that the recipes containing it were made regularly. However, frequent references can indicate the taste of the period, especially relating to spices. The most cited ingredient was sugar. This reflects the preponderance of recipes for conserves, preserves and fruit pastes, but it was also used in sauces to accompany meat; in broths and stews where it partly offset the sharpness of verjuice or vinegar; in boiled meats and fish, such as in the recipe for capon in white broth; and in vegetable tarts like spinach tart. It could also be scraped over a finished dish as a garnish.

In the seventeenth century there was a growing liking for adding scents to food, notably musk (from the gland of a musk deer) and ambergris (a secretion from the sperm whale usually found floating on the sea or washed up on the beach rather that derived directly from the creature).[37] Another widely used ingredient was rosewater. A spoonful or two, and even a pint or gill, were called for in puddings and cakes. It was also used to steep gumdragon, dissolve sugar, glaze cakes and pies and to prevent almonds from oiling whilst they were being ground, thus adding its distinctive flavour to a range of recipes. Gumdragon (gum tragacanth) and gum arabic were used as thickening agents in sugar work and banquetting stuff, as was isinglass, a gelatine derived from fish.

Of the spices, the most called-for in recipes were nutmeg and mace, followed by pepper, cinnamon, cloves and ginger. The order of preference in medieval recipes, led by ginger, pepper and cubebs rather than cloves, cinnamon and mace, suggests a sharper taste for the earlier period. Nutmeg had hardly figured then, and its increased use in the sixteenth and seventeenth centuries must reflect the expansion in trade, when English as well as Portuguese and Dutch merchants made direct contact with the East Indies. The preference for sweeter spices, along with rosewater and greater use of sugar, defined the taste of the period 1575–1675.

Another characteristic is the number of different ingredients going into one dish, with fruit, sweet spices and sugar being added to meat in both stews and pies. This habit can be traced back to similar mixtures in medieval times, and was a style of cooking that would find less favour in the eighteenth century.[38] An extreme example is the olio, acknowledged to be of Spanish origin. Markham's version in *The English House-wife*, 'an excellent Olepotrige' (1631 edition, pp. 81–82) includes a whole range of ingredients: beef, mutton, pork, venison, veal, kid, lamb, pullet, partridge, chicken, quails, rails, blackbirds, larks and sparrows; potatoes, turnips, carrots, scalions, spinage, endive, lettuce, succory, buglosse, marigold, violet and strawberry leaves, seasoned with sugar, cloves, mace, cinnamon, ginger and nutmeg. It was served on sippets of bread along with prunes, raisins, currants, almonds and orange and lemon slices. *The Compleat Cook* offered a more restrained 'Spanish Olio', being 'utterly against those confused Olios', and suggested that the broth was drunk separately out of a porringer (pp. 92–93).

There is no indication in the period under review, to 1675, of what is now perceived as the traditional combinations of meat and sauce. Neither recipes nor menus give roast beef and Yorkshire pudding, although the batter used for basting during spit roasting would fall into the dripping pan and could be used as a garnish. Pork was not served with apple sauce, but a variety of sauces for roast meats are described. Mutton and mint sauce are not paired, but MS 621 has a sauce for roast mutton consisting of chopped meat and gravy with onions, *parsley* and vinegar. Perhaps the more simple combinations awaited the habit of eating with a knife and fork.

The printed books and surviving manuscripts afford a detailed view of domestic cookery unavailable from written sources before the sixteenth century, describing both cooking methods and the combination of ingredients. Some recipes have survived the centuries, and others are well worth reviving, offering a taste of traditional English cookery.

DOMESTIC ENGLISH COOKERY AND COOKERY BOOKS 1575–1675

NOTES

References are given to the earliest edition held in the Leeds University Library Collection, and to modern facsimiles and editions.

1. Some idea of this range at a particular moment can be obtained from the inventory of John Foster's bookshop in York, taken on 26 November 1616: York Minster Archives, L1(17)38. A transcription was published by Robert Davies, *A Memoir of the York Press* (Westminster: 1868), pp. 342–374, which includes an identification of the books listed. Only a small proportion covered domestic or agricultural/horticultural topics, but it includes *Delightes for Ladies* and what is identified only as Markham's *Husbandry*.
2. F.N.L. Poynter, *A Bibliography of Gervase Markham, 1568?–1637* (Oxford: The Oxford Bibliographical Society, 1962), pp. 128–77. *The English House-wife* was part of a composite volume, first as *Countrey Contentments* then as *A Way to Get Wealth*.
3. Gervase Markham, *The English House-wife* (London: 1631), p. 78.
4. W.M., *The Queens Closet Opened* (1655), title-page.
5. *A Proper newe Booke of Cokerye*, facsimile edition, edited by Anne Ahmed (Cambridge: Corpus Christi College, 2002); *A Booke of Cookry very necessary for all such as delight therin*, gathered by A.W. (London: 1584; 'newly enlarged' edition, 1587); John Partridge, *The Widowes Treasure* (London: 1585); Thomas Dawson, *The good huswifes Iewell* (London: new edition, 1596) and *The Second part of the good Hus-wifes Iewell* (London: 1597); facsimile edition *The Good Huswifes Jewell 2 parts* (Amsterdam and Norwood, New Jersey: Theatrum Orbis Terrarum, 1977).
6. Sir Hugh Plat, *The Jewell House of Art and Nature* (London: 1594; other editions in 1613 and 1653); *Delightes for Ladies* (London: 1602; 1605 and subsequent editions) – the 1611 edition in Leeds University Library includes the additional *A Closet for Ladies and Gentlewomen*; G.E. Fussell and Kathleen Rosemary Fussell, eds., *Delightes for Ladies by Sir Hugh Plat* (London: 1948).
7. W.M., *The Queens Closet Opened*, made up of *The Queens Cabinet Opened: or, The Pearl of Practise*; *A Queens Delight, or, The Art of Preserving, Conserving, and Candying*; and *The Compleat Cook* (London: 1655). See also *The Compleat Cook and A Queens Delight* (London: Prospect Books, 1984), a facsimile edition of the 1671 edition.
8. *The Closet of the Eminently Learned Sir Kenelme Digbie, Kt., Opened* (London: 1669; third edition corrected, 1677; Jane Stevenson and Peter Davidson, eds., *The Closet of Sir Kenelm Digby Opened* (Blackawton: Prospect Books, 1997).
9. For a full description of Markham's works and their subsequent editions, see Poynter, *A Bibliography of Gervase Markham*. References here to *The English House-wife* are from the 1631 edition in Leeds University Library. Charles Estienne, augmented by Iean Liebaut, *L'Agriculture et maison rustique* (Paris: 1570). *Maison Rustique, Or, The Countrey Farme*, compiled in French by Charles Stevens and John Liebault, translated by Richard Surflet, and augmented by Gervase Markham (London: 1616).
10. References are to *Murrels Two Books of Cookerie and Carving* (London: 5th edition, 1638). A facsimile version of this edition was published by Jacksons of Ilkley in 1985.
11. Robert May, *The Accomplist Cook, or the Art and Mystery of Cookery* (London: 1660; second edition with additions, 1665). The fifth edition of 1685 has been published in facsimile: *The Accomplisht Cook*, Robert May (Blackawton: Prospect Books, 1994). 'A short Narrative of some passages of the Authors Life' by W.W. follows Robert May's introductory Epistles to Lord Montague and others, and 'To the Master Cooks, and to such young Practitioners of the Art of Cookery, to whom this Book may be useful'.
12. William Rabisha, *The Whole Body of Cookery Dissected* (London: 1661; the Leeds University

edition is 1673). The edition of 1682 has been published in facsimile (Blackawton: Prospect Books, 2003).

13. Hannah Wolley, *The Queen-like Closet or Rich Cabinet* (London: 1670; second edition 1672; third edition 1675). See *The Gentlewomans Companion or, A Guide to the Female Sex* attributed to Hannah Woolley (the spelling of her name in this book), text of the 1675 edition (Blackawton: Prospect Books, 2001). The Introduction by Caterina Albano discusses the authorship of Hannah Woolley, and provides a biography (pp. 7–50).
14. *Delightes for Ladies* (London: 1605), section C, end of recipe 22; Fussell edition (1948), p. 79.
15. For a modern publication based on a manuscript collection, see Hilary Spurling, *Elinor Fettiplace's Receipt Book* (London: 1986).
16. Leeds University Library: Manuscripts, MS 621, f. 160v. Other inventories from this manuscript have been discussed by Peter Brears, 'York and the Gentry', in *Feeding a City: York*, edited by Eileen White (Blackawton: Prospect Books, 2000), pp. 154–159.
17. Leeds University Library: Manuscripts, MS 506, f. 78v. Several eighteenth-century hands are interspersed through the book, with dates including 1732 and 1758, but these have not been examined for this study.
18. George Weddell, ed., *Arcana Fairfaxiana Manuscripta* (Newcastle-on-Tyne: 1890). Although the original manuscript is lost, the facsimile does seem to represent a genuine collection. The facsimile was obtained partly by photography and partly by meticulous tracing of the original.
19. Note also the section on plagiarism in the introduction to the Prospect Books edition of *The Accomplisht Cook* (1994), pp. (18)–(20). Plagiarism in the eighteenth century was examined by Fiona Lucraft, 'A Study of the *Compleat Confectioner* by Hannah Glasse (c 1760)', in three parts, in *Petits Propos Culinaires* 56 (September 1997), 23–35; 57 (December 1997), 13–24; and 58 (May, 1998), 25–30. Further thoughts on the subject can be found in other issues of *PPC*: Stephen Mennell, 'Plagiarism and Originality – Diffusion in the Study of the History of Cookery', *PPC* 68, 29–38, and Henry Notaker, 'Comments on the Interpretation of Plagiarism', *PPC* 70, 58–66.
20. Comfit-making: see Malcolm Thick, chapter 3 above, Hugh Plat, *Delightes for Ladies* (1605 and 1611; Section A, 54; Fussell edition (1948), pp. 42–47; Hannah Wolley (1672), pp. 137–139.
21. Brears, 'York and the Gentry'. p. 158. T.D. Whitaker, *The History and Antiquities of the Deanery of Craven in the County of York* (London: 2nd edition, 1812), pp. 103 and 108.
22. May, *The Accomplisht Cook* (1665), pp. 156 and 171. Ivan Day explained at the Food Symposium on 24 March 2001 that the effective way to grind mustard seed with a cannon bullet is to hold the bowl and rotate it so that the bullet rolls around and crushes the seeds, but he advised that the bowl and bullet should not be carried together in a car being driven along roads in the Cumbrian hills.
23. The biography of Robert May is given in the (unnumbered) introductory section of *The Accomplisht Cook*. Further information on his career and employers can be found in the introduction to the Prospect edition (1994), pp. (10)–(18).
24. *The Court & Kitchin of Elizabeth, Commonly called Joan Cromwel, The Wife of the late Usurper* (London: 1664). A modern spelling edition with a preface by Douglas Clinton, *Mrs Cromwell's Cookery Book*, was published by Cambridgeshire Libraries in 1983. The references quoted from the 1664 edition are on pp. 12, 36, 43, 83, 44 and 47 of this modern version.
25. *Court & Kitchin*: How to souse a Pig (1664), p. 50; (1983), p. 45. To stew a Carp (1664), p. 141; (1983), p. 80. *Arcana*, To boil a Carp (pp. 115–116).
26. *The Closet of Sir Kenelme Digby, Kt., Opened* (1671 edition), pp. 188–189; Prospect (1997), p. 163.
27. This section is based on reading recipes in all the books cited above, and specific references are too numerous to detail. In particular, Hugh Plat's advice on heating the oven uniformly

28. Thomas Dawson, *The good huswifes Iewell*, first part, 'To make fine bisket bread', f. 13–13v.
29. *A Queens Delight*, 'To dry Apricocks' (1655), pp. 232–233; (Prospect, 1984), pp. 38–39.
30. A summary of York inventories was given in 'The Domestic Scene', in *Feeding a City: York*, pp. 123–137.
31. *A Queens Delight* (1655), p. 268; (Prospect, 1984), p. 74.
32. Wolley, *The Queen-like Closet* (1672 edition), pp. 82–83.
33. *A Queens Delight* (1655), p. 222; (Prospect, 1984), p. 28.
34. John Gerard, *The Herball* (London: 1597), p. 782; Rabisha (1672), p. 170; *The Closet of Sir Kenelme Digby, Kt., Opened* (1671 edition), pp. 124–125; (Prospect, 1997), pp. 198–199; Wolley, *The Queen-like Closet*, Part I, Item 163 (1672 edition), pp. 90–91. The potato could be the potato 'of Virginia', or the sweet potato 'of Peru'; both appear in Gerard's *Herball*.
35. *Court & Kitchin* (1664), p. 38, (1983), p. 39.
36. C. Blair, 'Introduction to the History of Cutlery' in the Victoria and Albert Museum Exhibition Catalogue, *Masterpieces of Cutlery and the Art of Eating* (London: 1979), pp. x–xiii. Early forks were usually used to eat sticky sweetmeats. See also Peter Brown, ed., *British Cutlery: An illustrated history of design, evolution and use* (Philip Wilson Publisher, 2001), especially David Mitchell, 'The Clerk's View', pp. 19–29.
37. Alan Davidson, *The Oxford Companion to Food* (Oxford: Oxford University Press, 1999), p. 14. Ambergris is defined in the Glossary of *Mrs Cromwell's Cookery Book* (1983), as 'a grey substance like dried putty, produced from a secretion of the sperm whale. It has a perfume like the blending of new-mown hay with the scent of violets'(p. 85).
38. In the preface to a transcription of the medieval cookery book *The Forme of Cury* (London: 1780), the editor Samuel Pegge commented: 'Many of them are so highly seasoned, are such strange and heterogeneous compositions, meer olios and gallimawfreys, that they seem removed as far as possible from the intention of contributing to health; indeed the messes are so redundant and complex, that in regard to herbs, in No. 6, no less than ten are used, where we should now be content with two or three' (pp. xvi–xvii).

CHAPTER FIVE

From Murrell to Jarrin:
Illustrations in British Cookery Books,
1621–1820

Ivan Day

Seductive high-resolution photographs of beautifully 'styled' food are one of the most important selling points of modern cookery books. Dramatic improvements in the past few decades in printing technology have created vast markets for colourful and highly pictorial recipe collections. The pooled expertise of the specialist food photographer, home economist and food stylist are now as important to the success of a book as the culinary and literary skills of the author. Recipes written by (or ghosted in the name of) a preferably attractive celebrity chef, illustrated with eye-catching photography and backed up by a television series, all combine to make the perfect formula for a best seller. This design-led approach has elevated some cookery texts to the status of 'coffee table book', with images of dishes that are more likely to be admired for their pictorial beauty than replicated in the reader's kitchen. Recently, cookery and other domestic arts have become television spectator-sports, with entire channels and networks devoted to so-called life-style programmes. The books emanating from these productions are just one aspect of the huge merchandizing machine created around the culinary high priest or 'domestic goddess' and are just as likely to be illustrated with stills of the great man or woman at work, as with photographs of their handiwork.[1] What a contrast this highly artificial situation is to that which prevailed during the formative years of cookery book publication when, with the exception of a few decorative title-pages, early English printed recipe collections contained very little pictorial material. When the first illustrations do start to appear during the course of the seventeenth century, their function is purely instructive and they rarely have any intrinsic artistic merit. Some, such as table plans and carving diagrams, belong to the realm of the steward, housekeeper and other servants concerned with laying the table and serving food. Others, such as trussing diagrams and pastry designs, belong to the world of the kitchen and its ancillary offices. Careful study of these humble woodcuts and engravings can reveal important clues about our ancestors' eating habits, which are often not apparent in recipes. Illustrations were copied from one book to another in much the same way as were recipes and this brief essay traces some of these influences. It also aims to illuminate a few other shady corners of culinary history and offers some thoughts on links and parallels with the European mainstream. It only briefly touches on the subject of frontispieces and decorative title-pages, which are a large subject in their own right and have been dealt with elsewhere.[2]

The first English printed cookery texts published during the sixteenth century are little more than slim chapbooks of a few signatures. They were cheaply produced and lacked illustrations. In these matters English publishers lagged well behind their Continental colleagues, who had been producing lavishly illustrated cookery texts since the early days of printing. Sixteenth-century editions of the first German printed cookery book, the *Kuchemeysterey* (first edition Nuremberg 1485) include a number of attractive woodcuts such as the kitchen scene in figure 19.[3] Books on sweetmeats and confectionery were occasionally illustrated in the tradition of the great European herbals, an outstanding work in this genre being Walther Hermann Ryff's *Confect buch und Hausz Apoteck* (Frankfurt 1567), which includes appropriate full-page illustrations of fruits and medicinal flowers by Jost Amman. Marx Rumpolt's encyclopaedic work *Ein new Kochbuch*, printed in Frankfurt in 1581, contains over 140 woodcuts by Amman, Virgil

Figure 18. One of the few illustrations to appear in a sixteenth-century culinary text printed in England. This woodcut shows a set of manica (jelly bags) for straining the spices out of hippocras. Girolamo Ruscelli, The Secrets of Maister Alexis of Piedmont *(London: 1558).*

Figure 19. Illustration of a kitchen scene from the Koch und Kellermeisterey *(Frankfurt: 1547). Genre scenes like this are common in German, French and some Italian books of the sixteenth century, often appearing among the text as vignettes. Similar illustrations of domestic scenes do not appear in English cookery books until the 1650s and are restricted to frontispieces and decorative title-pages.*

Solis, Hans Weiditz and other important Northern-school artists. Many of the images in these early texts are very much in the miniature tradition of the medieval illuminated manuscript and include kitchen and feasting scenes as well as illustrations of the tasks of the months. Their aim is essentially decorative.

South of the Alps, a more didactic approach to cookery book illustration starts to emerge in the last thirty years of the sixteenth century and vignette-style genre scenes give way to more detailed engravings illustrating culinary procedures and utensils. Twenty-seven engraved plates in Bartolomeo Scappi's *Opera – Dell'Arte Del Cucinare* (Venice 1570) give us an unparalleled insight into Renaissance cookery equipment and kitchen layout (figure 35). Scappi had an illustrious career, including a spell in the Vatican kitchens as *cuoco secreto* to Pius V. Later editions of the *Opera* were frequently combined with Vicenzo Cervio's *Il trinciante* (Venice 1581), one of a number of illustrated works solely devoted to carving and the art of serving. The woodcuts of dissection diagrams and carving tools in this important book acted as a model for many later monographs on the subject, including the highly influential *Li tre trattati* (the three treatises) of Matthias Giegher, published in Padua in 1639. Giegher's work features numerous diagrams for carving fish, flesh, fowl and fruit. It combined two earlier works by the same author – *Il trinciante* (the carver) of 1621 and *Lo scalco* (the steward) of 1623 – with a new treatise on napkin folding and table decoration. Giegher, (possibly an Italian attempt at spelling Jäger) was a member of the expatriate German community in Padua and worked as a professional carver. After his death from plague, a local publisher, Paolo Frambotto, bought Giegher's copper-plates at an auction and printed *Li tre trattati* to prevent spurious versions of the earlier two works, which were already beginning to appear in pirated editions. Complex procedures, such as pleating a napkin to resemble a tortoise, or carving a citron into the form of a lobster, are difficult to explain in written descriptions and Giegher's forty-eight detailed engraved plates give essential visual instructions to the would-be practitioner. These images were to be slavishly copied in many countries over the next two centuries, derivatives of them finding their way to England in the late seventeenth century (see figure 37).[4]

Designs for dining: Table plans

In addition to its extraordinary plates depicting carving and napkin-folding, Giegher's book seems to be the first European work to offer annotated table-layout diagrams. In this respect it is well ahead of its time, pre-dating the first French work to incorporate this feature by more than fifty years.[5] Among them is a scheme showing how plates of sweetmeats and fruit were to be arranged on the table for the *ultimo servitio*, or final course of the meal, which had become known in England at this time as the banquet (figure 23). Some large chargers, with the typical wide rims of this period, are labelled *marzapane* (marchpane), while smaller surrounding dishes are laid out with fruits and various comfits, including cinnamon, almond, fennel and coriander. The scheme is very similar to English descriptions of banquet settings from this period. In fact it could almost be an illustration to Gervase Markham's oft-quoted instructions for 'Ordering of Banquets' given in *The English House-wife* of 1615, in which we are told that 'March-panes have the first place, the middle place, and last place'. Giegher's much-imitated plates were considered to be the most up-to-date word on this subject in the early

Figure 20. Frontispiece of Hannah Wolley's The Ladies Delight *(London: 1672). This engraving (which had first appeared in the same author's* The Ladies Directory, *London: 1662) shows a gentlewoman in a room that seems to be functioning as a pastry or confectionery. Note the oven on the extreme left and the sugar cones on the shelf above the door. The highly ornamented metal apparatus on the charcoal brazier is puzzling. Is it meant to represent some kind of still? If so, it is probable that the artist had never seen one, as this is unlike any known from this period. It cannot be a water heater as the spout is coming from the top. If it is meant to be a still, the gentlewoman's use of a jug rather than a luted receiver is strange. This unusual image is one of the earliest English cookery book illustrations to depict a domestic scene, a fashion that seems to have started with the frontispiece of La Varenne's* The French Cook *(London: 1653), which shows a* cuisinier *at work in his kitchen.*

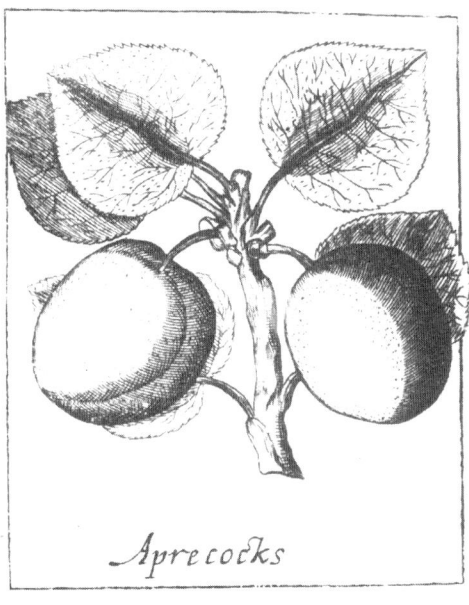

Figure 21. A woodcut illustration from A Book of Fruits and Flowers *(London: 1653), the only English illustrated work in the 'Herbal' tradition of Walther Hermann Ryff's* Confect buch und Hausz Apoteck *(Frankfurt: 1567).*

seventeenth century, so England does not seem to have been behind in these matters. The evidence of Markham's description would suggest that the conventions of the sweet after-course were very well established in England among the nobility, though less familiar to those somewhat lower in status.[6]

Markham's book was targeted at gentlewomen and housewives from the rural gentry and better-off yeoman class, aiming to give them an insight into the 'secrets' of table-craft as practised at court and by the nobility. The fashionable sweetmeat banquet of this period was an amplification of the void, the medieval court ceremony at the end of a meal when the monarch drank hippocras and ate spices, comfits and wafers. It was also to some degree modelled on the *ultimo servitio di credenza* of the Italian Renaissance *banchetto*, like the example illustrated in Giegher's table plan.[7] The influence of the Low Countries with their strong associations with Spain and its food traditions was also of great importance in stimulating English awareness of luxury sweetmeats of Mediterranean origin. Although these 'banqueting matters' had been essential treats at the English court for a long time, the growing availability of cheaper sugar was helping to create a market for luxury sweetmeats and preserves lower down the social scale. Publishers recognized a need for collections of banqueting recipes and a flush of specialist books emerged from the London printers in the first two decades of the seventeenth century. The public interest in small volumes of this kind was so intense and sustained that some of these works became best-sellers over a long period of time. For instance, Sir Hugh Plat's work on the subject, *Delightes for Ladies*, ran into numerous editions between 1600 and 1656. The closely related *A Closet for Ladies and Gentlewomen* (1608) was also re-printed at least nine times.

Apart from some attractive decorative borders, none of these works included illustrations. However, in 1621 John Murrell, an English contemporary of Giegher, incorporated eleven plans of sweetmeat arrangements in a small treatise on luxury banqueting foods entitled *A Delightfull Daily Exercise for Ladies and Gentlewomen* (figure 24). Unlike Giegher's plans, these arrangements hardly qualify as illustrations, since they are composed purely of text and lack the circular shapes that represent the plates and bowls. However, the plans clearly indicate where the various dishes are to be located on the table. The author instructs us to 'Serve your banqueting stuffe in Silver or Guilt Boules, or Glass Plates, and set your Boules on the Table as you see in these following examples'. They are in fact the precursors of the

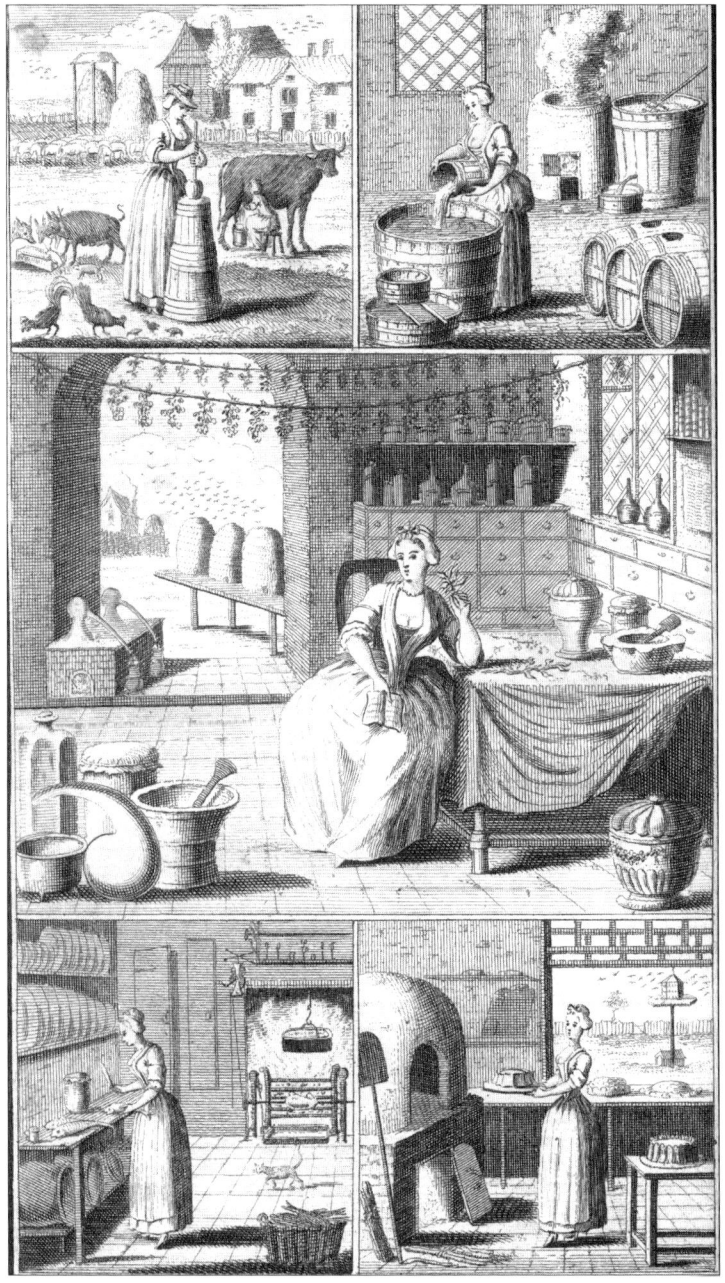

Figure 22. Engraved frontispiece from Nathan Bailey's Dictionarium Domesticum, *published by Charles Hitch (London: 1736). This fine plate showing a variety of domestic tasks, continues the tradition started by Hannah Wolley's frontispieces of the 1660s and '70s. In 1749, Hitch recycled the plate to create the frontispiece of* The London and Country Cook, *a spurious work claiming to be a collection of recipes by the celebrated court cook Charles Carter.*

text-only plans published nearly a century and a half later in works like Hannah Glasse's *The Complete Confectioner* (1760) and Charlotte Mason's *The Lady's Assistant* (1775).

Murrell's humble plans are the earliest English table-layout schemes, their publication predating Giegher's more pictorial diagrams by two years (*Lo scalco* 1623). Murrell, an entrepreneurial teacher of cookery and comfit-making based in London, in total authored four small household books. One of these, his first book, *A Daily Exercise for Ladies and Gentlewomen* (1617) also deals with banqueting foods. It has a very similar title to *A Delightfull Daily Exercise* of 1621, but its content is different. This slim volume was printed for the widow Helme in St Dunstan's Churchyard in Fleet Street, who also sold 'the moulds wherin any of the formes specified in the Booke following are made'. In the same year, the widow's neighbour John Browne published Murrell's *A New Book of Cookerie*. His last cookery compilation, *Murrel's Two Bookes of Cookerie and Carving*, appeared in 1631.[8]

In the preface to *A Delightfull Daily Exercise*, Murrell tells us of his 'travels when I was in France, Italy, the Low-Countries, and divers other places'. The title-page of his first cookery book also boasts of his grand tour – *A New Book of Cookerie… All set forth according to the now, new, English and French fashion. Set forth by the observation of a Traueller. I. M.* (i.e. John Murrell). The evidence of the recipes in his books supports these claims, as many describe how to prepare foods of Continental origin. For instance, in *A Daily Exercise*, Murrell gives a recipe for the little biscuits in the form of letters of the alphabet, which start to appear in Netherlandish paintings at this time. These 'Sinnamon letters by Art' also feature in two of his table schemes. Clara Peeters, Osias Beert and other Antwerp-school artists frequently depict them in confectionery still-life paintings. Sir Hugh Plat also mentions them in passing, but Murrell's recipe is the only one to appear in an English household text.[9] One of his table plans is for 'A Bill of Service for a Banquet on the Dutch fashion'. As well as sweetmeats, this arrangement includes anchovies, parmesan and caviar. This setting agrees well with the content of many Dutch 'banquet' still-life paintings of this period, which often have cheese and fish on the table as well as sweetmeats. He also gives a number of receipts for sweetmeats of Italian origin, with names like *callishones*, *muscachones*, *muscadinoes*, *gentillisoes* and *novellissoes*. His cookery texts are also rich in dishes dressed 'in the French manner'.[10]

It would seem that Murrell's focus was to make his exotic foreign recipes

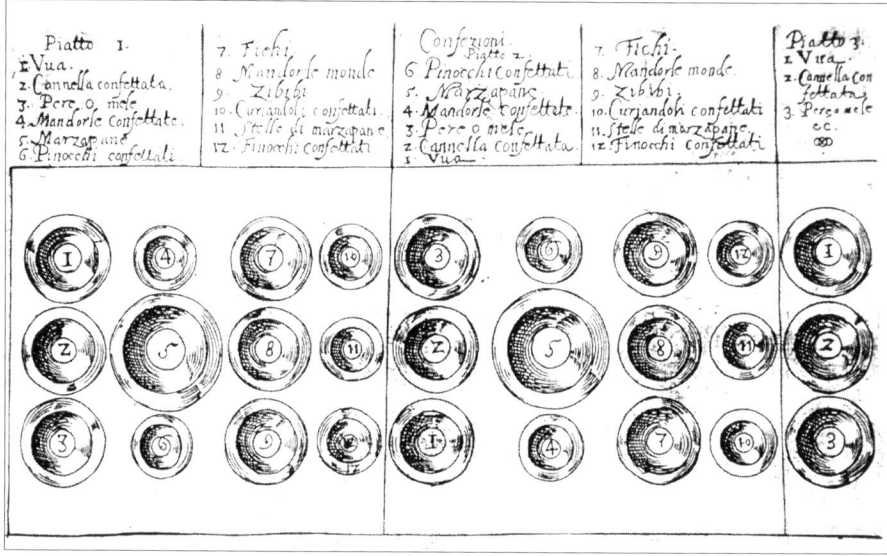

Figure 23. Table plan to show how sweetmeats and fruit were to be arranged for the ultimo servitio *of an Italian feast. From Matthias Giegher's* Li tre trattati *(Padua: 1639). The nature of the sweet foods on this table agrees well with those which appeared during the English banquet course. The items on the table are: 1, Grapes; 2, Cinnamon comfits; 3, Pears or apples; 4, Almond comfits; 5, A marchpane; 6, Pinenut comfits; 7, Figs; 8, Shelled almonds; 9, Raisins; 10, Coriander comfits; 11, Marchpane stars; 12, Fennel comfits.*

important selling points. This 'professor' of 'the secrete misteries of the purest preservings in Glasses and other Confrictionaries [*sic*]' seems to have been well aware of recent Continental trends, and was a well-qualified authority to teach English gentlewomen how to lay out their banquets in the most fashionable Italian and Dutch manner. It is puzzling that nothing like his little diagrams would be printed in a cookery text in England for another sixty-one years.

When table settings do next appear, it is not in a truly native English text, but in the 1682 translation by Giles Rose of *L'escole parfait des officiers de bouche* (*A Perfect School of Instructions for the Officers of the Mouth*), a collection of six little treatises first published in Paris in 1662. One of these, entitled 'A Master of the Household', is aimed at the steward and it features three table plans copied from the French work. These are easily recognized as debased copies of Giegher's schemes (figures 25 and 27). Although Rose includes the same numbers on the circles representing the dishes, he fails to include a key identifying the food items they contain. He also refers mistakenly to Giegher's banquet setting as a representation of 'the furnishing of an ordinary table – with a Reserve of three dishes for any Persons that may come at the time of Serveing'.[11] Rose's translation does not seem to have been a success in England, as it only appeared in one edition. Its copies of Giegher's table plans are decidedly old-fashioned, even for 1680s England, where new French modes of dressing the table were just beginning to take over from the earlier Italian and Dutch schemes, at least at the Stuart court.

Three years after Rose's book appeared, London experienced its most lavish entertainment for many decades. This was the coronation feast of James II in Westminster Hall on Thursday 23rd April 1685. Francis Sandford, the Lancaster Herald of Arms, received £300 from the King for writing a detailed account of the coronation ceremonies, published in 1687.[12] It contains a chapter devoted to the feast, illustrated with table plans and a perspective of Westminster Hall. Unlike the few sketchy plans of idealized meals and banquet settings that had appeared in print so far, the illustrations in this work are records of an actual event. The King and Queen's table is dressed *à l'ambigu*, with the banquet gracing the middle of the table throughout the two courses, rather than appearing as a separate third course after the meal (figure 26). One hundred and forty five dishes in the first course are arranged round three tall pyramids of sweetmeats, followed by a further thirty during the second course. A more old-fashioned method of service had been used at Charles II's coronation feast twenty-five years earlier, when 'the Banquet was served in 12 great Gilt Basons, and in each Bason 20 Boxes of several Confections dryed, in all 240 Pound, and betwixt the Basons 12 Dishes of choice Confections liquid, with 4 Basons of Creams'.[13]

Although the manner of service at James II's feast was based on more up-to-date French court dining protocol, the content of the meal was predominantly English in character. Apart from a few luxury items of foreign origin, such as caviar and mangoes, most of the dishes were not so different to those that had graced important English feasts since the Tudor period. The King and Queen sat alone at the heavily-laden table under their canopies of state (figure 26). Which of the dishes they chose from this overwhelming selection is not known. However, it is recorded that the King tasted one special item that does not appear in Sandford's long 'Catalogue of the several Meats.' This was a humble mess of *dillegrout*, a sacramental oat potage served to medieval monarchs at their coronation feast and specially revived for the occasion. Prepared by the King's master-cook Patrick Lamb, it was presented to the newly-crowned monarch by John Leigh of Addington in Surrey, whose family had an ancient claim to serve the dish at coronation feasts. The King

Figure 24. Two table layout diagrams from John Murrell's A Delightfull Daily Exercise for Ladies and Gentlewomen *(London: 1621). These plans for laying out banquets with sweetmeats are the earliest table plans to appear in an English cookery book. The author includes a total of eleven plans in his book, each showing nine typical sweet foods of the period.*

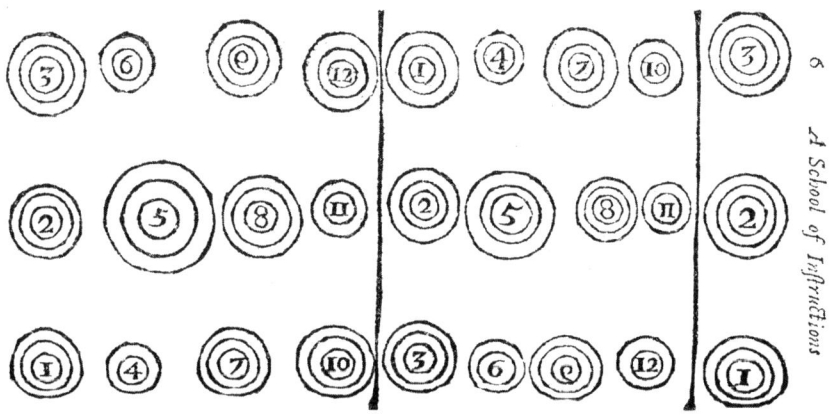

Figure 25. A rather debased woodcut copy of Giegher's banquet table (figure 23), printed in Giles Rose's A Perfect School of Instructions for the Officers of the Mouth *(London: 1682).*

must have approved, as Leigh received a knighthood a few days later. Lamb was not so lucky, as three months after the feast he was demoted to second master cook and yeoman of the pastry, and was replaced by the French cook Nicholas Fourment. During James's long exile in the interregnum years, he had become familiar with the new style of cookery at Louis XIV's court and was probably happier with a Frenchman in charge of his kitchens. *Service à l'ambigu,* with its tall pyramids of confectionery, became the preferred method of dressing English coronation feasts, being used at Westminster Hall for those of William and Mary (1689) Queen Anne (1702) and George II (1727).[14]

In the first year of Queen Anne's reign, the new French style of service was summarized in an English translation of François Massialot's *Le cuisinier roïal et bourgeois* (published in Paris in 1691 – first illustrated edition 1698). The English language version – *The Court and Country Cook* – was launched in London in 1702 and is illustrated with a number of engraved plates showing

Figure 26. Top, a detail of the King and Queen's table from an engraved plate by S. Moore in Francis Sandford's The History of the Coronation of James II *(London: 1687). Bottom, Sandford's table plan of the same table. These illustrations of James's coronation feast in Westminster Hall on St. Georges Day 1685 demonstrate how the French-style* ambigu, *with its pyramids of sweetmeats and fruit, was adopted at court well before the publication of Massialot's* The Court and Country Cook *in London in 1702.*

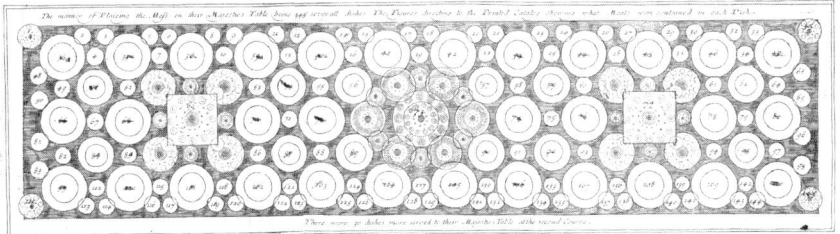

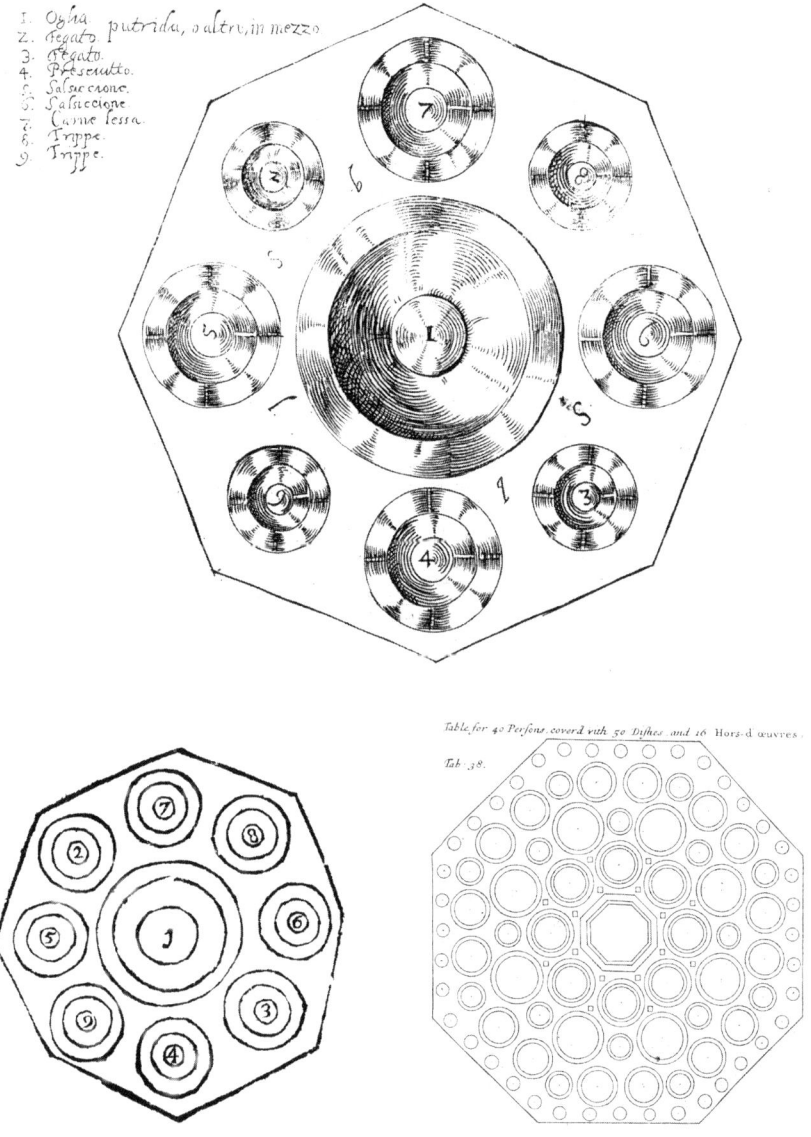

Figure 27. (Top) A plan for a table from Giegher's Li tre trattati *(Padua: 1639). The meal is dominated by a large charger of* oglia putrida, *a complex mixed meat stew of Spanish origin known in England as* olio. *It is surrounded by a symmetrical arrangement of other typical Italian dishes of the period. 1, Olio or another similar dish; 2, Liver; 3, Liver; 4, Ham; 5, Sausages; 6, Sausages; 7, Boiled meat; 8, Tripe; 9, Tripe. (Below left) A woodcut of an identical table plan from Rose (London: 1682). (Below right) A similar, though more complex table-layout from Patrick Lamb's* Royal Cookery *(London: 1710).*

table settings, including a dessert table complete with pyramids. Like Giles Rose's book, it only appeared in a single edition, but was to prove a much more influential work in this country. In her essay 'Ideal Meals and their Menus', C. Anne Wilson has shown how this work marked a watershed in the evolution of table plans.[15] After its publication, they became a much more common feature in native English cookery books. They appear initially in the works of cooks whose impressive *curricula vitae* included employment either at court or in the houses of the nobility. Their plans reflect the triumph at this high stratum of English society of the new French style of regulating a table. For instance, Henry Howard's *England's Newest Way* of 1703 (the first native work since Murrell to include table-layouts), shows how the soup was to be replaced with a *remove* – the English name for the *relevée* of French dining protocol. *Royal Cookery* (1710) by Patrick Lamb, who had prepared James II's coronation *ambigu*, contains numerous illustrations of *à la française* settings, featuring French soups, olios and bisques and their removes. Perhaps the most elegant engraved table plans of this period are those in *The Compleat Practical Cook* (1730) by Charles Carter which, like Lamb's, record actual meals, all arranged in flamboyant *à la française* style. The elaborate 'show-off' settings published by these culinary grandees are in marked contrast to the much more practical schemes that start to appear in the works of female cookery authors from 1727 onwards. Fiona Lucraft has examined this issue in her essay 'The Fine Art of Eighteenth-Century Table Layouts' and the reader is referred to it for a detailed analysis of the table plans of this period.[16]

Despite the strength of French influence, some early eighteenth-century plans still continued to display faint echoes of Giegher's pioneering schemes. Copies of his engravings had been circulating around Europe in numerous plagiarized versions of *Li tre trattati* for the best part of a century. Many English kitchen professionals would have known them through Giles Rose's translation of *L'escole parfait*. For instance, Giegher's plan of an octagonal dinner table has more than a passing resemblance to a similar, though much more ambitious scheme illustrated in Lamb (figure 27).

Giegher's choice of centrepiece for this setting, a large charger of *Olla potrida* (known in England as olio), is echoed in another of Lamb's table plans for a first course (figure 27). Lamb's plans frequently feature this dish, but he more usually places it among the bisques and soups in the new French manner and not in the middle of the table (figure 28). To feature it as a centrepiece is rather old-fashioned for this period. Charles Carter also illustrates a similar scheme with the olio in the middle of the table, though he, too, more usually puts it among the soups. Originally a meat and chickpea stew of Spanish origin, this truly heroic dish was adopted throughout sixteenth-century Europe as a symbol of ostentatious hospitality. Combining the products of farmyard, game park, decoy pond and kitchen garden in one enormous pyramid of boiled meat and fowl, this substantial dish was the culinary equivalent of those monumental paintings of game and butcher's meat by Frans Snijders and other Flemish artists.

Both Scappi and Rumpolt included recipes in their collections, indicating that it had become embedded in the Italian and German court tradition by the second half of the sixteenth century. A detailed recipe, probably of sixteenth-century provenance, was included in Markham's book of 1615, so it also appears to have been well known in England at this early period.[17]

Lamb had overseen the preparation himself of an 'Oglio hot' for James II's coronation feast in 1685. A very thorough recipe in his book outlines the elaborate preparations that would have taken place on the morning of the feast. He instructs the cook to start at six o' clock in the morning by boiling together a leg of beef, six pounds of brisket, a neck of veal, a neck of mutton and half a pig. A variety of vegetables were added and then we are told to 'get the Fowls following, or what the Country can afford, viz. Two Chickens, two Pigeons, two Woodcocks, four Snipes, two Teals or widgeons, two dozen of Larks'. The resulting broth was strained off and served at the beginning of the meal as potage. This was served from a large dish with a rim that had been raised with a collar of pastry. The assemblage of boiled meats was arranged in the form of a sugarloaf-like pyramid and enriched by pouring a rich cullis over the top. The olio's strong associations with the chase and the pastoral fecundity of the country gentleman's estate, made this monumental 'citadel' of flesh and fowl a highly appropriate dish for the landed nobleman's table. Its form was frequently echoed later in the meal by the dessert pyramids of sweetmeats.[18]

By the end of the seventeenth century, conspicuous extravagance of this kind was considered a little too coarse for the urbane culinary sensibilities of the French aristocracy. As a result, the number of the ingredients in Gallic versions of the dish (known in French as *ouille* or *pot pourri*) tended to be scaled down. These more refined adaptations became well established among the *grosses entrées* at French court entertainments. Instead of a large pyramid

Figure 28. Two table plans from Lamb (1710). That on the left shows the mode of serving an olio as a first course centrepiece, almost certainly in 'the form of a sugarloaf', as described in Lamb's recipe for the dish. This approach is close to that in Giegher's diagram and was the standard way of serving an olio until the late seventeenth century, though in England the olio as centrepiece seems to have continued until the 1730s. The plan on the right shows an olio terrine as one of the grosses entrées *of a much more up-to-date arrangement based on French court dining protocol.*

of carnage dominating the centre of the table, soups and stews of this kind were served from two specialized vessels – a round *pot d'ouille* and an oval *terrine* (later tureen) – usually arranged in pairs around a *surtout de table*. By the late 1720s, precious metal vessels to serve *ouille* were beginning to emerge from the workshops of important French silversmiths such as that of Thomas Germain and his son François-Thomas Germain.

In London, the Huguenot craftsmen Paul de Lamerie and Paul Crespin were producing very similar vessels for English aristocratic customers who wished to impress their guests with full service *à la française*. Notable among these was the 4th Earl of Chesterfield (1694–1773), who employed the French cook Vincent La Chapelle as his *chef de cuisine*. La Chapelle's cookery book, *The Modern Cook*, was first published in English in London in 1733, two years before a French language edition was issued in The Hague. It gives 'instructions for preparing and ordering publick entertainments for the tables of princes, ambassadors, noblemen, and magistrates etc.' It is illustrated with

Terrine *or* Olio.

Figure 29. Two copper-engraved plates from Vincent La Chapelle's The Modern Cook *(London 1733). These illustrations of silver vessels for serving the olios, terrines, bisques and potages of the first course were first published in London, when La Chapelle was cook to the 4th Earl of Chesterfield. Vessels by the French craftsman Thomas Germain dating from the late 1720s, and almost identical to those illustrated by La Chapelle, can be seen in the Paul Getty Museum in Los Angeles. The London-based Huguenot silversmith Paul de Lamerie also produced very similar vessels for wealthy English clients in the 1730s.*

lavish engravings of table settings and equipage. Among these are detailed images of a *pot d'ouille* and a *terrine* (figure 29). A scheme to show how they were placed on the table in pairs appeared in later French editions of the work (figure 30). This gives no doubt as to how the olios and other rich stews of the first course should be served in the most fashionable rococo style, rather than the earlier baroque approach of heaping up the meat in the form of a pyramid. It is possible that La Chapelle's sumptuous illustrations were based on actual items from Lord Chesterfield's remarkable collection of plate. Though these have not survived into modern times, very similar vessels by both Germain and de Lamerie have endured and can be seen in a number of public collections.[19]

The Modern Cook incorporates some table plans that are very ambitious in scope. 'A Royal Table of sixty Covers' (figure 31) gives us a useful insight into dining at the very highest level, with its great variety of dish shapes and arrangements of *surtouts de table*. The accompanying key to this plate informs us that among 'the 106 dishes great and small' are six pots of olios, each of them different, with only one being dressed *à l'Espagnole*. Recipes for all six are given in the cookery section of the book – one olio is of rice with crayfish, another is based on green peas. Versatility was one of the key charac-

Figure 30. This plan shows how the terrines *and* pots d'ouille *were to be arranged on the table for the first course. It appeared in the first French edition of La Chapelle's book published in the Hague in 1735.*

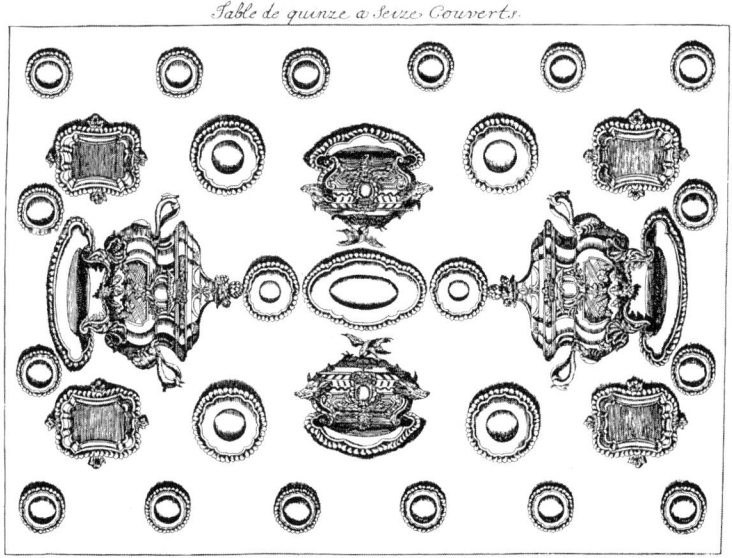

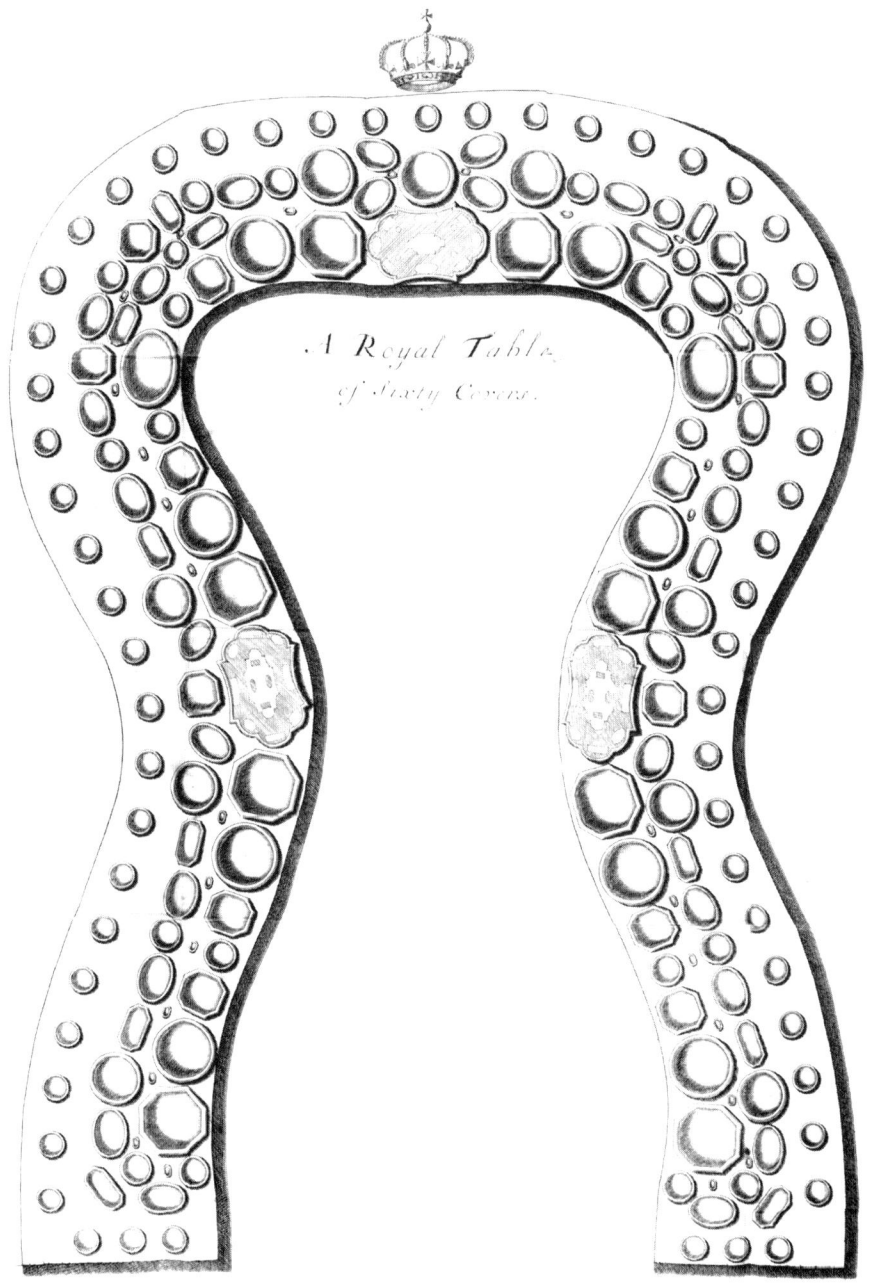

Figure 31. A Royal Table of sixty covers with three surtouts de table, the 'engines' originally designed for condiments, which often featured candle holders at this period. By the 1740s they had evolved into much larger table plateaux and were used for displaying the ornamental items of the dessert course (see Figure 58).

teristics of the new French court cuisine and this is reflected in these imaginative variations on an old and well-established theme.

Diagrams like this had real 'snob value' and provided a rare glimpse of the extravagance of regal dining for those whose lives were remote from court society. Their occasional inclusion in household books specifically aimed at the gentry and merchant class almost certainly had a voyeuristic intention. A good example of this is the illustration of an 'Instalment Dinner at Windsor' (figure 32) included in Charles Carter's second book *The Compleat City and Country Cook* (1732). Unlike his grander work on court cookery, the target audience for this more prosaic volume was a rung or two further down the social scale. Clues to the identity of its readership are provided by the recipes for the first-course stews, which are headed 'Spanish Olio, the cheap Way' and 'Spanish Tureene the easy Way'. The title-page boasts that the work contains a number of large copper-plates including 'The *Horse-shoe Table* for the Ladies at the late Instalment at *Windsor*; the *Lord Mayor's Table*; and other Hall Dinners in the City of *London*; with a Fish Table &c.' These must have been included for their curiosity value, in the hope that they would increase the appeal of the book and therefore sales. The same spectacular plates were used again in 1749 to illustrate a spurious work published posthumously under Carter's name – *The London and Country Cook*. This compilation of fairly ordinary domestic cookery and medicinal recipes is aimed at an even lowlier readership – the burgeoning middle class of Georgian England and their cooks and housekeepers. Similar 'souvenir' plates of regal tables were to appear later in the century in works like William Gelleroy's *The London Cook* of 1762.[20]

La Chapelle commenced his work with 'Directions for the House Steward', the officer who not only had responsibility for his master's precious plate, but also for the overall organization of household meals. One of his most important domestic duties was the drawing up of table plans: 'Moreover, a Steward of the Household must be able to form the Plan of an entertainment, to draw up a Bill of Fare, and to order the Courses for every different Table, according to his Master's Will and Pleasure…The Steward must form a Plan of the whole Service beforehand, ranging every Thing in its proper Place, observing well the different sizes of the Dishes, and what everyone is to contain. – He ought to be well provided with Plate, and must form his Plan, and make a Draught of all as regular and beautiful as possible.'[21]

It would seem, then, that stewards sketched their own table diagrams

Illustrations in British Cookery Books, 1621–1820

Figure 32. A large folding engraved plate from Charles Carter's The Compleat City and Country Cook *(London 1732). This work was aimed at a less well-off readership than the same author's sumptuous court cookery text of two years earlier. This 'show-off' illustration was probably included to impress those who could not aspire to this scale of entertaining.*

when planning an important entertainment, closely liaising with the cook. In many noble households it is likely that this practice was carried out on a daily basis for straightforward day-to-day meals, as well as for feasts for special occasions. Countless sketches of this kind must have been pinned up in the kitchen, thrown away as soon as the meal had been served, and consequently lost forever. In England, the only ones that don't seem to have perished in this way are in a small collection of documents drawn up in 1684 by the clerk of the kitchen to James Cecil, 4th Earl of Salisbury (1666–1694). This archive consists of about 85 lists of food for daily meals and among them are four table plans.[22] Each is dated and has been drawn on a single sheet of paper used on both sides. The first course of the meal is sketched on the front, the second course on the back. What makes these very early examples so different from most of the printed plans is that we can be sure that the meals recorded actually took place. They also represent fairly undistinguished meals rather than the sumptuous entertainments illustrated in the works of Lamb and Carter three or four decades later. The family dinners they depict are rather similar to some of the more modest bills of fare printed in the 1685 edition of May's *Accomplisht Cook*. Unfortunately, all are in very poor condition and some are so badly water-stained that parts of them are illegible. These plans would have enabled the clerk of the kitchen to manage the necessary provisioning and to discuss the content of the meals with his master or mistress. They were also essential to the cook, who could see at a glimpse how to structure his working day.

Plans for a dinner on Thursday January 20th 1684 are illustrated in figures 33 and 34. The first course consists of nine dishes typical of the period arranged symmetrically on the table. The second course features just five dishes. One of the Hatfield plans is so badly damaged that it is impossible to identify the main dishes ranging down the middle of the table. However, in the other three (drawn up for quite different times of year) there is a remarkable uniformity in the first-course foods. Potage is placed at the top end of the table, a dish of fish in the centre and roast beef at the bottom in all three. There is a little more variation in the main dishes on either side of the fish, but venison pie features in two, and scotch collops in three of the four table arrangements. The dishes of the second course offer more variety, with some seasonal foods such as asparagus and a fricassee of lamb appearing in a setting for May. Both the plans and the lists indicate that the diet of Lord Salisbury's household was English in character, with little hint of the new French influence, other than the odd fricassee. Lord Salisbury was only eighteen years old in 1684 and, since he had only succeeded to his title the previous year, had probably not had any experience of court life with its French fashions and food. In fact, he was still too young in 1685 to be ranked among those peers eligible to attend James II at his coronation, so both he and his Countess missed out on the great feast in Westminster Hall on St George's Day that year.[23]

One 'Thursday Dinner' (no month given) indicates that the Countess (Frances Bennett, *d.* 1713) dined separately from her husband on that day – 'My Lady's Table' is laid with a potage, a roast neck of mutton, a roast haunch of venison and a sallet for the first course. The second consists of three chickens, 'pease' and tarts. Lady Salisbury's table is laid in a much more modest fashion when compared to that of her husband. Some of these plans and accompanying lists also give us an insight into the hierarchical nature of the servants' meals. On Monday 15th September 1684, the male servants, who sat at the clerk of the kitchen's table, had one course only of three dishes:

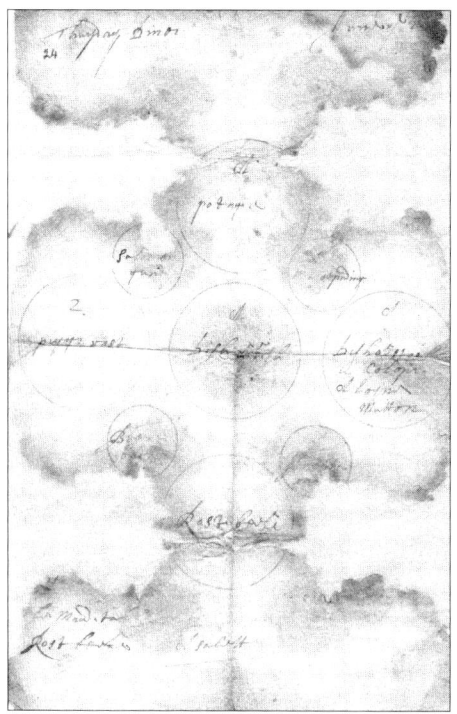

Figure 33. A manuscript table plan for the first course of a dinner served to James Cecil, 4th Earl of Salisbury on Thursday January 20th? 1684 at Hatfield House (Hatfield General 6/24 recto). The meal consists of a potage, a dish of fish, roast beef, a dish of scotch collops, a loin of mutton, 2 roast pigs, a salmagundy, a marrow pudding, beans and bacon and a fricassee of mutton? The sheet is badly water-damaged and at some time has been folded. Although it is not possible to read what the male servants were fed, the maids' table was laid out with 'rost beefe and a salett'.

Figure 34. The second course of the same Hatfield dinner (Hatfield General 6/24 verso). Only five dishes were served in this course – the potage of the first course was replaced with a large charger of ducks, rabbits and chickens. The centre of the table was graced with bacon and tongues. The other dishes were tarts and custards, 3 lobsters and 'a dish of pease'.

boiled beef, a breast of pork and a shoulder of mutton. The maids' table was also laid with one course, but this time with just one dish – a shoulder of veal.[24]

Planning meals for a large household was a demanding task, requiring a great deal of skill and experience. Availability of foodstuffs according to season and the need to offer variety one day after another, are just two of the many things that needed to be taken into consideration when sketching out a plan for a meal. The choice of second-course foods that could be quickly cooked while the first course was being consumed was also important. It was the steward's responsibility to ensure that the clerk of the kitchen, cook, butler and housekeeper worked together to make the system function smoothly. Carefully thought-out table plans and bills of fare were the best way of doing this. The origins of table plans in printed English cookery books are probably in these hand-drafted schemes, put together by countless stewards, clerks and housekeepers during the course of their daily duties. Most of the cookery authors whose books featured table plans had worked in great houses or other prestigious establishments. They would have used sketches similar to the Hatfield House plans to regulate the tables of their employers. It is possible that at least some of the settings they published for

Figure 35. A figure showing an Italian cook carving a joint in alto, *while his assistant uses a duck press to extract gravy. From Bartolomeo Scappi's* Opera *(Venice: 1570).*

Illustrations in British Cookery Books, 1621–1820

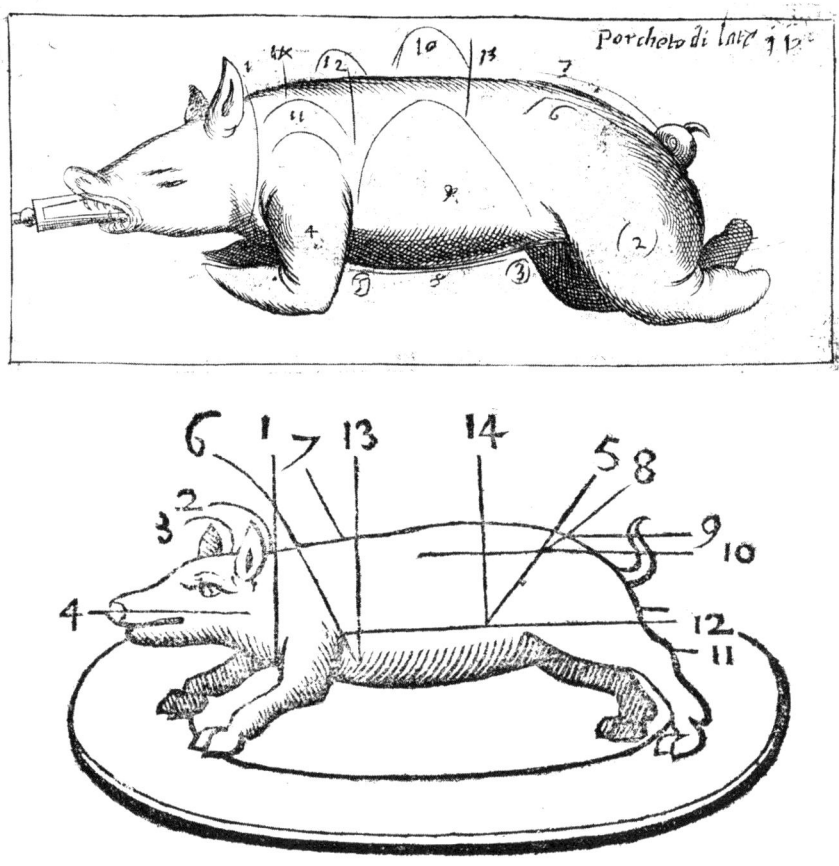

Figure 36. Dissection plans for carving a roast pig in the Italian manner. The etching at the top of the page is from Giegher (1639). The woodcut below is from Rose (1682), which is clearly a copy of the former. The native English style of carving and serving a suckling pig is shown in Figure 40.

the benefit of their readers were based on hand-drafted diagrams they had kept in their possession.

Carving diagrams

John Murrell may have had the foresight to include innovative table plans and fashionable continental recipes in some of his books, but despite its name, his *New Booke of Carving and Sewing* (1630) is a very old-fashioned work. The complex system of carving it describes is wholly medieval in character, being achieved entirely without the aid of a carving fork. Murrell's text is in fact a plagiarized version of Wynkyn de Worde's *Boke of Kervynge* of 1508, a small treatise summarizing the system of aristocratic table service used in medieval English royal palaces and noble households. Practical instructions for carving everything from a pike to a peacock are given in considerable detail, with hints on the *modus operandi* of serving food and drink at a noble table. It belongs to the medieval tradition of the courtesy book and derives ultimately from fifteenth-century manuscript sources such as John Russell's *Boke of Nurture* (1440), which describes a court dining protocol that had already been codified for the best part of a century and a half.[25]

During the fifteenth and sixteenth centuries, carving was considered an important social accomplishment and was taught to young noblemen at their parents' table through practical experience. Some young boys were boarded out to court as 'henxmen' to learn the craft from professional carvers. Courtesy books were written by 'maisters of the henxmen', like Russell, and were frequently composed in rhyme to help scholars learn the terminology of table service more easily by rote. This is why the 'Tearmes of a Carver' reprinted in Murrell's book are listed in 'sing-song' repetitive form such as, 'Breake that Deere, leach that Brawne, reare that Goose, lift that Swan' etc.[26]

Giegher's work on carving, published in the same decade as Murrell's reprint, comes from an entirely different world. It is a profusely illustrated account of a new system of carving developed in Renaissance Italy, which is based on the skilful use of specialized forks and carving knives. It not only shows would-be practitioners how to carve a wide range of flesh, fish and fowl, but also to whittle fruits, such as citrons, into the most extraordinary shapes (figures 36 to 38). It illustrates a set of carving forks and knives of various sizes in a large folding diagram. Supplementary plates show how these were used. Italian carving forks had very long tines and were triangular in section, allowing the carver to securely impale the bird or joint. He was then able to carve the meat with the aid of a razor-sharp knife in mid-air. This impressive procedure, known as carving *in alto,* is perfectly illustrated in an engraving in Scappi's *Opera* (figure 35). It was conducted at the tables of popes, prelates and princes with virtuoso skill and high ceremony. After his death, Giegher's text and illustrations were enthusiastically copied and

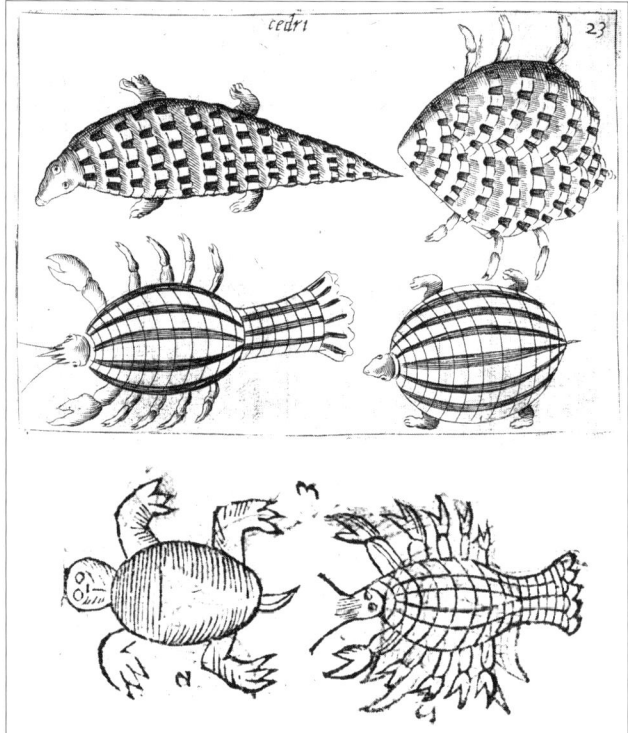

Figure 37. One of two plates from Giegher which show how to carve citrons in the form of animals. Below are two of Rose's much more primitive woodcuts, clearly showing the influence of Giegher's illustrations.

formed the basis of almost every European work on the subject over the next two centuries.

Conservative resistance to the fork in England in the first half of the seventeenth century meant that ostentatious Italian carving methods never caught on in this country. For many years English carvers continued to secure their master's meat on the plate with the first two fingers and thumb of the left hand while they sliced it according to art with the knife held in their right hand. While the rest of Europe moved on in these matters, this medieval mode of cutting up meat became marooned in England. Cookery books, such as those of Robert May (1660), William Rabisha (1661) and John Nott (1723), continued to include the ancient terms of carving and service.[27] Ironically, May, like Murrell, dishonestly describes these centuries-old procedures as '*The most Exact, or A-la-mode Ways of Carving and Sewing*'. These ancient instructions may have been included for curiosity value, reflecting the growing interest in antiquarianism during this period. Carving as it was actually practised in the seventeenth century was probably much simpler than the medieval system outlined in these books. By the closing decades of the eighteenth century, carving instructions in some works still include guidelines for *lifting* swans, *displaying* cranes and *dismembering* herons. So durable was this conservative English tradition that many of these instructions agree word for word with those written by John Russell in the 1440s.[28]

Complex procedures for cutting up the different joints of meat and birds are difficult to describe in words. The often-ambiguous instructions given in works like Murrell's would have been easier to follow if they had been accompanied by illustrations. However, the first carving diagrams to be published in England do not appear until 1682. They are in fact woodcut copies of Giegher's plates and surface in Giles Rose's translation of *L'escole parfait* (figures 36 and 37). They illustrate a Continental system of carving that was quite alien to most Englishmen, a factor which may explain why the book was not terribly successful. Although Italian carving protocol was widespread throughout Europe, national variations appear to have survived in some countries as well as in England. Rose advises the professional carver to be flexible and to conform 'himself to the use and custom of the Country, where he shall happen to serve, that he may know how to learn their ceremonies'.[29]

There is some evidence that carving schools existed in London at this time, where scholars were instructed in the native English style. It would seem that a number of curious teaching strategies were used in these establishments. In 1693, an unusual work on the subject was 'Set forth by several of the best Masters in the Faculty of Carving, and Published for publick Use.' This was a little 48-page booklet called *The Genteel House-Keepers Pastime: Or, the Mode of Carving at the Table Represented in a Pack of Playing Cards*. Although a number of copies of the book have survived, no set of the playing cards engraved with carving diagrams has come to light. It is likely that these were the earliest illustrations of carving procedures in the native English tradition. According to the author of *The Court & Kitchin of Elizabeth… Cromwel* (1664), wooden models of birds and joints were also at one time used to instruct would-be carvers in the mysteries of the art.[30]

In addition to the carver himself, other kitchen professionals such as cooks and confectioners required some carving skills in the course of their daily work. An accomplished cook in the seventeenth century needed to be able to carve fruits and vegetables into attractive shapes for garnishing plate rims and decorating salads and dishes of brawn. Robert May instructs us to

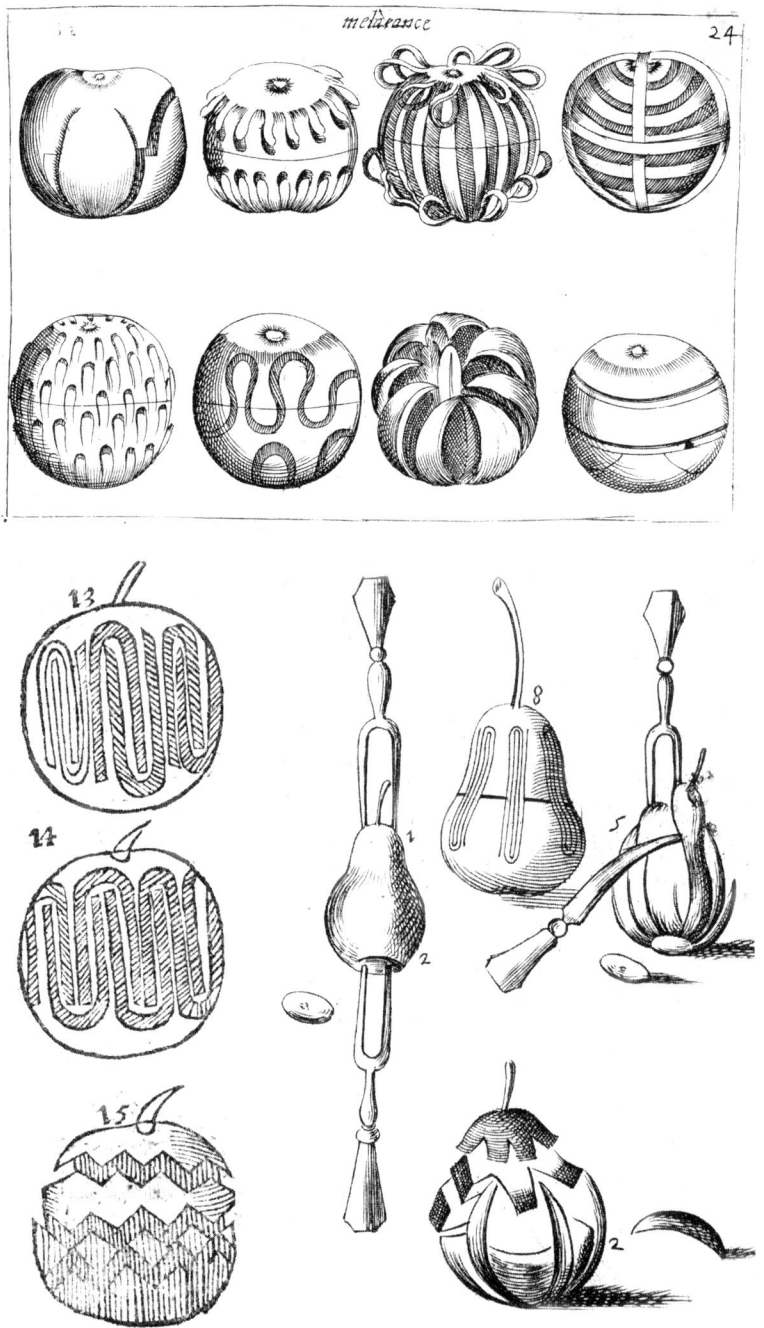

Figure 38. Designs for carving oranges from Giegher. (Bottom left) Three designs for carved apples from Rose. (Bottom right) A detail of Giegher's illustration showing the method to carve pears.

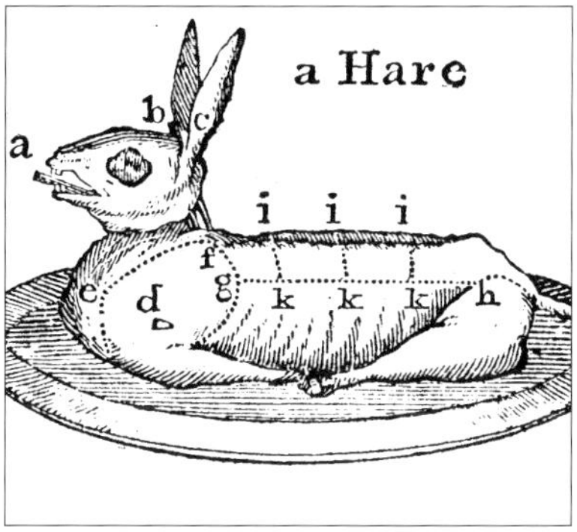

Figure 39. A dissection diagram showing how a roasted hare was to be carved in the native English style. Woodcut from John Trusler's The Honours of the Table *(London: 1788). The ears, roasted crisp, were especially esteemed, but had to be protected from the fire in the early stages of roasting by enclosing them in paper.*

Figure 40. The diagrams on this engraved carving plate from Collingwood and Woollams' The Universal Cook *(London 1792) was copied from Trusler's little book of four years earlier. Versions of them also appeared in William Augustus Henderson's* The Housekeeper's Instructor *(London ca. 1790). Trusler's plates were to form the basis of most carving diagrams well into the nineteenth century.*

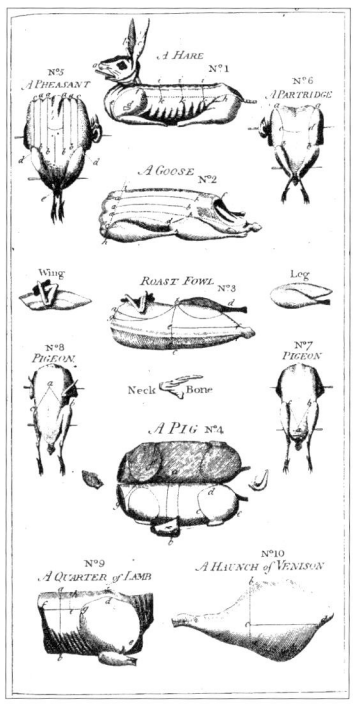

garnish brawn with 'carved lemons, oranges and barberries, bay-leaves gilt, red beets, pickled barberries, pickled gooseberries, or pickled grapes'.[31] Oranges and lemons were also carved with intricate designs and then preserved in syrup, a tradition first described in English confectionery texts in the eighteenth century.[32] The only designs that ever appeared in England for creating these delightful decorations are those in Rose's book. Again most of these are derived from Giegher's engraved plates, though some seem to be new. Even a variety of Giegher's stunning illustrations of carved *cedrati* (citrons) appear in debased versions (figure 37).

When the carving fork did eventually come into common usage in England after the Restoration, it differed considerably from the Italian-style fork used for *in alto* carving performances. It was furnished with short round tines and was used solely for stabilizing the meat on the plate. It in fact replaced the two forefingers and thumb of the medieval system. Surviving examples from this period are almost identical with those we use today. Their adoption meant that it was now unacceptable for the carver to touch the meat. In 1670, Hannah Wolley tells us 'the neatest carvers never touch any Meat but with the Knife and Fork; he must be very nimble lest the Meat cool too much, and when he hath done, return the Carving Napkin, and take a clean one to wait withal.'[33]

Carving seems to have become an acceptable practice for women some time after the Restoration. However, most of the female cookery writers of the eighteenth century do not offer carving instructions in their works.[34] No illustrations of the art appear in any eighteenth-century English cookery book until the publication of John Trusler's *The Honours of the Table* in 1788 (figure 39). The simple, but very clear woodcuts of carving procedures in this work are entirely original and owe nothing to Giegher's designs, which continued to be published in France until a decade after the Revolution.[35] Trusler's schemes, entirely English in character, were immediately plagiarized, copies of them first appearing in Henderson's *The Housekeeper's Instructor* (ca. 1790) and then in Collingwood and Woollams' *The Universal Cook* (1792) (figure 40). In a kitchen scene depicted in the frontispiece of early editions of Henderson, a male servant is being instructed to carve by a steward or butler who is pointing to carving illustrations, presumably in a copy of Henderson's book. Versions of Trusler's diagrams continued to be reproduced over the next hundred years, finding their way into numerous Victorian household guides and cookery books, including those of Eliza Acton (1845) and Isabella Beeton (1861).

Designs for the cook: Pie and pastry designs

In 1658, two years before Robert May's *Accomplisht Cook* appeared in the London bookshops, the publisher Nathaniel Brookes printed a list of 'Books, in the Press and ready for Printing'. This appeared in a small supplement to his third edition of *The Queens Closet Opened*. Among these advertisements was a short entry singing the praises of May's forthcoming work, with its 'All-

Figure 41. Designs for bride pies (left) and mince pies (right), from Robert May's The Accomplisht Cook *(London 1660). These compound pies were made up from symmetrical arrangements of a number of small shaped pies, a tradition that does not seem to have been confined to England alone.*

a-mode curiosities, together with the lively illustrations of such necessary figures, as are referred to practise'.[36] When the book was launched, these 'lively illustrations' proved to be the very first images of actual food to appear in an English printed cookery book. They provide a unique insight into food presentation in Stuart England, particularly in pastry work, and start a trend in cookery illustration that lasts for almost a hundred years. The enlarged fifth edition of 1685 boasts of 'two hundred Figures', most of which are printed on four large folding plates, though there are also a number of small in-text illustrations scattered throughout the work. A few of these are naïve woodcuts of fish and decorations for blancmangers and whitepots, but most are representations of various kinds of pastry work. A huge variety of pies, pasties, cut-laid tarts, florentines, custards and cheesecakes are illustrated in this unique work (figure 41).

The spectacular tradition of the pastry cook displayed in these simple cuts was already well established when May worked in the early 1600s as a young apprentice to Arthur Hollinsworth, master cook to the Grocer's Hall and Star Chamber. Like most traditional art forms, pastry decoration during this period seems to have been subject to a degree of convention. For instance, pies were frequently given a particular shape in order to enable the diners to identify their contents. There is evidence that this tradition was not just confined to England, though no European culinary professional during the course of the seventeenth century produced illustrations comparable to those published in May's book. However, a number of early Netherlandish artists

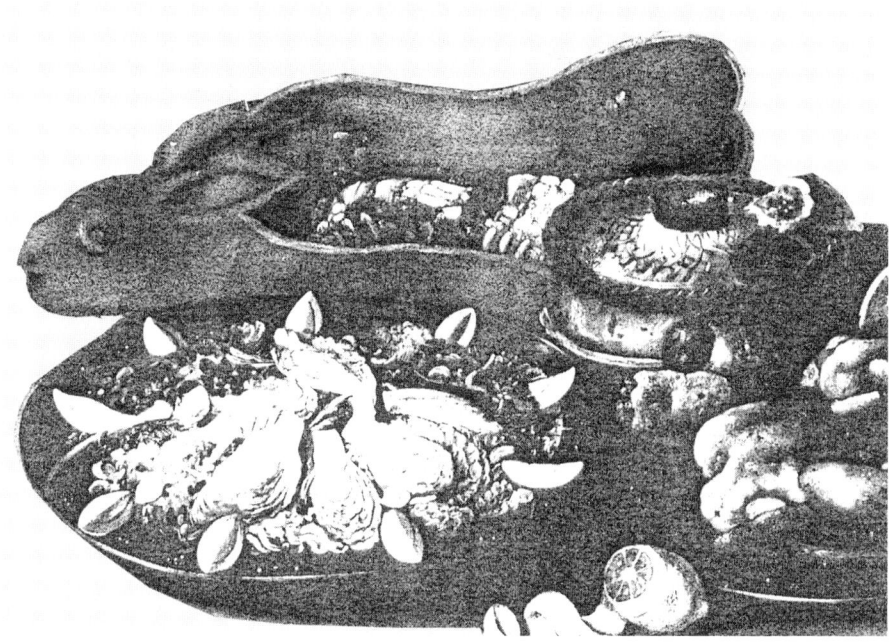

Figure 42. School of Osias Beert. A detail from a still life showing a rabbit pie and other foods on a table. Oil on panel, early 17th century. (Current whereabouts unknown.)

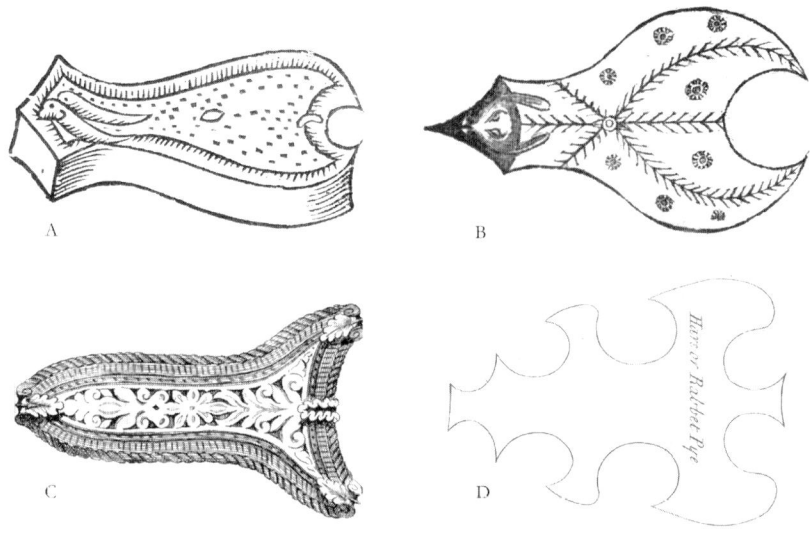

Figure 43. Designs for rabbit and hare pies relating closely to the pie depicted in the Beert still life. A. May (1660). B. Thacker (1758). C. Hagger (1719). D. Kidder (ca.1720).

do depict pies and pastries in their paintings with close similarities to those represented in May's little woodcuts.

A still life by a follower of the Antwerp artist Osias Beert (*ca.*1580–1623), painted when Robert May was a young man, depicts a table setting with a pie in the form of a rabbit or hare (figure 42). The pastry coffin is fiddle-shaped and is ornamented with a realistic pastry sculpture of the animal's head, complete with ears. It is very similar to a small primitive woodcut in *The Accomplisht Cook* printed above a recipe 'To bake a Hare with a Pudding in his belly' (figure 43A). The author tells us to 'Make your Hare-Pie according to the foregoing form'. The close resemblance of these two pies could be a coincidence, but there is evidence that similar hare and rabbit pie designs were widespread in Europe. In some places they seem to have endured well into the following century. The German cook Conrad Hagger included a large number of designs for pies and pastries in his encyclopaedic *Neues Saltzburgisches Koch-Buch* (1719). Hagger was born on the Rhine in 1666 and trained in St Gallen in Switzerland. He worked as a military cook in the Balkans before taking up various posts in Austria, Germany and Northern Italy. For the last twenty-seven years of his career he worked as the *Stadt- und Landschafft Koch* to the Bishop of Salzburg.[37] The fine engravings of pastry work in his profusely illustrated book are of very high quality. Many have striking similarities to May's more primitive woodcuts, some of them representing hare and rabbit pies baked in comparable fiddle-shaped coffins (figure 43C). John Thacker, master cook to the Dean and Chapter of Durham Cathedral, also illustrates a very similar rabbit pie in his cookery book of 1758 (figure 43B).[38] In European cities as far apart as Antwerp, London, Salzburg and Durham, over a period of about one hundred and forty years, we see the same approach to decorating a rabbit pie.

The similarity between other designs in May to those in Hagger's book is striking and would support an argument for a pan-European school of pastry design. For instance, their illustrations of fish pies and pasties are very close in spirit. Both authors include a number of designs for pastry coffins with unusual asymmetrical shapes, suggesting that a number of them were to be put together to form a pleasing pattern (figure 49). That this happened in practice is borne out by some woodcuts of mince and bride pies in May's illustrations, showing how they were arranged to create a kaleidoscopic effect (figure 41). Similar compound arrangements of mince and egg pies also appear in eighteenth-century cookery texts. An illustration from *The Queen's*

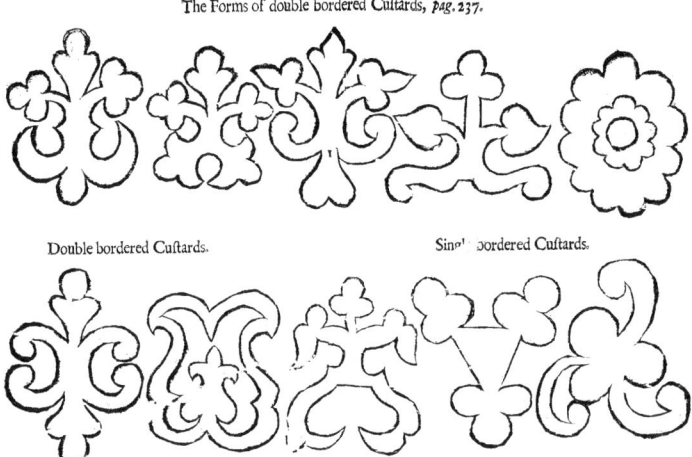

Figure 44. Custard designs from May (1660). A number of double-bordered custard shapes were used to surround one single-bordered custard to create similar arrangements to those illustrated in Figure 41.

Royal Cookery (1710) shows how these shaped mince pies were arranged on a salver (figure 48). Another, in Edward Kidder's *Receipts in Pastry and Cookery* of ca. 1720 shows a decorative arrangement of egg pies (figure 51).

May illustrates some particularly complicated designs for baked custard tarts in the form of sinuous cants and volutes (figure 44). Some of these are irregular in form and are labelled 'double bordered custards'; others are entirely symmetrical and are 'single bordered'. It would seem that the latter were surrounded by an arrangement of the double-bordered variety in order to create a pattern rather like the beds of a knot garden. These complex custards are alluded to in a poem dedicated to May by James Parry: 'A City Custard doth so subtly wind,/That should Truth seek, she'd scarce all corners find.'

They appear on the bills of fare of city livery company feasts in the sixteenth century, which is probably why Parry calls them city custards.[39] They were also familiar to Ben Jonson, who refers to them in *The Staple of News* of 1631, in which Lickfinger the cook:

> Mounts marrow bones, cuts fifty-angled custards,
> Rears bulwark pies, and for his outer works,
> He raiseth ramparts of immortal crust;

May gives a recipe for the pastry used for the coffins of these eccentric custard tarts. Made from flour, a little sugar and boiling water, it is in fact a hot-water paste without shortening. It was rolled thin and the shaped base of the form was cut out, probably with the aid of a paper template.[40] May's designs were almost certainly intended as patterns for templates of this kind. Gervase Markham outlines the rest of the process: 'raise it in pretty works or angular forms, which you may do by fixing the upper part of the crust to the nether with the yolks of eggs'. The coffins were pricked to stop them blistering and then hardened in a cool oven to a pale white. To prevent the walls and corners from collapsing, we are instructed by another author to 'stuff the Corners with brown Paper'.[41] The egg and cream custard mix was poured into the coffins without removing them from the oven, via a special custard funnel with a long pipe. After gentle baking, they were ornamented with colourful caraway comfits and muskadines. Although the custard fillings made very good eating, the 'fifty-angled' pastry coffins were inedible – their role was purely ornamental. Since they were so much trouble to make, it is possible that once the custard had been consumed, the ceramic-hard coffins may have been used again.

The popularity of these improbably shaped tarts endured well into the eighteenth century, when they became known as 'set custards' (figure 51). Their convoluted forms are very much in the style of the decorative strap work of the 1570s and they must have looked oddly out of place on tables set in the elegant manner of the 1730s. They are in fact survivors of a very old food tradition that emphasized the decorative merits of pastry rather than its eating qualities. Although May's book contains an excellent range of perfectly appetizing pastry recipes, his custard paste is identical to modern children's 'play dough' and about as edible. However, it was ideal for its ornamental role, which could not be achieved with short or puff paste.

May's contemporary La Varenne, whose *Le Cuisinier François* had appeared in translation in England during the 1650s, rarely refers to pastry ornamentation, other than the odd *chapiteau* for the top of a *pâte*.[42] In truth, La Varenne's range of pastry recipes is more limited than May's, who gives five excellent receipts for puff paste, all of which work extremely well when properly followed. In addition his three recipes for 'paste royal' for tarts are also excellent. The English at this time could be justly proud of the quality of their pastry work. It would be a generation or so before the whole accent of the French approach would be on eating quality achieved through carefully controlled pastry-room procedures. Initial English reaction to French pastry recipes was predictably conservative. Parry, who was full of admiration for May's 'City Custards', is scathing of *Le Pâtissier François* (traditionally ascribed to La Varenne), which had appeared in London in 1656 as *The Perfect Cook*:[43]

> A Good *English* Cook,
> Excellent Modish Monsieurs, and that Book
> Called *Perfect Cook*, *Merete's* Pastery
> Translated, looks like old hang'd Tapistry,
> The wrong side outwards: so Monsieur adieu,
> I'm for our Native *Mays* Works rare and new

Even Marnette, the translator of *Le Pâtissier François* and of French extraction himself, expressed embarrassment at presenting a collection of French pastry recipes 'to this Nation, where every Matron and young Damsel are so well vers'd in the Pastry Art, as that they may out-vie the best Forreign Pastry Cooks in the World besides'.[44]

No passage in 'Native Mays' book is more resonant of the old style of cookery than the oft-quoted *Triumphs and Trophies in Cookery* passage in his

Figure 45. Designs for pies in the form of stag (top right) and an alpine chamois (bottom right). The instructions explain how the underlying superstructures were made out of twisted wire, while the necks were formed carefully from wood. Forms of other animals, such as lions, were made in the same way before the whole skeleton was covered in pastry. Conrad Hagger, Neues Saltzburgisches Koch-Buch *(Augsburg: 1719).*

introductory section. In this, the author nostalgically recollects Twelfth-day entertainments, which were 'formerly the delights of the Nobility, before good House-keeping had left England'. He describes a performance featuring pastry sculptures of a castle, a ship and a 'Stag made of coarse paste with a broad Arrow in the side of him'. The stag's body was filled with claret, so when the arrow was pulled out, what appeared to be blood poured onto the table. Two pies on either side of the stag were filled with live birds and frogs, which when released caused 'the Ladies to skip and shreek'.[45]

This naive interlude was very much in the tradition of the *entremets mouvants* of medieval and Renaissance court entertainments. In fifteenth- and sixteenth-century England, these pastry sculptures would have been called *sobtelties* or *warners*. In May's lifetime, embellishments of this kind were normally referred to as *standards*. His use of the word 'triumph' was a reference to the current Italian term – *trionfi di tavola*. He fails to illustrate any of his 'triumphs', but in 1719 Hagger, his German counterpart, does include a number of engravings of pastry sculptures of this kind among his illustrations. In a remarkable group of plates, which include a pie in the shape of a double-headed eagle, Hagger not only illustrates a pastry stag like that described by May, but also shows how it was made (figure 45). These images are incredibly old-fashioned for the eighteenth century and may reflect a conservative style of cookery favoured by high-ranking clerics. This could have been the case in the palace of the Bishop of Salzburg, where Hagger worked for twenty-seven years. In contrast to the Church, princely households were much keener to embrace new fashions and were therefore faster to adopt the new French dining protocol. This may explain why similarly old-fashioned pie illustrations lingered in Thacker's cookery book of 1758, a compilation of recipes prepared for the Dean and Chapter of Durham Cathedral.

Hagger's beautiful book is a curious fusion of both old and new approaches to cookery. Sitting rather uncomfortably alongside images of sixteenth-century-style pies and marchpanes, are also a few engravings of the most up-to-date items of table equipage, such as French dessert ornaments and *surtouts de table*.[46] No such modish items appear among the illustrations in Edward Kidder's *Receipts of Pastry and Cookery*, an attractive little book, almost contemporary with Hagger's *magnum opus*, published in London in 1720.[47] Kidder's wonderful engravings are stylistically close to Hagger's – the foliage embellishments in both authors' representations of pastry decorations

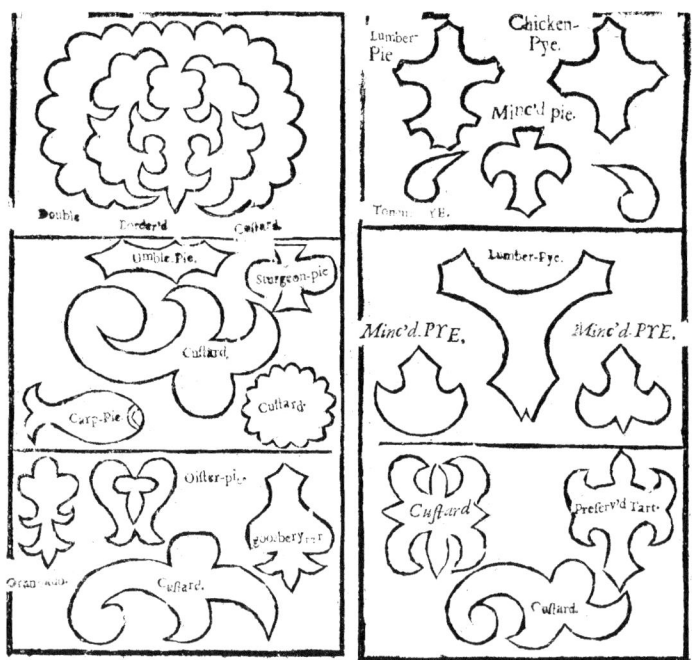

Figure 46. Two woodcut pages of shaped pie designs from T.P., The Accomplisht Ladies Delight *(London: 1675).*

Figure 47. Engraved pie designs from Henry Howard, England's Newest Way *(London: 1703).*

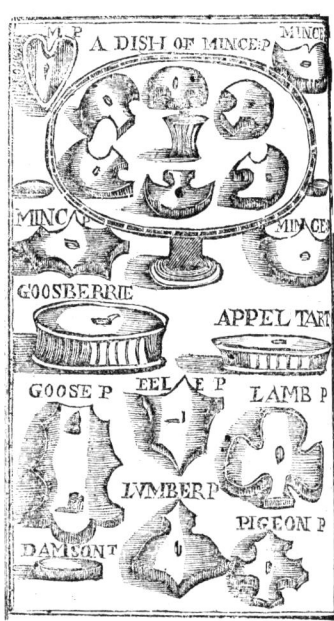

Figure 48. Woodcut pie designs from T. Hall, The Queen's Royal Cookery *(London: 1709).*

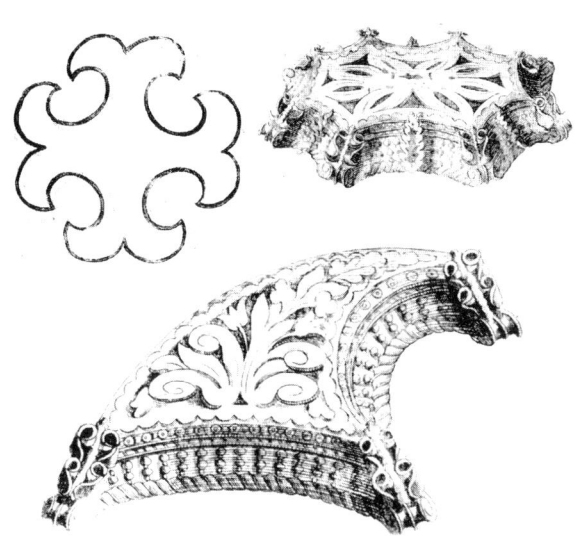

Figure 49. Three designs for pies from Hagger (1719).

are very similar. Compare for instance, the leaf ornaments on Hagger's large asymmetrical pasty in figure 49, with those decorating Kidder's two pasty designs in figure 50.

Between May and Kidder, only a few other English authors went to the trouble of including pie designs in their books. In 1675 *The Accomplish'd Lady's Delight*, a compilation put together by the as yet unidentified T.P., included a double-page spread of crudely printed woodcuts (figure 46). There are shapes for mince and lumber pies, tarts, and a particularly eccentric form for a double-bordered custard.[48] Like May's designs, they are two-dimensional in character and were probably intended to provide the readers with shapes for templates. Henry Howard (1703) and T. Hall (1710) both published single pages of designs representing these pies in a more three-dimensional manner (figures 47 and 48). Howard, who chose to illustrate his work with engravings rather than the more primitive medium of woodcut, mentions his copper plates of 'the Newest Fashions of Mince-pies' on his title-page.[49] That these highly embellished pastries were really produced in late Stuart England is borne out by a skilfully engraved invitation card printed for Nathaniel Meystnor, the proprietor of a late seventeenth-century London cookery school (figure 52).

Kidder also ran various cookery schools in London in the first three decades of the eighteenth century. His detailed engravings are by far the clearest and most beautiful designs of their kind published in England, even

Figure 50. Designs for a lamb pasty and a venison pasty. From Edward Kidder's Receipts of Pastry and Cookery *(London: ca. 1720). The bird on the lamb pasty may represent the first cuckoo of spring.*

rivalling those of Hagger. However, like those of his German contemporary, they appear to be stylistically about a hundred and fifty to a hundred years out of date. Kidder's design for a venison pasty looks almost like it has been based on an Elizabethan plaster over-mantle (figure 50). His lamb pasty could almost be a pattern for a Jacobean stump-work cushion (figure 50). The plates in Kidder's book appeared again in the anonymous compilation *The Whole Duty of a Woman* first published in 1737. The versions in this book are exact mirror-images of Kidder's original plates, suggesting that they were copied from them. They continued to be published in an enlarged version of *The Whole Duty* called *The Ladies Companion* until 1753.

The inclusion of pie designs in cheap little works like *The Accomplisht Ladies Delight*, as well as in the books of cookery-masters like Kidder and Thacker is interesting. It is a similar publishing phenomenon to the fashion for books of secrets in the early seventeenth century among gentlewomen anxious to keep abreast of stylish court practice. Both the banqueting recipes and the pie designs' purpose was to reveal the fashionable foods of the very rich to a less privileged audience. By the time these secrets had been 'discovered', the wealthy had moved on to something new. A similar phenomenon can be seen in the late nineteenth century, when cookery authors like Agnes Marshall were teaching young middle-class wives to make moulded ices identical to those fashionable at court in the previous century. What the designs in May, Hagger, Kidder and Thacker actually represent is a long-established international style of food which probably had its origins in the sixteenth-century European courts. Its sheer visual splendour ensured its survival for the best part of two centuries and it was only partially eclipsed by the new French cuisine of the Enlightenment, lingering on in some parts of Europe like England and Austria well into the eighteenth century.

Figure 51. Designs for set custards and egg pies. Kidder (ca.1720).

TRUSSING AND BUTCHERY DIAGRAMS

In addition to its plagiarized copies of Kidder's attractive pastry designs, *The Whole Duty of a Woman* also offered its readers some useful illustrations of how birds, rabbits and hares were to be trussed for both the pot and spit

Figure 52. A late 17th-century trade card in the form of a dinner invitation to a cookery school. Note the array of decorated pies, florentines and custards at the bottom of the card. These have a great deal in common with the designs in May (1660) and Hagger (1719). The gentlewoman on the right is holding a chocolate mill and a tray of drinking chocolate in cups. Her companion is carrying a pyramid of fruit. Note also the beautifully trussed game and poultry in the top right-hand corner.

(figure 53). These were also copied from an earlier work, this time from the second part of Richard Bradley's *The Country Housewife and Lady's Director* of 1732. Bradley, who described himself as professor of botany at Cambridge University, had first published trussing instructions in his *Weekly Miscellany* of 1727, obtaining the information from an acquaintance who worked as a butcher.[50] His diagrams give us an interesting insight into how poultry and game were prepared for cooking at this period. Unlike today, many birds were cooked with both their heads and legs intact. These parts were enjoyed by many and were also valued because they produced collagen-rich gravy. In addition, birds, suckling pigs and other small animals could sometimes be secured to the spit by tying their legs on with string. However, this was not always successful, so skewers were used to ensure that the animal did not remain motionless while the spit rotated, causing one side to burn. Rabbits and birds to be boiled needed to be trussed in such a way that their limbs did not protrude and therefore make it difficult to put them in the pot. Bradley's two diagrams of how rabbits were prepared for boiling and roasting explain

Figure 53. A diagram to show how a hare was trussed. From The Whole Duty of a Woman *(London: 1737).*

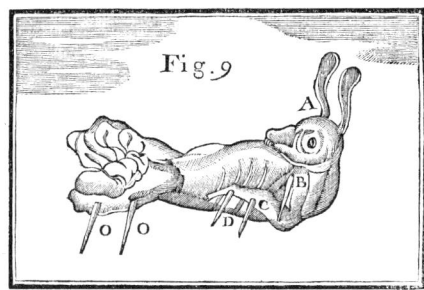

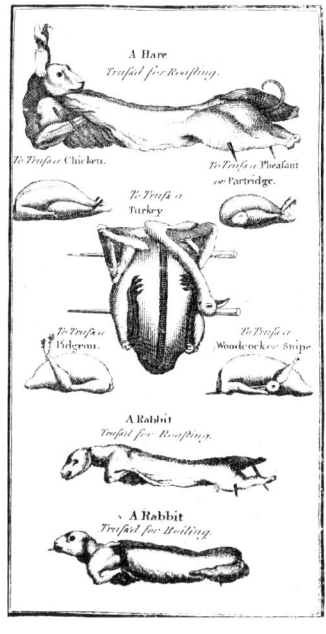

Figure 54. A plate of trussing diagrams from Mrs Frazer The Practice of Cookery, Pastry, Pickling, Preserving, &c. *(Edinburgh: 1791). These illustrations are based on those in the second part of Richard Bradley's* The Country Housewife and Lady's Director *(London: 1732).*

Figure 55. Trussing designs from Bradley (1732). The two diagrams at the top show how rabbits were prepared for the spit and the pot. Unlike hares, their ears were removed. Below is a chicken prepared for the spit. Most poultry and game were cooked with their heads and legs intact. Geese were roasted headless and without their feet. Ducks had their heads removed, but not their feet. The livers and gizzards of the birds were roasted under their pinions (wings), a feature which can frequently be seen in early Dutch still-life paintings of food.

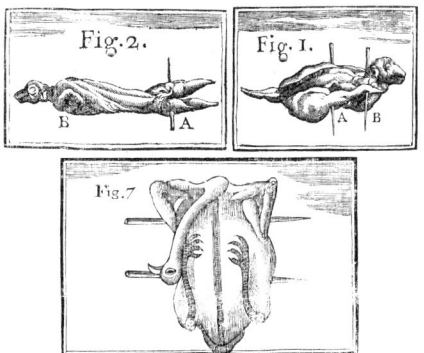

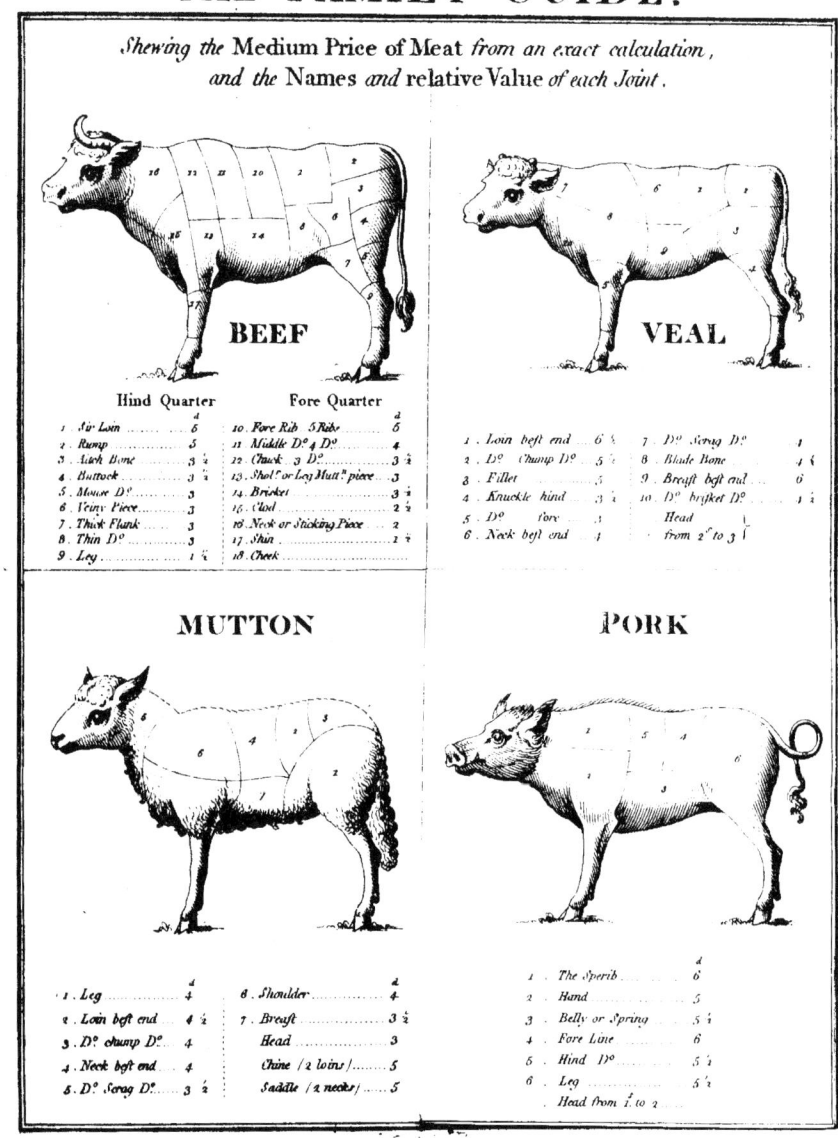

Figure 56. A printed broadside showing the cuts of meat and their prices in the London markets on December 8th 1792. Printed by W. Simpkins of Clements Inn, London. Note the high cost of a calf's head, a delicacy at this period – from two to three shillings each. Veal appears to have been more expensive than any other meat, though some pork cuts were also not cheap. Even belly pork, known as 'spring', cost five pence halfpenny a pound, compared to only five pence a pound for sirloin of beef. Prints like this were the precursors of the butchery diagrams that were commonly included in Victorian household books like those of Beeton (1861) and Jewry (1890s).

these principles in a way that a word-only description could not (figure 55). Versions of Bradley's innovative illustrations appeared in other cookery books of the eighteenth century, such as Mrs Frazer's *The Practice of Cookery, Pastry, Pickling, Preserving, &c.* (Edinburgh 1791) (figure 54). Like Trusler's carving diagrams, Bradley's illustrations were to form the basis of a number of major nineteenth-century treatments of the subject.

Large nineteenth-century cookery compendiums and household books frequently include butchery diagrams illustrating the precise nature of the joints and cuts obtained from each animal. These usually show a carcass divided up into its constituent parts and are labelled *The Joints of Beef, Veal, Pork* etc. During the eighteenth century a few marketing tables for calculating the cost of the various meats were printed in some cookery books, but no diagrams of cuts of meat appeared until the following century. However, single sheets of paper printed with diagrams showing animals divided up into the correct joints, were sold by butchers in the late eighteenth century (figure 56). These little prints, which are the precursors of the illustrations in the later household books, usually indicate the current prices for each joint. They must have been an invaluable resource for both innkeepers and housekeepers when calculating the cost of provisions for large establishments.

ILLUSTRATIONS FOR THE CONFECTIONER

By the 1740s, the baroque dessert with its pyramids of fruit and sweetmeats was giving way to miniature tabletop gardens in lively rococo style. Vivid chenille parterres filled with coloured sugars dominated the fashionable table plateaux of this period. These extraordinary arrangements included garden buildings, fountains, trellises and little figures all moulded from sugar paste. Although this fashion seems to have initially emerged from the French court, it quickly became a craze throughout Europe. By the middle of the century, a number of Continental confectionery texts featured copper-plate engravings of plans for these settings. The most notable of these were Menon's *La Science de maître d'hôtel, confiseur* (1749) and *Le cannameliste français* (1750) by Joseph Gilliers, former confectioner to the deposed king of Poland.[51] England was not slow to take up this vogue for desserts with a horticultural theme and settings of this kind became *de rigueur* for those who could afford them. However, nothing like the complex table plans of the

Figure 57. A wood engraving of a pièce montée made by the Yorkshire confectioner Joseph Bell for the Prince of Wales. From Bell's A Treatise of Confectionery *(Newcastle: 1817). Since all of the wooden moulds needed to make this still survive in various museums and private collections, it is possible to re-create this ornament exactly in this form.*

French texts appeared in any English book of this period, though we know that confectioners' shops in both London and the provinces were happy to provide the necessary sugarwork and equipage.[52]

Nevertheless, one English work, more or less contemporary with Menon and Gilliers, does offer illustrations of two different styles of rococo table plateaux, though it fails to show the actual decorative features used to dress them. This was *The Modern Method of Regulating and Forming a Table* (ca. 1760), a work devoted entirely to table settings. In 1789, Frederick Nutt, a professional London confectioner, also provided a series of table plans for desserts, ranging in scale from simple to magnificent in his *The Complete Confectioner* of 1789 (figure 58).[53] Although he clearly indicates the nature of the sweet foods on the table, he too offers us no clue to the appearance of the ornaments to be placed on the plateau. It is not until 1817 that an English confectionery text actually illustrates this kind of sugarwork, though by this time the style of presentation had changed from a sinuous rococo to a more formal neo-classical. These were the designs for *pièces montées* that appeared in *A Treatise of Confectionery* by Joseph Bell, formerly confectioner to the Prince of Wales and Duke of York. Bell, whose book was published in Newcastle, had run confectionery shops in York and Scarborough. He tells us that he was persuaded to write a work on ornamental confectionery by the Duchess of Bolton while she was visiting his shop. His Bewick-style wood engravings include designs for *pièces montées* and sugar fountains (figures 57 and 59). These were built up on a base of sponge cake and decorated with sugar paste features 'printed' from carved wooden moulds. In his introduction he tells us, 'Nothing can give so much pleasure at an entertainment, as to observe a table sumptuously decorated with elegant and appropriate devices; they give splendour to the fete, an appetite to the most delicate, and amusement to all.'[54]

Wooden moulds like those used by Bell to decorate his devices are illustrated by one of his contemporaries, the much better-known G.A. Jarrin, formerly ornament-maker to Gunter's of Berkeley Square. His *The Italian Confectioner* (1820) contains two engraved plates showing a wide range of confectioner's tools and equipment (figure 60). Other than a small engraving of a biscuit syringe in Nutt's book of 1789, these illustrations are the first images in an English culinary text to show kitchen utensils. They are in the tradition of the illustrations of the French *encylopédie* of the eighteenth century, owing a great deal to the plates of equipment in Gillier's work of 1750. Jarrin not only illustrates the tools required to engrave the moulds, but also offers some diagrams to show how drawings of figures could be scaled

Figure 58. Engraved table plan for a dessert setting with a plateau consisting of three frames. From Frederick Nutt The Complete Confectioner *(London: 1789).*

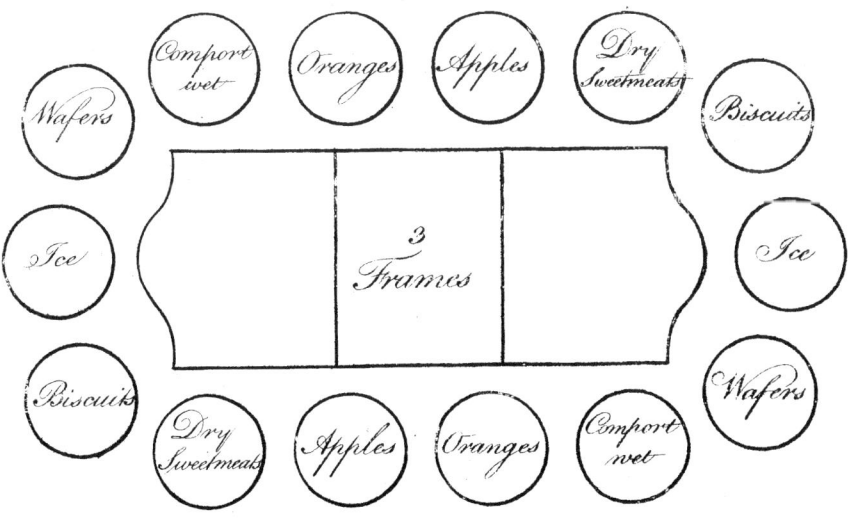

Figure 59 (above). A sugar paste fountain from Bell (1817).

Figure 60 (below). A detail from a folding plate of confectionery equipment from Jarrin's Italian Confectioner *(London 1820). Illustrated in this detail are 1. A biscuit syringe with its dies. 2. A balancing pan for making comfits. 4. A carved wooden walnut mould. 5. A set of wafering irons. 6. The manner of making sugar paste petals with a confectioner's balling tool.*

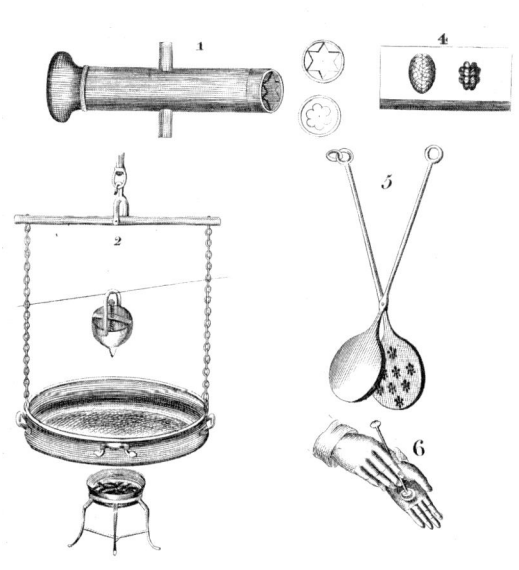

down to fit the wooden block. In his text, he tells us that he 'has laboured for sixteen years, and has made himself particularly perfect in the figure; and he can assure his readers, that they may succeed in the art of engraving on wood without the assistance of masters, by copying good models, and particularly by accustoming themselves to examine the reverse of objects, and the effect will then be apparent.'[55] Readers of this paper should be able to judge Jarrin's skills for themselves, as a mould carved by Jarrin has recently come to light in a private collection and is illustrated in figure 61.

The works of Bell and Jarrin mark a watershed in English cookery book design. They look forward to the culinary illustrations of the later nineteenth century, when chromolithographs of elaborately prepared food and steel engravings of kitchen equipment were to become commonplace features of many Victorian cookery books.

Figure 61. A recently discovered mould signed by Jarrin. Boxwood ca. *1820s. (Private Collection.)*

Illustrations in British Cookery Books, 1621–1820

Notes

I would like to thank the following for their help and invaluable advice – Harlan Walker, Stuart Peachey, Gillian Riley, Robin Harcourt-Williams and Jennie Walsh.

1. The multifaceted issues relating to contemporary cookery book illustration have been explored in depth by Lynette Hunter, who recognizes how many recent trends are 'rooted in developments surrounding the presentation of food in advertising'. Lynette Hunter, 'Illusion and Illustration in Cookery-books since the 1940s', in C. Anne Wilson (editor), *The Appetite and the Eye* (Edinburgh: 1991), pp. 141–160.
2. Many English cookery-book frontispieces and decorative titles show kitchen scenes. Pamela A. Sambrook and Peter Brears (editors) in *The Country House Kitchen 1650–1900* (Stroud: Alan Sutton, 1996) have used a number from eighteenth- and nineteenth-century works to illustrate the evolution of the English kitchen. A useful series of reproductions of these images can also be found in *Petits Propos Culinaires: PPC* 64 (April 2000), 20–27 and C. Anne Wilson, 'Frontispieces II' *PPC* 66 (February 2001), 23–38.
3. A later version of the *Kuchenmeysterey*, adapted to include another work on wine, beer and other drinks and called the *Koch und Kellermeisterey* (Frankfurt: 1547) contains 49 woodcuts in the text. Figure 19 is from this edition.
4. Matthias Giegher, *Li tre tratatti* (Padua 1639). All of the European carving books of the seventeenth century are heavily dependent on Giegher's work. Notable among these are Georg Harsdörfer's *Vollständiges Trincer-Büchlein* (Nuremburg: ca.1640), Anon., *De Cierlyke Voorsnydinge aller Tafel-Gerechten*, (Amsterdam: ca.1668) and even the anonymous Swedish work *Myket Nyyig Och Förbettrad Trenchier-bok* (Vesterås: 1696). The earliest surviving illustrated carving book is the *Arte Cisoria* of Enriques de Aragón (1423). There are drawings of carving forks in this work, together with other tools resembling Arab surgical instruments. A useful transcript of the original manuscript was published in the eighteenth century – Enrique de Aragón, Marqués de Villena, *Arte cisoria, ò del tratado del arte del corter del cuchillo* (Madrid: 1766). A very early Italian illustrated manual of carving dedicated to the Duke of Ferrara – *Refugio over ammonitorio de gentilhuomo* by Giovanni Francesco Colle was published in Ferrara in 1532. This was probably the original model for Cervio's work and therefore of Giegher's *Il trinciante* section of *Li tre trattati*.
5. The first table diagrams to appear in a French work are those in *L'escole parfait* (Paris: 1662), but these are copies of Giegher's Italian settings. The 1698 illustrated edition of François Massialot, *Le Cuisinier roïal et bourgeois*, which also includes his *Nouvelle instruction pour les confitures etc.* seems to be the first French work to include original table plans.
6. Gervase Markham, *The English House-wife* (London: 1615) pp. 97–98.
7. Bartolomeo Scappi gives many examples of these 'ultimate courses' of sweetmeats in his *Opera* of 1570.
8. John Murrell, *Murrels Two Bookes of Cookerie and Carving*, (London: 1631)
9. Murrell in fact gives different recipes for these letters in both his banqueting books. That below is from *The Daily Exercise for Ladies and Gentlewomen* (London: 1617) p.89.
   'To make Cinamon Letters
   Take paste made as for Gemillisoes *(jumbals)*, colour it with cinnamon, and rowle it in long rowles, as neere as you can all of a bignness, and therof make faire capitall Romane letters, according to some exact patterne, cut in thinne board or in white plate, gild them and make a crosse in the beginning of them.'
10. John Murrell, *Murrel's Two Books of Cookery and Carving* (London: 1631). In the first book of this work, Murrell includes 16 recipes for French-style dishes.
11. Giles Rose (translator), *A Perfect School of Instructions for the Officers of the Mouth* (London: 1682). pp. 6–8.
12. Francis Sandford, *The History of the Coronation Of the Most High, Most Mighty, and Most*

Excellent Monarch, James II (London: 1687).
13. Sandford, op. cit., p.5.
14. An illustration of William and Mary's coronation feast in Westminster Hall is included in a large commemorative etching by Romeyn de Hooghe published in Amsterdam a few months after the coronation – Romeyn de Hooghe , *H. Mai. Willem III en Maria Gekroont tot Koning en Koningin van Engelant, inde Abdij van Westminster in het groote koor den 21 April Anno 1689* (Their Majesties William III and Mary Crowned as King and Queen of England, in Westminster Abbey in the great choir on 21 April, 1689) Amsterdam: 1689. Charles Carter includes a table plan of George II's coronation feast in *The Complete Practical Cook* (London 1730). Both feasts are dressed as ambigues with pyramids of sweetmeats in the middle of the table.
15. C. Anne Wilson, 'Ideal Meals and their Menus from the Middle Ages to the Georgian Era', in C. Anne Wilson (editor), *The Appetite and the Eye* (Edinburgh 1991) pp. 98–122.
16. Fiona Lucraft, 'The Fine Art of Eighteenth-Century Table Layouts' in Walker, Harlan (editor), *The Meal – Proceedings of the Oxford Symposium on Food and Cookery 2001.* (Totnes: Prospect Books, 2002).
17. Markham, op. cit., pp. 63–4.
18. Lickfinger, the cook in Ben Jonson's *Staple of News* (London: 1631) was probably referring to the two components of the olio in the lines telling us that he,
    'Makes citadels of curious fowl and fish,
    Some he dry-dishes, some motes round with broths'.
19. The Paul Getty Museum in Los Angeles has some superb examples of Germain's work, which agree very closely to the olio and terrine illustrated in La Chapelle's plates.
20. William Gelleroy, *The London Cook, or the whole art of cookery made easy and familiar* (London: 1762). In this work there is a large copper-plate engraving, 'representing his Majesty's Table, with its proper Removes, as it was served at the Guild-Hall, on the 9th of November last, being the Lord Mayor's Day'.
21. Vincent La Chapelle, *The Modern Cook* (London: 1733) Vol. I p. vi.
22. Hatfield House General, 6/5, 6/7, 6/12, 6/24.
23. Sandford, op. cit., p.13.
24. Hatfield House General, 6/12 recto.
25. John Russell, 'The Boke of Nurture' in F.J. Furnival (editor), *Early English Meals and Manners,* Early English Text Society (Oxford: OUP 1868).
26. Peter Brears, *The Boke of Keruyinge (The Book of Carving) Wynkyn de Worde* (Lewes: Southover Press, 2003). See also Ivan Day, 'The Honours of the Table' in Peter Brown (editor), *British Cutlery* (London: Philip Wilson, 2001).
27. Robert May, *The Accomplisht Cook* (London: 1660), William Rabisha, *The Whole Body of Cookery Dissected* (London: 1661) and John Nott, *The Cook's and Confectioner's Dictionary* (London: 1723).
28. Richard Briggs, *The English Art of Cookery* (London: 1788) pp. 477–9.
29. Rose, op. cit., p. 23
30. Anon, *The court & kitchin of Elizabeth, commonly called Joan Cromwel, the wife of the late usurper: truly described and represented, and now made publick for general satisfaction* (London: 1664) p. 39. This is a classical allusion. The author of the political tract that precedes Mrs Cromwell's recipes is scathing about her frugality. He alleges that she once ordered her cook to roast a half capon on the spit, causing a great deal of vexation to her carver – 'how it puzzled her Ladyship's Carver, to hold him to the knife, and to apportion half and quarter Limbs according to Art.' 'Much more do I wonder what those Fellows at Rome did, or what they would have done here, who kept carving Schools *ludi fructorii*, and had all manner of Fowl and Fish, and such other Festival meat carved in Wood, which they marked out in Wooden Knives with very great curiosity, and instructed their scholars.'

31. May, op. cit., p. 194.
32. Elizabeth Raffald, *The Experienced English House-Keeper* (London: 1769) p. 210.
33. Wolley, Hannah *The Queen-like Closet* (London: 3rd edition, 1674) p. 337.
34. Both Elizabeth Cleland and Martha Bradley give carving instructions in their books. Slightly smaller carving forks, designed with ladies in mind, start to appear from the mid-eighteenth century onwards. Elizabeth Cleland, *A New and Easy Way of Cookery* (Edinburgh: 1759); Martha Bradley, *The British Housewife* (London: 1760).
35. Anon., *L'Art de découper les alouettes* (Paris: 1796).
36. W.M., *The Queens Closet Opened* (London: 1658).
37. Conrad Hagger, *Neues Saltzburgisches Koch-Buch* (Augsburg: 1719).
38. John Thacker, *The Art of Cookery* (Newcastle: 1758).
39. May, op. cit.
40. Markham describes using paper templates to cut shapes for pastry decorations, 'having patterns of paper cut into divers proportions, as Beasts, Birds, Armes, Knots, Flowers and such like: Lay the patterns on the past, and so cut them accordingly.' Markham, op. cit., p. 84.
41. Anon, *The Whole Duty of a Woman* (London: 1737) p. 528.
42. François Pierre de La Varenne, *Le Cuisinier François* (Paris: 1651). An English translation was issued by Robert May's publisher Nathaniel Brookes as *The French Cook* (London: 1653).
43. *Le Pâtissier François* (Amsterdam 1655). This appeared in a translation in the first part of Marnette's *The Perfect Cook* (London: 1656). Marnette is presumably the Merrete mentioned in Parry's poem.
44. Marnette, op. cit.
45. May, op. cit.
46. Hagger, op. cit., plates 222 and 223.
47. Edward Kidder, *Receipts of Pastry and Cookery* (London: ca.1720).
48. T.P., *The Accomplisht Ladies Delight* (London: 1775).
49. Henry Howard, *England's Newest Way* (London: 1703).
50. Caroline Davidson, (editor) *The Country Housewife and Lady's Director,* by Richard Bradley. Parts I and II, first published in 1727 and 1732 respectively (London: Prospect Books, 1988).
51. Menon, *La Science de maître d'hôtel, confiseur* (Paris: 1749) and Joseph Gilliers, *Le Cannameliste français ou nouvelle instruction pour ceux qui desirent d'apprendre l'office* (Nancy: 1751).
52. See Peter Brown and Ivan Day, *The Pleasures of the Table* (York: York Civic Trust, 1997).
53. Frederick Nutt, *The Complete Confectioner* (London: 1789).
54. Joseph Bell, A *Treatise of Confectionery in all its Branches* (Newcastle: 1817) pp. iii–iv.
55. G.A. Jarrin, *The Italian Confectioner* (London: new edition, 1831) p. 236.

CHAPTER SIX

WILLIAM ALEXIS JARRIN AND *THE ITALIAN CONFECTIONER*

Laura Mason

When I first began researching the history of sugar confectionery, the work of one author stood out: that of William (Guglielmo) Alexis Jarrin, whose book *The Italian Confectioner* was first published in 1820. Initially, I viewed it in the general context of cookery and confectionery books published between about 1750 and 1850. From Mrs Raffald's *Experienced English Housekeeper* (1769), through Borella's *Court and Country Confectioner* (1770) to W. Jeanes's *Modern Confectioner* (1861), a slow progression in the types of confections discussed, the techniques for making them, and the presentation of recipes could be discerned. I became especially fascinated by books which showed some association with the business established in Berkley Square during the mid-eighteenth century by the confectioner Domenico Negri, which later became Gunter's. These included Robert Abbot's *Housekeeper's Valuable Companion* (*ca.* 1780); Frederick Nutt's *Complete Confectioner* (1789); and William Gunter's *Confectioner's Oracle* (1830). Jarrin, too, worked for Gunter's, and *The Italian Confectioner* was first published whilst he was still employed there: the frontispiece tells us that he was 'confectioner and ornament-maker at Mr Gunter's.'

My first meeting with Jarrin's work was through the handlists of the Blanche Leigh and Preston Collections in the Brotherton Library at the University of Leeds. From these it was apparent that *The Italian Confectioner* ran into several editions. This in itself was not unusual: a number of earlier books dealing principally with confectionery had gone into numerous editions. Examination of *The Italian Confectioner*, however, showed that Jarrin's work had more to offer than the earlier works. His book is exceptionally well organized. The recipes are carefully sorted according to method, a feature which other writers were often inconsistent about. They are also precise and detailed compared with the somewhat hit-and-miss nature of some earlier works.[1] An unusual feature[2] is the short definitions and general notes, offered at the start of most chapters, giving the reader specific

William Alexis Jarrin and *The Italian Confectioner*

Figure 62. The four ages of William Jarrin: the portraits from successive editions of his work, dated 1820 (top left); 1827 (top right); 1829 (bottom left); 1844 (bottom right).

information about the type of confection in the following recipes. Jarrin's book is also comprehensive, covering much that a confectioner working at the top of his profession would need to know. Comparing editions revealed considerably more. They had been regularly updated, with information about new fashions, techniques and implements added. For some years, the revisions appear minor (although in terms of additional information about techniques, they are often significant) but by 1844 there had been a major change in recipes. Bibliographical detail suggests the book was reprinted eleven times; the contents were updated at least five times.[3] Jarrin considered he had brought his work to perfection, commenting that

> I am thankful that my life has been prolonged, so as to enable me to make these corrections, and thus leave the world a work which cannot vary for many centuries to come; because the general principles will always be the same, – the description of an art being nothing more than the history of what is practised; or, if I may so express it, the map of what exists, raising all intelligent artists to the same degree of knowledge; and a kind of light-house to guide the young beginner.[4]

An aspect of Jarrin's character which comes through strongly is an enquiring mind. Over the years, editions of his book include observations on ice wells, saccharometers, thermometers and Nicholas Appert's method for bottling fruit. He comments on the quality of ices served in London confectioners' shops, saying they were often badly mixed so that the sugar sank to the bottom, and were full of lumps, and of a 'disagreeable, dirty red colour'.[5] Allusions to other craftsmen occasionally appear, often in tones of respect, but sometimes derogatory. For instance, the first edition contains an effusive dedication which, whilst addressed to Robert Gunter, is actually intended for his father James Gunter who died in 1819. Jarrin speaks of James's 'fostering care' and says that, 'without such assistance it would have been in vain for me to have projected, and impossible to have completed, so arduous a work.'[6]

There is also a cutting remark about pastry cooks, couched in terms that make one suspect that his contemporaries knew who was intended (Carême is a possible target). Jarrin says:

> The making of gum and other pastes ... was once in great vogue, and the most magnificent and costly ornaments have been made of gum

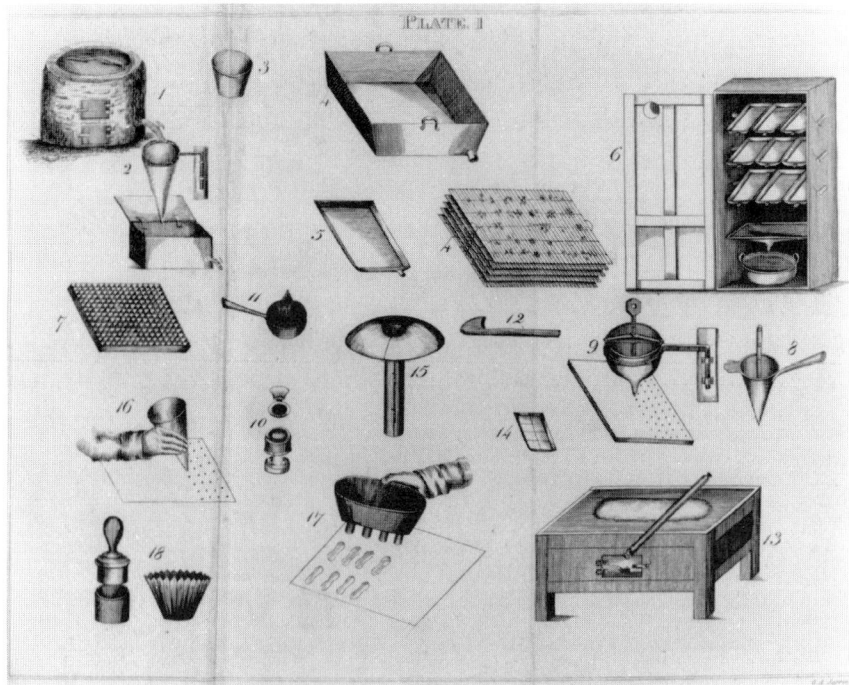

Figure 63 One of two folding plates (drawn by Jarrin himself) showing confectionery equipment, from the 1820 and subsequent editions of The Italian Confectioner.

paste; but it has fallen comparatively into disuse, and what is worse for the confectioner, the fragments of the art have been transferred to pastry-cooks, and cooks, who have at once disfigured, if not destroyed, the most beautiful flower in the banquet of the confectioner. To make gum paste properly, great care and dexterity, much patience, some knowledge of mythology, of history, and of the arts of modelling and design, are requisite – qualifications seldom possessed by the mere pastry-cook.[7]

Carême and Jarrin were born within a year of each other, and would almost certainly have heard about each other's work. There is strong possibility that they met; Jarrin shared with Carême a history of work in the most important households of Napoleonic France. He drops a hint about this in *The Italian Confectioner*, mentioning a figure of Napoleon made for the Emperor after he had returned victorious from his German campaigns,[8] and in a later edition comments,

…when France saluted her Napoleon with the title of "the Great"… I was seized with so much enthusiasm for my profession, which I practised both in the Household of the Emperor, and at the Town Banquets.[9]

Such training and experience no doubt contributed substantially to the chapters Jarrin devoted to materials and techniques used by confectioners in making *pièces montées*. As far as I am aware, the techniques for the elaborate sugar, gum and wax decorations which had been a feature of the aristocratic European dessert table since the Renaissance had never been fully described in print before. In addition, there are several descriptions of moulds for making confections in the shape of fruit and other novelty shapes, and references to the importance of items such as sieves of different types – silk for powdered sugar, lawn for flour, wicker for pulping fruit, and pierced leather for grading comfits.

And then there were the plates. The two fold-out ones of implements at the back of the book contain many interesting details but remain unchanged through the editions. Some layouts for desserts were added in 1829. The frontispiece portrait, however, shows Jarrin at four stages: a bright-eyed enthusiastic youngster in Regency cravat and broadcloth (1820), a man in the prime of life wearing a medal (1827),[10] and a grey-haired but still vigorous figure (1829). The final one showed an elderly, grey-haired man, but one whose eyes still glow with life (1844). The 1823 edition tells the reader that Jarrin had established a shop at 123 New Bond Street in London, and underneath the 1827 portrait was the information that he was born in 1784 in Colorno. An atlas revealed this to be in northern Italy, in the Po valley. Jarrin really was an Italian confectioner.

This much I knew for several years, until serendipity led me back to the university library catalogue and research into a different field. I was looking for descriptions of shops in the eighteenth and nineteenth centuries. A book called *Retailing in England during the Industrial Revolution*[11] sounded promising. When I found it, the index showed that Jarrin was mentioned several times. The relevant pages gave me a shock: Jarrin had been registered bankrupt in 1828, and the file survived in the Public Record Office at Kew. It was not extraordinary that Jarrin went bankrupt. Numerous tradesmen did, partly through bad management and partly through the generally louche attitude of Regency society towards paying bills. What the reference did show me was that there was another source about Jarrin's work beyond *The Italian Confectioner*, and one apparently unknown to the handful of food historians interested in him.

The reference took me off to the PRO at the first available opportunity. On arrival, I discovered that fate had truly been on my side. Firstly, because most bankruptcy records had been destroyed, apart from a sample of 5 per cent kept for future generations, and Jarrin's was one of the sample. Secondly, because although I was warned by the PRO staff that most bankruptcy files contained only the sketchiest details, such as a list of names and amounts owed, Jarrin's file was not one of these.[12] Compiled in November and December 1828, it was a substantial and detailed account of his business, containing lists of debtors, of creditors and their businesses, notes of losses, estimates of his profits, some valuations of equipment and, bound in as evidence, accounts from two merchants with whom he dealt. There were references to leases on property, to a lawsuit and a patent, to his household and to *The Italian Confectioner*. Most of it was written in a beautifully clear hand. The figures concerned revealed the kind of money to be made through a high-class confectioner's. Jarrin's profits were estimated as at least £13,969 2s 6d over the six years he had been trading independently. This is probably an under-estimate, as it appears to make no allowance for bills which had been paid during this time. Jarrin owed £4,060 11s 7d; and was owed £836 11s 1d. He held leases to the value of £1231, and reckoned to have made losses of over £4000 through making experiments and losing money on catering for various events. In modern terms, it was as if a high-profile medium-sized business – say one of the better-known London restaurants – had gone spectacularly bust.

The contents of this file gave me numerous leads about Jarrin's personal and business life.[13] The source of his downfall appeared to be a change in the nature of his business away from confectionery towards dealing in wines and spirits. The list of clients who owed money to him showed that he supplied the *bon ton*, as well as a few people who sounded like scoundrels. The list of his creditors gave some impression of the scope of his business and an idea of how his Bond Street shop must have appeared – sparkling with mirrors and glass in a tradition of confectionery shops which went back at least a century, but also featuring innovations such as the newly-available gas lighting (at a cost of £36 per annum). It was evidently well equipped with china and glass, at a cost of over £700, and silver and plate had cost £250.

Figure 64. Drawing of Jarrin's Patent Water Cooler, 1827.

The recipes in *The Italian Confectioner* show that the quality of the edible stock matched the surroundings: almond caramel baskets, drops flavoured with perfumes such as coffee, vanilla, and orgeat, capillaire syrup, fruit pastes, ices, jellies, biscuits, liqueurs. No doubt the atmosphere was similar to that in another fashionable confectioner, Farrance's, which was described in *The Epicure's Almanack* in 1815:

> in this temple Pomona and Ceres hold daily a levee of beauty and fashion; and you may observe at all hours in the forenoon a whole nidus of little Cupids and Psyches feasting in terrene nectar and ambrosia. In plainer terms, ladies generally regale their younger friends and relatives here with the incomparable bon-bons...[14]

On a more practical level, coppersmiths, ironmongers and a cooper are all mentioned in the accounts. Jarrin's stock of copper utensils were valued at £150 when new, tin ones at £160, and pewter ones at £200. 'Moulds, tools and different apparatus' cost another £200, and a reservoir, for syrup, was

£143, implying a substantial object. £50 a year went on paper and string; initial advertisements, taken when the business began in 1822 cost £60, with a subsequent cost of about £10 per annum; and 'Copper Plates for Ornaments Bills Tickets and Charities for Christmas' came to a total of about £150 over the same time.

Jarrin's innovative mind was further revealed in his patent.[15] This was for a water cooler which worked on a similar principle to the modern cool box, with the ice and salt mixture in a sealed container inside a larger vessel. Supporting evidence for his interest in technology came from references scattered through *The Italian Confectioner* to inventions and improvements he had made to implements for confectionery processes, such as an improved funnel for making drops, a cupboard with tilting shelves for draining confections, and a press designed for dealing with the large quantities of soaked gum tragacanth which any confectioner working extensively with sugar paste was obliged to handle. Another item of interest was the reference to his ice well, the location of which was listed in Cromer Street, along with the considerable sum that had been expended on mending it. With this knowledge in mind, a re-reading of the section on ice wells in the 1827 edition of *The Italian Confectioner* suddenly brought Jarrin's statements about their management into focus; he had updated his book according to his experience.

The tradesmen's accounts revealed some details of how much Jarrin's business spent on ingredients such as fruit, dairy produce and eggs. Between 1825 and 1828, he had accumulated a debt of £245 for the latter alone; it was when his egg merchant, Edmund Chambers, lost patience that Jarrin was declared insolvent. Regrettably, the detail I would have really liked – on quantities of sugar purchased – is unclear. Although it is a substance which features heavily in a grocer's account which is bound into the file as evidence, the quantities recorded are not large and do not tally with what one would expect to find for a confectioner who was evidently working on a large scale (in the 1840s, William Finemore, a journeyman confectioner working in Walworth, south London, recorded in his notebook that two hundredweight of sugar was a day's boiling).[16] Eventually, I concluded that Jarrin must have had an alternative supplier whose account has gone unrecorded.

An item for foreign travel, correspondence from foreign merchants, and references to Continental confectioners in *The Italian Confectioner* suggest that Jarrin kept up his contacts abroad. It can be inferred from statements in his book that Jarrin made his way from his birthplace in Italy, via France to

England, and the PRO file indicates that he arrived in London in 1817. I found the Italian aspect of his background both fascinating and tantalizing, to the extent that I eventually visited Colorno on the off-chance of gleaning some extra information (without, it has to be said, knowing any Italian beyond that necessary for ordering a cup of coffee). The visit showed me a sleepy little Italian town which had one claim to fame: a palace formerly belonging to the Dukes of Parma. It also presented me with another conundrum: the realization that Jarrin is not an Italian surname. The origin of the name (my best guess is Spanish) and the presence of Jarrin's family in this backwater remain a mystery, although I speculated about the possibility of their being in service at the ducal palace, which had devolved on one of the Spanish Bourbons in the mid-eighteenth century.

Transactions which had found their way into the file because they were financially contentious offered other leads. The lawsuit with the Horticultural Society over a 'breakfast' provided for their exhibition at Chiswick in 1827 was a detail which sent me scuttling off to examine minute-books in the Lindley Library at The Royal Horticultural Society,[17] and to consult *The Times* newspaper. Between them, these sources intimated a culture-clash as the Horticultural Society wanted good plain food and lots of it, English style, whilst Jarrin's mind seems to have run on a loftier Continental plane which featured champagne and ices. Jarrin had contracted to supply a 'collation' at a fixed price per head, but evidently the guests felt no obligation to consume a fixed amount and Jarrin reported during the hearing that:

> all the ladies and gentlemen came with remarkably good appetites. Two of them in particular stood eating and drinking for an hour and ten minutes, and would make way for nobody. After they had finished at one table, they went to another and looked out for something fresh. Many of the other ladies and gentlemen acted in a similar manner. Their conduct was like that of the Goths and the Vandals.[18]

It was an event on which Jarrin considered to have made a loss of £400, a considerable sum and a blow to his already delicately balanced finances. Other references to losses which intrigued me remain untraced, for instance, catering for masquerade nights at the Argyll Rooms and supper for a ball given in aid of the Spanish refugees in 1825, both of which I should have liked to know more about.

Through Palmer's *Index to The Times*, Robson's *London Commercial*

Figure 65. Recreations of Jarrin's ices. Above: a composition of several pieces; below left and right: the pineapple and the melon in detail. (Photographs, Laura Mason.)

Directory, and other miscellaneous sources I was able to piece together some of Jarrin's later career. He resurrected his business at 123 New Bond Street, and one January the display caught the eye of William Sandys, who described the shop as 'filled with French bean-cakes' and,

> that beautiful frosted, festooned, bedizened, and ornamented piece of confectionery, called, par eminence, Twelfth-cake, with its splendid waxen or plaster of Paris kings and queens, the delight and admiration of school-boys and girls.[19]

The Times also contained an exchange of letters between 'an Opera-Goer' and Jarrin, alleging that his wife and her staff were overcharging customers for refreshments at the King's Theatre.[20] In 1833 or '34 Jarrin moved from New Bond Street to 77 Regent Street Quadrant:

> where he established what he calls a "Café et Restaurant," conducted after the manner of such establishments in Paris; it has been much frequented...[21]

He was once again declared bankrupt, on 19 April 1834; the notice appears in *The Times*, but this time, to my frustration, the file did not survive.

After the second bankruptcy, Jarrin appears to have tried to re-establish his business again, this time in Tichbourne Street, but disappears from the directories in 1836. It is unclear what he did to earn a living during the last fourteen years of his life. Perhaps he acted to some extent as a consultant: when writing about saccharometers, he remarks that 'this instrument can be obtained of the author',[22] or made some money through his book (the 1828 file records a profit of £400 on the sale of copyright of this); or perhaps he concentrated on outside catering. He died in 1848 from stomach cancer,[23] a cruel death for anyone, but especially for a man who appreciated the finer things in food and drink. He had a wife and children. Mrs Jarrin is mentioned in the Horticultural Society lawsuit, and again in the correspondence relating to the theatre. She evidently worked alongside her husband and I would like to know more about her and what she thought about the bankruptcies. Evidently there were children as well; the upkeep of his family is referred to in the 1828 file, and one of the creditors listed is a Mrs Hasard, schoolmistress in Mornington Crescent, but details about number, genders and ages do not survive.

With the benefit of hindsight, I re-read some of the works of his contemporaries. William Gunter warns in his *Confectioner's Oracle* (a work much inferior to *The Italian Confectioner*) against being too much interested in innovation:

> You should ... study the art, with a view to come up to the excellence of your contemporaries, than to *invent*; in which last attempt you may injure your health, and render your character ambiguous; – and instead of being a respectable and thriving professor in Regent Street, Bond Street, St James's Street or Berkley Square, – you may end your days in a prison, after having pined away for years, with scarcely the means of keeping body and soul together.[24]

He may well have had Jarrin's career in mind. In the 1860s, William Jeanes, also a graduate from the Gunter business, commented on Jarrin's book, which by then was considered out of date,[25] but, from a twenty-first century viewpoint, it has to be said there was nothing published to rival it during the four decades from 1820 to 1860.

Together, the sources provide a fascinating insight into the work of the high-class confectioner at a point just before the dread hand of industrialization compromised the need for skilled handwork, and cheap sugar removed the exclusivity. They also show the scope of such luxury businesses as they flourished in late-Georgian London. Since so few records survive, it is not possible to know if Jarrin's misfortune brought other tradesmen to the point of bankruptcy as well, but his debts to some were so large (over £1,000 to his grocer, for instance) that the possibility must be considered. The records also cast a little light on an important but largely unknown aspect of the confectioner's business, outside catering. The life of Jarrin himself shows how international the careers of some of these men were, carrying ideas and techniques from country to country. Finally, perhaps we should thank Jarrin for being both insatiably curious and arrogant enough to consider that he had written the ultimate confectionery manual. A more cautious man would have left a far less interesting legacy.

Notes

The following institutions and individuals have all been most helpful during this research: The Public Record Office, Kew; the Bishopsgate Institute, the British Library, the Guildhall Library, the Lindley Library at the Royal Horticultural Society, the Theatre Museum (all in London); the Brotherton Library, Leeds University; the Patent Office, York Road, Leeds; Craig Barclay at the Yorkshire Museum, York; A.W. Scott at the Poulters' Guild; Andrew Millward at the Manchester Museum; Philip and Mary Hyman; Ivan Day.

1. Though it has to be said that Frederick Nutt's book is relatively well organized and clear, as is Joseph Bell's *Treatise on Confectionery* (1817); the latter had no known link with the Gunter business.
2. At least in English; I have not been able to make comparison with many Continental texts.
3. I have seen editions from 1820, 1823, 1827, 1829, 1831, 1836, 1837, 1844 and 1861, and found definite evidence for an 1834 edition. Internal evidence in the 1844 edition suggests an 1843 edition, but I have not located a copy.
4. W.A. Jarrin, *The Italian Confectioner*, a new edition revised and enlarged (London: E.S. Ebers and Co, 1844) p. viii.
5. G.A. Jarrin, *The Italian Confectioner*, 1st ed. (London: John Harding, 1820) p. 123.
6. ibid, pp. v–vi.
7. ibid, p. 215.
8. ibid, pp. 215–6.
9. Jarrin (1844) p. ix.
10. For all his admiration for Napoleon, this appears to be The Order of the Cross of Fidelity, established by Louis XVIII for those who had remained faithful to the royal cause during the reign of Napoleon I. I am grateful to Craig Barclay, Keeper of Numismatics and Decorative Art at the Yorkshire Museum, York, for identifying this medal.
11. David Alexander, *Retailing in England During the Industrial Revolution* (London: Athlone Press, 1970).
12. Public Record Office PRO B 3/2739.
13. A deeper analysis of this and some aspects of Jarrin's life can be found in Laura Mason, 'William Alexis Jarrin: an Italian confectioner in London', in *Gastronomica*, I: 2 (2001), 50–64.
14. Anon., *The Epicure's Almanack* (London: 1815) p. 103.
15. British Patent number 5539.
16. William Finemore, *Confectionery* (unpublished MS in possession of Andrew Millward, ca. 1840).
17. Minutes of the Horticultural Society, 17.5.1827; 29.6.1827; 7.7.1828; 21.8.1828.
18. *The Times*, London: Court of King's Bench, Jarrin v. Elliot and another.
19. Cited in Bridget Ann Henisch, *Cakes and Characters* (London: Prospect Books, 1984) p. 143.
20. Letters dated March 5th, 7th, 8th and 9th 1832, *The Times*, London.
21. 30.4.1834, *The Times*, London.
22. Jarrin (1844) p. 4
23. According to his death certificate.
24. William Gunter, *Gunter's Confectioner's Oracle* (London: Alfred Miller, 1830) p. xxxii.
25. William Jeanes, *The Modern Confectioner* (London: John Camden Hotten, 1861) p. iv.

Appendix

The material presented below represents part of Jarrin's bankruptcy file, PRO B3/2739 (the remainder is concerned with the sequence of events as they unfolded when Jarrin was declared insolvent). Although the bulk of the record is written in a clear hand, in places the ink has faded. Occasionally notes have been scrawled by other hands which are difficult to read, so some words remain illegible, or the reading uncertain.

Nevertheless, the file is interesting for many reasons: the sums involved, the range of tradesmen mentioned, and the list of names who owed money to Jarrin. As William Thackeray commented in *Vanity Fair*, the whole of society ran on debt. Several of Jarrin's fellow-tradesmen seem to have had little idea of how much he actually owed them, leading to some readjustment in their statements. The amount of detail is, apparently, unusual; why Jarrin's affairs should have been recorded in such depth is not clear to me, but it is obvious that they were complex and involved sums which were substantial in the context of the 1820s.

The beginning of each folio in the record is marked by [f.].

[f.]

BALANCE SHEET

Bankrupt		£	s	d		£	s	d
1822 to 1828	Amount due by the Bankrupt as for sheets 2 and 3	4060	11	7	Amount due to the Bankrupt as per sheets 1 to 11 inclusive	836	11	1
1822	Capital	1000	0	0	Property as per sheet 12	1231	—	—
1823 to 1828	Received Rent of House 15 in Lincolnshire Court 5 ½ years at £26 per annum	143	—	—	Losses as per sheet 13	4013	3	—
1825 17 Jany	Received on Account of £100 which was to have been paid as a premium with an Apprentice but in consequence of Mr John Louis Lin dying I did not receive the remaining £80	20	—	—	Expences as per sheets 14 to 15	14,467	—	—
1827	Received by Sale of Copyright of Italian Confectioner	400	—	—				
	Received in 6 ½ years about £100 per Annum for Instruction in making Confectionery	650	—	—				
1824	Received with an Apprentice	105	—	—				
1822 to 1828	Received from various persons for Board and Lodging and teaching them the business of Pastry Cook and Confectioner, about	200	—	—				
	Profits Not having kept any regular Accounts I am unable to state accurately the Profits of my business but to have covered the charges per contra the same must have been	13969	2	6				
		20,547	14	1		20,547	14	1

[f.]   Debts due by the Bankrupt

Creditor	£	s	d
Mr Blackburn, Avery Row, Bond Street Carpenter	60	—	—
Mr Richard Wilson, Saint Martins Court Paper Merchant	54	16	1
James Stow, 123 Fenchurch Street City Wine Merchant	211	—	—
Bakes and Lee, Oxford Street, Butter Merchants	3	9	4
Messrs Claude Scott & Company, Cavendish Square Bankers	200	—	—
Mr Giblett, Bond St, Butcher	114	—	—
Mr Fricour, George Street, Hanover Square Wine Merchant	95	10	10
Mr Thomas, Bond Street Silversmiths about	200	—	—
Mr Norwood, Maddox Street Cream Merchant	132	5	4
Mr Phillips, Oxford Street Chinaman	343	14	8
Mr Johnson, Conduit Street Copper Merchant	92	7	—
Mr Le Faure, Paris Wine Merchant	47	—	—
Mr Wainright, Conduit Street Looking Glass Maker	67	15	10
Messrs Calton and Son, Great Marylebone Street Furniture Warehouse about	108	—	—
Mr Dill, Oxford Street, Baker	60	—	—
Mr Chambers, Old Compton Street Egg Merchant	245	15	8
Mr Mecklam, Wells Street Oxford Street Tailor	40	—	—
Mr John Wright Oxford Street Grocer	1025	—	—
Mr Bott, Allsops Buildings Edgeware Road Carpenter	450	—	—
Mr Francis Lewin, Tyas Street, Coal Merchant	60	—	—
Mr Plowman, Covent Garden Fruiter	30	—	—
Mr Stowell, Grosvenor Street Upholsterer	20	—	—
Mrs Hasard, Mornington Crescent Schoolmistress	60	—	—
Mr Stevens, Duke Street Plumber	10	—	—
Mr John, Ironmonger Bond Street	34	2	—
[f.] Mr Barthes, Great Marlborough Street Wine Merchant	15	15	—
Messrs Barker, Carter and Allen, 29 City Wharf, Salt Merchants	7	6	3
Mr Crawcour, King Street Covent Garden Gentleman	66	—	—
Mr Gall, Fieres, Biberai in Wilhemburg Merchants	10	—	—
Mr Hackett, Gold Square City Agent	16	19	11
Mr Hodgkinson, 86 Snow Hill Druggist	14	3	6
Mr Haswell, Robert Street Oxford Street Cooper	8	8	8
Mr Charles Hindley, 52 Berners Street Floor Cloth Manufacturer	8	10	8
Mr Augustin John, Regent Street Liquor Merchant	2	4	—
Mr Nilkens, Holland Wine Merchant	35	7	—
Messrs Levy and Salmon, Oxford Street Fruiters	15	—	—
Mr Allen, Avery Row Bond Street Glaziers	11	—	—
Mr Stroud, Lower Grosvenor Street Poulterer	25	—	—
[Carried Forward	£4000	11	9]

Debts due by the Bankrupt

[Brought Forward]	£4000	11	9]
Sundry small debts about	20	–	–
Mr Leftwich, Strand	40	–	–
Sawyer	14	3	3
Dover	16	16	5
	£4060	11	7

[f.]

Debts due by the Bankrupt

Mr Johnson debt stated at 92.7.0 should be	£108	19	10
Mr Francis Lewin debt stated at 60 0 0 should be	85	–	–
Mr Johns debt stated at 34 2 0 should be	45	14	–
Mr Allen Debt stated at 11 0 0	41	18	10
Mr Sawyer	14	3	3
Mr [illegible]	100	–	–

[Here are listed a few minor debts, none more than fifteen shillings, and without names of creditors.]

[f.] ## Debts due to the Bankrupt

Good | Mr H Wilkins, 43 Broad Street Golden Square	–	6	6
Good | Mr Ainsworth, 8 Sussex Place New Road	3	10	2
Good | Mr Thelluson, 82 Gloucester Place	–	16	–
Good | Mr Womwell, 16 George Street Hanover Square	3	13	11
Good | Mr Douglas, 28 Bruton Street Bond Street	5	8	4
Good | Mr Ure, Grosvenor Street	2	6	3
Good | Mr Holass, Dover Street Piccadilly	4	12	–
Good | Mr Moore, Cleveland Row, St James's	–	18	–
Good | Mr Parnther, Grafton Street, Bond Street	–	10	3
Good | Mr Ausly, 7 Langham Place	–	19	2
Good | Mr Hope, Dutchess Street [illegible]	19	4	7
Good | Lady East, Stratford Place	34	1	6
Good | Mr Fitzgibbon, 28 Berkley Square	–	10	6
Good | Mr Levy, Saville Street, Piccadilly	4	4	6
Good | Lady Glengall, 54 Grosvenor Street	7	14	3
Good | Mr Hatton, 48 Harley Street	2	18	7
Good| Mr Raining 48 Berkley Square	–	10	–
Good | Mr Burton, 15 Park Square	5	5	1
Good | Mr Martell, Brussels	2	9	–
Good | Mr Meyers, 136 Bond Street	–	12	–
Good | Mr Wainwright, 6 Harley Street [?]	5	1	–
Good | Mr Smith, 20 Saville Row	–	6	2
[Carried Forward]	£124	1	1]

Debts due to the Bankrupt

	[Brought Forward	£124	1	1]
Good | Mr Phillips, Oxford Street [?] set off		7	15	—
[f.] Good | Mr Hitchcock, Davies Street, Berkley Square set off		30	—	—
Good | Mr Fraser, Bury Street		40	5	6
Good | Mr Brand, 8 Portland Place		1	18	—
Good | Mr Stevens, Duke Street Plumber and Glazier sett off		10	10	—
Good | Lord Maryborough, Saville Row		—	15	4
Good | Lady Fitzpatrick, Grosvenor Place		—	14	6
Good | Mr Williamson, 25 Bond Street		—	12	6
Good | Captain Cunningham, 19 Maddox Street		—	10	—
Mr Hale, Welbeck Street		—	16	—
Good | Mrs[?] Wyatt, Foley Place		6	13	8
Good | Mr Beddingfield, Grosvenor Square		—	3	6
Good | Sir G Bamfylde, Grosvenor Square		2	2	—
Good | Mr Strachan, Cadogan Street		4	14	6
Good | The Countess de [?] Martin		—	1	6
Good | Mr Matthew, Cavendish Square		—	16	—
Good | Lady Stewart, Conduit Street		—	16	—
Good | Mr Ebers, Bond Street		2	5	6
Good | Mr Gillers, Connaught Place		8	—	—
Good | Mr Dermague, 42 Albermarle Street		2	6	8
Good | Mr Gregory, 13 Clarges Street		—	13	—
Good | Mr Nevill, 16 Park Lane		3	3	—
Good | Mr Addison, 1 Curzon Street		1	4	2
Good | Mr Mivart, Mivarts Hotel, Brook Street		1	16	—
Good | Lady Keith, Piccadilly		1	14	—
[f.] Good | Mr Simpson, Hampstead		—	6	6
Good | Earl Bathurst, Mansfield Street		24	11	3
Good| Mr Ealcraft, 6 Hanover Square		—	5	6
Good | Mr Jones, 149 Bond Street [?]		21	2	—
Good | Mr Alfred, 26 Surrey Street		—	16	—
Good | Mr Collier, Dutchess Street		—	16	3
Good | Mr Stroud, Poulterer, Grosvenor Street		9	4	—
Good | Mrs Stapleton, Mereworth Castle		1	15	—
Good | Mr Touri Golden Square		10	12	—
Good | Countess St Germains, Park Crescent		—	13	6
	[Carried Forward	£324	8	5]

Debts due to the Bankrupt

[Brought Forward	£304	8	7]
Bad | Mr Arnant, 27 Grosvenor Street	1	5	—
Bad | Mr Augustus, 67 Regent Street	—	11	6
Good | Countess of Aylesford, Audley Square	—	7	—
Good | Mr Albertz, Bookseller, 72 Charlotte Street	—	9	—
Good | Mr Thomason, Burlington Street	—	5	—
Bad | Mr Benfield (dead)	—	5	—
Good | Mr Bonfil, 19 Bedford Square	—	5	—
Doubtful | Mr Barry	—	6	—
Bad | Mr Barrow, Horse Guards	4	7	2
Good | Mr Bilton, Richmond	1	12	—
Doubtful | Mr Brett, Brompton	—	14	—
Bad | Mr Brown, 3 Wyndham Place	—	12	—
Good | Mr Brisset	4	3	—
[f.] Bad | Mr Ballow, 34 Sackville Street	—	15	9
Good | Mr Barnett, Poland Street	2	5	9
Good | Lady Brownlow, 30 H[?]ll Street	1	6	—
Good | Captain Chambre	8	11	—
Doubtful | Mr Cosway, 13 Berkley Street	1	—	—
Good | Mr Casey, Fulham	1	2	6
Bad | Mr Chadron,	1	—	—
Good | Mr Colombine, Bayswater	2	5	9
Good | Madam Charlow, 26 Surrey Street, Strand	1	6	—
Good | Mr Chatfield, 42 Welbeck Street	2	1	6
Bad | Mr Chasson, 3 Tichfield Street		15	—
Good | Miss Conyer, Duke St Albans	2	10	—
Bad | Madame De Costa, 3 Hereford Street	3	17	4
Good | Mr Digwell, at Lady Coopers	2	7	—
Good | Mr de Witte, Stamford Hill	—	15	—
Bad | Mr Draines	2	1	—
Good | Mr Dews[?]	—	15	—
Bad | Count Delaganti[?]	1	1	2
Good | Lord Dorchester, 20 Lower Brook Street	1	5	6
Bad | Sir William Elliott	—	13	—
Bad | Miss Gooch	6	2	4
Good | Doctor Goddard, Kew	4	4	—
Bad | Mr Foscolo	1	14	—
[f.] Good | Mr Game, 55 Doughty Street	1	18	2
Good | Captain Garth	7	8	—
Good | Mr Gill, 21 Bruton Street	—	12	—
[Carried Forward	£393	16	3]

Debts due to the Bankrupt

[Brought Forward	£393	16	3]
Good | Madame Goldsmith, Italy	—	13	—
Good | Mr Hulton, Lincolnshire	5	7	—
Good | Mrs Halsey, Hemsley	4	11	—
Bad | Mr Holding, York Street	2	10	—
Doubtful | Mr Hicks, Somerset Street	2	10	—
Doubtful | Mr Handlem, Connaught Terrace	—	8	—
Good | Mr Hermitage, 42 Montague Square	2	13	2
Good | Mr Higgins, Northampton	5	17	—
Bad | Mr Hamilton	2	7	—
Good | Mr Harrison, Berkley Street Solicitor	1	17	—
Doubtful | Mr Hornblow, 7 Ebury Street, Pimlico	1	7	6
Good | Mr Hare, Devonshire Terrace	2	—	10
Bad | Mr Hicks, 99 New Bond Street	1	1	—
Bad | Mr Holmes, Grosvenor Street	6	—	—
Doubtful | Mr Jones, York Terrace	—	7	10
Good | Madame Jannett, Paris	3	16	—
Bad | Mr Jerrett, Hertford Street, May Fair	—	10	—
Good | Count D Offalia, 61 Wimpole Street	2	9	10
Good | Mr Johnson, Ironmonger, Conduit Street set off	1	13	—
[f.] Bad | Mr Grame, Doughty Street	1	9	—
Good | Lady Lindsey, 30 Albermarle Street	1	15	3
Good | Dutchess of Leinster		14	6
Doubtful | Mr Kendrick, 4 Dutchess Street	1	2	6
Bad | Mr Levien	4	10	10
Doubtful | Mr Lascelles, 69 Grosvenor Street	1	16	10
Good | Mr Locke, 81 Grafton Street	—	10	10
Good | Mr Leigh, Brook Street	1	14	9
Bad | Mr Kennett, Brompton	8	2	—
Good | Mr Lloyd at Paris	1	6	—
Doubtful | Mr Murray at Hick's Hotel	—	10	6
Doubtful | Mr Mitchell	1	11	10
Bad | Mr Marshall, 36 York Street	2	18	—
Bad | Mr Morris, Chandos Street	1	16	—
Good | Miss Maddox, Upper Seymour Street	1	9	3
Doubtful | Mr Martini, Brussells	3	2	11
Doubtful | Mr Cleay, Queen Square	—	8	—
Good | The Honorable Mrs Murray, Scafes Hotel	1	4	9
Good | Sir P McLeod, Woolwich	1	12	—
[Carried Forward	£479	8	8]

Debts due to the Bankrupt

		Brought Forward	[£479	8	8]
Good	Lord Newborough		12	4	6
Good	Mr North at Mr Coulsons		–	6	–
Good	Revd. C Orde, Reading		2	10	–
Good	Mr Phillips, Loughborough		2	4	6
Good	Mr Plenderleath, Ramsgate		6	–	–
[f.] Bad	Mr Prescott, Charles Street [? paid]		14	16	–
Doubtful	Mr Pemberton, Chappell Street		–	3	6
Good	Mr Pitt, Ironmongers, Great Portland Street		–	12	6
Bad	Mr George Price		3	12	–
Doubtful	Mr Piggott		–	9	9
Good	Sir G Puleston		1	5	–
Good	Mr Parkes, Woolwich		1	–	–
Doubtful	Sir S Raffles, 24 Lower Grosvenor Street		–	19	6
Doubtful	Sir William Rowley		1	10	–
Bad	Mr Reid, 8 Thayer Street		1	10	–
Doubtful	Mr Robertson		–	17	4
Bad	Mr Rovinelle		–	12	–
Good	Mr Reid, Grosvenor Street		20	9	–
Bad	Mr Siverack		–	15	3
Good	Mrs Scott		–	12	–
Bad	Mr Sparkes, 48 Baker Street		4	3	11
Good	Mr Solier, Fenchurch Street Wine Merchant		12	4	–
Bad	Mr Steward, Regent Street		11	6	1
Doubtful	Lady Seymour, 7 Henrietta Street		2	8	6
Good	Sir P Shee		–	9	–
Bad	Mr Sparrow		–	7	–
Good	Revd. E Thorlow, Norwich		6	4	–
Good	Sir H Tichbourne, Aylesford		4	8	–
[f.] Good	Mr Turton, Seven Oaks		1	3	3
Good	Mr Thomas, Bond Street		–	18	–
Bad	Mr Underwood		3	–	–
Bad	Mr Villerbois, 100 Gloucester Place		–	15	–
Good	Viscount Weymouth, Cumberland Street		4	9	6
Bad	Mr Walthem, Park Street		9	11	3
Bad	Mr Walton, Carleton Palace		2	10	–
Bad	Mr Willson		–	6	–
Good	Sir E Way		–	17	10
Good	Mr Williams		1	1	–
Good	Mr Webster		–	8	–
		[Carried Forward	£638	15	10]

Debts due to the Bankrupt

	[Brought Forward	£638	15	10]
Good	Mr Willmot, Bagshot Confectioner	3	18	4
Good	Mr Walpole, Charles Street, Berkley Square	–	6	–
Good	Earl Warwick, 2 Seymour Place		16	6
Bad	Mr Weymss	1	6	6
Bad	Mr Douglas, Artist, Berwick Street Soho	20	–	–
Bad	Mr Mayhew, Painter, Old Bond Street	80		
Bad	Mr Erveaux, Painter, Newman Street, Oxford Street	10	–	–
Bad	Madame Robine, Queen Street, Soho	20	–	–
Bad	Madame Deparden, Gaudier[?] Hotel, Haymarket	94	–	–
		£836	11	1

[f.]   Property

Lease of my present residence granted to me by Abraham Sunmonds for a term of 21 years of which 14 years are now unexpired at a rent of £255 per Annum – Cost me about – £30
This lease is in the possession of Messrs Claude Scott and Co as a collateral security for £200

Lease of House No 15 in Lincolnshire Court granted to me by Mr William Taylor for a term of 30 years of which 25 years are now unexpired at a rent of £30 per Annum – the same cost me £45
         this Lease is also in the possession of Claude Scott & Co

Lease of House No 13 in Lincolnshire Court granted by Mr Norwood for a term of which 4 years are now unexpired at a Rent of £25 per Annum – Cost me £100
         this Lease is also in the possession of Claude Scott and Co

Cost price of stock taken possession of by my Assignees £300 0 0

Value of Furniture Fixtures Silver and plated Articles and the whole of the Copper and other Implements used in my Business £756 0 0

                                                                                    £1231   –   –

[f.]   Losses

			about		
1824	By Suppers supplied on Masquerade Nights at the Argyll Rooms		80	–	–
1825	By Supper supplied on the occasion of the Ball given in Aid of the Spanish Refugees at the Opera House		120	–	–
June 1827	By Breakfast supplied to the Horticultural Society at Chiswick		405	16	–
1826	By Horse and Chaise		64	–	–

		£	s	d
1824	By Sale of a Debt of £576 due by Messrs Chambers of Bond Street for which I received 8/– in the pound	345	12	–
1822 to 1827	By various experiments in Preserving Fruit &c about	200	–	–
1827	By experiments in Iceing Water, about	50	–	–
1823	By Ice Melting in Ice Well in Cromer Street about	100	–	–

By difference between Cost price of the following
Articles and what the same are now valued at

	£	s	d
Gas Apparatus	80	–	–
Brass Work in Shop	63	–	–
Looking Glasses	334	4	–
Other Glasses and China	712	7	6
Furniture	500	–	–
Copper Utensils	150	–	–
Tin Utensils	160	–	–
Pewter Utensils	200	–	–
Moulds, tools and different Apparatus	200	–	–
Glass Cases and Fixtures in Shop	200	–	–
Silver and Plated Articles	250	–	–
Iron Work	411	3	6
Reservoir	143	–	–
	3403	15	–
Valued at about	756	–	–
	2647	15	–
	£4031	3	–

[f.]   Expences

May 1822 to November 1828

	£	s	d
Rent of House in Bond Street for 6 ½ years at £255 per Annum	1657	10	–
Taxes 6 ½ Years at about £60 per Annum	390	–	–
Housekeeping expences 6 ½ years at about £350 per Annum	2275	–	–
Servants Wages (in House and Business 10 in number) £430 per Annum	2795	–	–
Wearing Apparel for Self Wife and Family 6 ½ years at £60 per Annum	390	–	–
Education of Children 6 ½ years at about £100 per Annum	650	–	–
Doctors and Medicine in 6 years	60	–	–
Law Expences in 6 years / exclusive of the Lawsuit relative to the Horticultural Breakfast about	100	–	–

Insurance for 6 ½ years at £26 per Annum	169	–	–
Painting about £30 per Annum for 6 ½ years about	195	–	–
Gas Lights £36 per Annum for 6 years	234	–	–
Travelling Expences in 6 ½ years about	60	–	–
Paper, String, &c 6 ½ years at £50 per Annum	325	–	–
Rent of Ice House for 6 ½ years at £120 per Annum	700	–	–
Carriage of Ice 6 ½ years at about £100 per Annum	650	–	–
Wine and Spirits £20 per Annum for 6 ½ years	130	–	–
Washing 6 ½ years at £70 per Annum	455	–	–
Newspapers 6 ½ years at £20 per Annum	130	–	–
1827 Repairing Ice Well	21	–	–
1822 to 1824 Repairing House in Bond Street	1300	–	–
1824 to 1828 Repairs of House about £20 per Annum for 4 years	80	–	–
1827 Paid for the Kings Court Arms about	66	–	–
August 1827 Paid for obtaining a Patent in Iceing Water	125	–	–
1822 to 1828 Paid for Copper Plates for Ornaments Bills and Tickets and Charities for Christmas about	150	–	–
1827 Paid Advertisements relative to Horticultural Society about	45	–	–
1828 Paid Witnesses expences on the Trial of the Action brought by me against Messrs Elliott and Sabine relative to the Horticultural Societies Breakfast about	50	–	–
1828 Paid Mr Hitchcock Law charges on such Action	98	–	–
[f.] 1822 Paid Advertisements about	60	–	–
1823 to 1828 Paid Advertisements about £10 per Annum for 5 ½ years	55	–	–
1823 Paid Repairs of House No 15 in Lincolnshire Court about	100	–	–
1823 to 1828 Rent of House in Lincolnshire Court £30 per Annum for 5 ½ years	165	–	–
1823 to 1828 Taxes about £8 per Annum	44	–	–
1823 By Gifts to obtain possession of the House in Lincolnshire Court	20	–	–
1823 to 1828 Rent of House in 13 Lincolnshire Court 5 ½ years at £25 per Annum	137	10	–
— ,, — Taxes about £8 per Annum	44	–	–
Oil Cloth for Shop about £14 per Annum for 6 ½ years	91	–	–
Wear of Pewter Tin and Copper Utensils for my business about £30 per Annum for 6 ½ years	195	–	–
1822 Paid for Fixtures of House in Bond Street which became useless and not worth anything	175	–	–
	£14,467	–	–

CHAPTER SEVEN

BEYOND BEETON: SOME NINETEENTH-CENTURY COOKERY AND HOUSEHOLD BOOKS IN THE BROTHERTON SPECIAL COLLECTIONS

Valerie Mars

BEETON AND OTHERS: CONTEXT AND CONTINUITY

Although this paper is not primarily about Mrs Beeton's *Book of Household Management*,[1] I should offer an explanation for the title 'Beyond Beeton'. It is essentially a dip into the wider diversity of works available to nineteenth-century cooks and focuses on the tension between traditional and new styles of service, and the foreign influences and recipes that were increasingly directed at particular social constituencies. These provided for a new and expanding readership.

Isabella Beeton's *Book of Household Management* is popularly viewed as the quintessential Victorian cookery and household book. Victoria had been on the throne for twenty-two years when it was first published as instalments in 1859. It was published as a complete volume in 1861.[2] 60,000 copies were sold in the first year and 640,000 to 1898.[3] Unlike previous works, *The Book of Household Management* offered the novelty of coloured plates. Beeton's contemporary popularity, however, owed more to her feel for changing social attitudes than great cookery.

Mrs Beeton's book borrowed from many other people. She acknowledges help from correspondents to her husband Samuel's publication *The Englishwoman's Domestic Magazine* and to some private sources. She also claims to have 'made a diligent study of the works of the best modern writers'[4] and from these she selected what she required. Among her sources were Thomas Webster,[5] who wrote a comprehensive household encyclopædia, and Eliza Acton who wrote *Modern Cookery for Private Families*.[6]

Acton was a remarkable cookery book writer, who blended English and French bourgeois traditions at the same time as advising on new methods, equipment and ideas to incorporate from foreign cookery. Her fourteenth edition topically includes comment on the work of Liebig, the great German

Figure 66. A selection of decorative desserts set out, for added effect, on a mirrored pier-table, thus offering an ornamental small-scale display for middling Victorian households. From Mrs Beeton's Book of Household Management *(1861), p. 695.*

chemist.[7] Yet her books did not run to nearly as many editions as Beeton.

Like Delia Smith, Beeton caught a popular mood and taste. But the real secret of the book's fame is that it was continually re-edited and posthumously updated. Isabella Beeton died aged 28, four years after the first edition was published. Her husband, the publisher Samuel Beeton, was the first to ensure the work's long endurance. After its initial appearance in 1861, it was first revised in 1869. Later editions had more illustrations. Like *Persil*,[8] Beeton became a brand: a product that has nothing of the original content. Because the Beeton brand was in continuous production, it served to obscure the impact of the wider range of nineteenth-century works on cookery, servants, housekeeping, etiquette and eating and drinking.

The question is, if Beeton is not all, which books do reveal the range of nineteenth-century cooking and eating? This question is not easily answered. Many of the less well-known books, especially those without further editions and contemporary or later references, leave unanswered questions about their success or failure. This is especially so with those titles intended for particular niche markets such as *A Manual of Homeopathic Cookery, designed chiefly for such persons as are under homeopathic treatment* (1846).[9] For a less exclusive readership, Sidney Lear's 1884 *Maigre Cookery*[10] offered Continental fast-day dishes as a useful aid to health and economy.

The Book of Household Management has certainly given rise to some overarching generalizations, but the flight to gentility with which Beeton is associated was well established before her work was published. In this paper I shall attempt to outline some of the nineteenth-century preferences that showed a greater diversity of tastes than Beeton offers.

Nineteenth-century social revolution was reflected in the ways food was cooked and presented. A general increase in book production included more on these subjects than had ever been published before and many of the titles are to be found in the Blanche Leigh and the Preston collections in the Brotherton Library. They offer rich sources of social comment on consumption. Nearly all the nineteenth-century books cited in this paper are in these collections.[11]

Eighteenth-century cookery continues into the new century

How far were nineteenth-century styles of cooking and eating a product of what had gone before? Nineteenth-century cookery did not, of course, begin in 1800. Domestic cookery was a perpetuation of the ways of at least two previous generations' styles of cooking and eating. An historian's 'long eighteenth century' could easily describe the extension of eighteenth-century styles of cooking and eating into those which flourished during the first half of the nineteenth century. In the Leeds collections there are several books rooted in the eighteenth century extending eighteenth-century culinary style via editions published in the nineteenth.

Cooking techniques frequently have a much longer life than the life of the particular book in which they are written. They exist outside of texts, for cookery is essentially a craft. Texts follow practice so that day-to-day cookery is not usually text-based. As an example, for true roasting in front of a fire, necessary skills were being practised long before cookery books were written.

Some books had very long lives. For example, Hannah Glasse's *The Art of Cookery made plain and easy* was in print from 1747 to 1843.[12] Another work bridging the eighteenth and nineteenth centuries was Elizabeth Raffald's *The Experienced English Housekeeper*,[13] first published in 1769, and the last regular edition in 1834.[14]

The most constantly in-print work to carry an eighteenth-century traditional style into the nineteenth was *A New System of Domestic Cookery:*

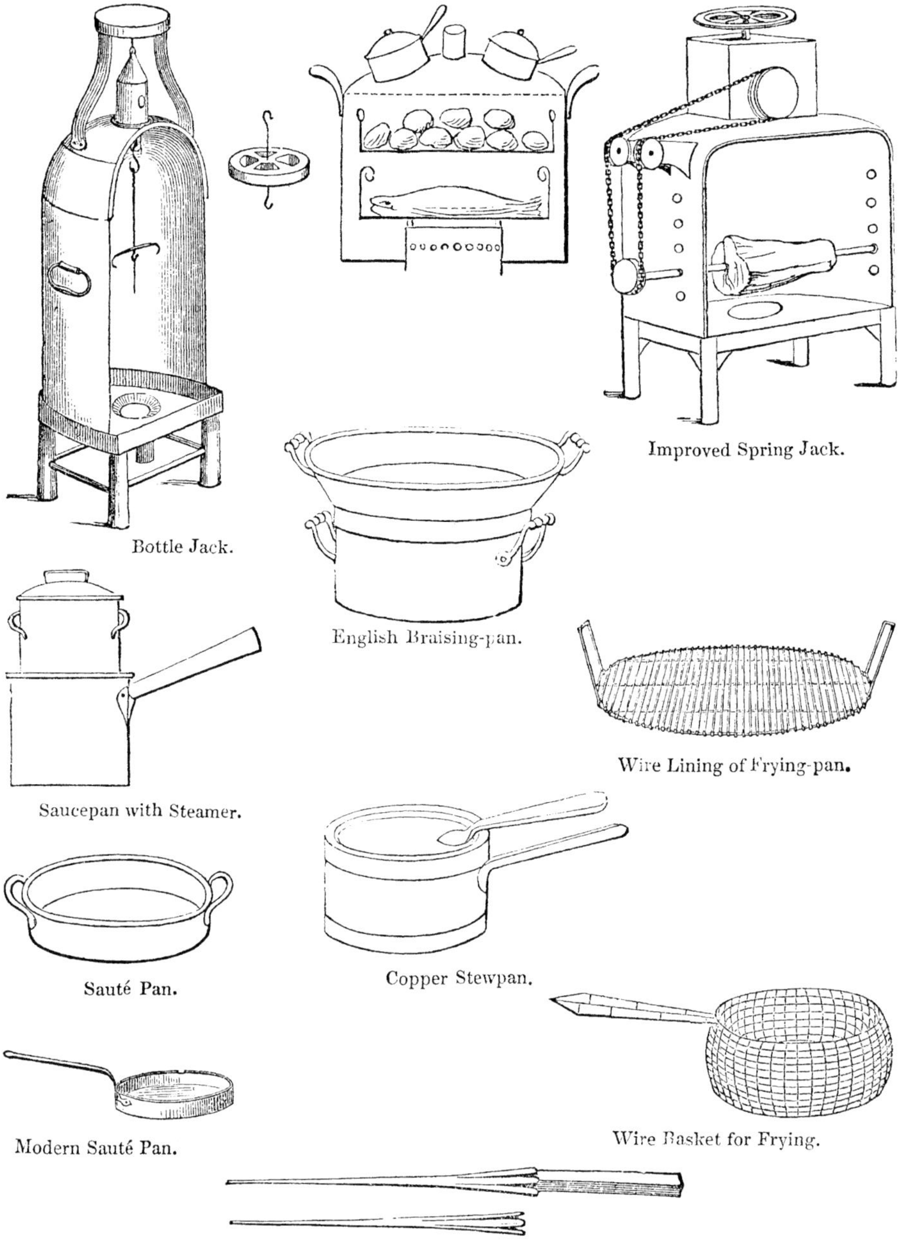

Bottle Jack.

Improved Spring Jack.

English Braising-pan.

Saucepan with Steamer.

Wire Lining of Frying-pan.

Sauté Pan.

Copper Stewpan.

Modern Sauté Pan.

Wire Basket for Frying.

Larding Pins.

Figure 67. Eliza Acton states: 'A thorough practical knowledge of the processes described, boiling, roasting, steaming, stewing, broiling, frying, baking, braising and larding … will form a really good cook far sooner and more completely than any array of mere recipes can do.' She not only explains technique, but also has illustrations of equipment that might be unfamiliar to her readers. Illustrations are drawn from Chapter IX, 'Boiling, Roasting, etc.', Modern Cookery for Private Families, *first published in 1845.*

Formed upon Principles of Economy, and Adapted to the Use of Private Families, written by Maria Eliza Rundell (née Ketelby) who was born in 1745.[15] She wrote up a lifetime's culinary repertoire when she was 60. It was published in 1806 and Mrs Rundell died in 1828. *A New System of Domestic Cookery* has 63 editions and titles in the Leeds collections, dating from 1806 to *circa* 1876.

The 1856 edition is published as *The English Cookery Book Comprising Mrs Rundell's Domestic Cookery revised with several modern dishes added thereto, carefully selected and simplified* by Frederick W. Davis, head cook of the Freemasons' Tavern in London. The Freemasons' was a well-known place for all-male dinners. Rundell's unfussy style appealed to traditional male taste. Davis states in his introduction, his 'aim has been to furnish the women of England with an English Cookery Book, that, while it contained nothing too difficult for a female cook, should embody all that might be required for a gentlemanly repast.'[16]

Classical values, associated with rural simplicity in the eighteenth-century, were embodied in the idea of a 'gentlemanly repast' and are quoted repeatedly for most of the rest of the nineteenth-century. This may explain why The Reverend Hugh Reginald Haweis, a fashionable London clergyman, chose Mrs Rundell as the source of two booklets of selections for 'Routledge's World Library' in 1886: the first relating to meats, the second to sweet and vegetable recipes. This series of assorted literature at sixpence or a shilling was intended to improve the poor and, he hoped, 'if not a complete cure for indolence and vice, may at least prove a powerful catechism'.[17] These were the only cookery books in the series and were chosen for women readers. His purpose was to 'vary the monotony of the ordinary dinner-table, and to prevent waste.' Haweis notes that the writer has drawn on her predecessors' and her own lifetime's practical experience. Conservative practice is a favourite validation for traditionalists, among whom were many of these male gastronomic commentators.

Haweis recommends the unabridged edition of Mrs Rundell for those living in the country where meat is killed on the farm and hens are kept. Eighteenth-century and early nineteenth-century cookery was closer to the sources of production and nature, whereas food distribution in the expanded later-Victorian cities was separated from its rural context. In 1855 London acquired central slaughterhouses in Islington and a meat market at Smithfield. In 1876, frozen stores were installed below Smithfield for Argentine meat.[18]

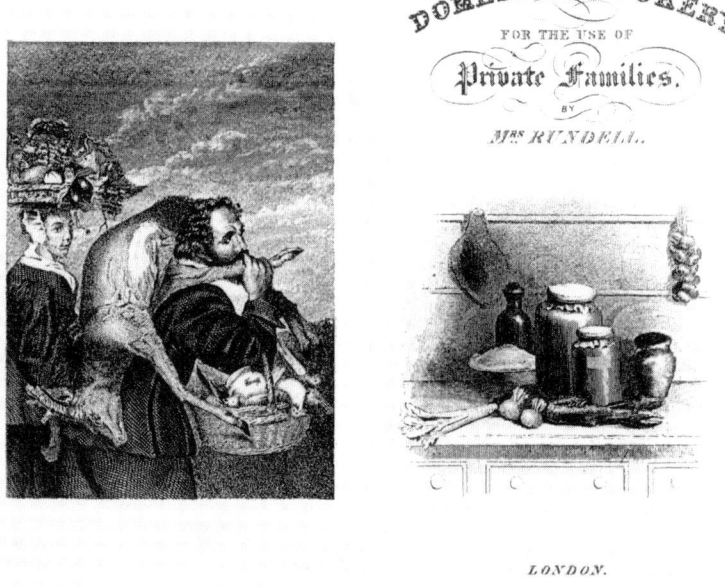

Figure 68. These two front plates from Mrs Rundell embody eighteenth-century housekeeping values. The period hunter with game and the woman with a basket represent a classic view of nature's plenty for human provision. The message opposite reflects nature as judiciously preserved. A kitchen dresser displays the cook's competence at preserving, with a ham, preserve jars and a pie. Summer plenty is thus captured for later needs. Skills like pastry-making were increasingly replaced during the nineteenth century by commercially manufactured products.

From unadorned nature to gentle disguise

Rundell's natural, unadorned cuisine was a style often in conflict with a refined Victorian feminization of cookery that transformed simple ingredients into decorative displays. Unadorned calves' heads did not appear on later Victorian menus for genteel dinners and suppers, yet they persisted as colour plates in later editions of Mrs Beeton, just as they had been included in the first edition. The book was designed from the outset to appeal to a range of tastes, both plain and fancy. However, the editors of later issues of the book included illustrations that suggest a wider readership than is supported by the accompanying recipes. There are dishes included in the colour plates that are well beyond the abilities of a domestic cook or kitchen maid.

Some of these illustrations catered to a need to know how to compose and arrange elaborate and fashionable dishes. For example, from the 1880s, there is a colour plate showing a 'Timbale Milanaise Maccaroni'. Eliza Acton does not recommend *timbales* as a dish for the domestic kitchen: 'We have inserted here no receipts for these, because unless very skilfully prepared they are sure to fail, and they are not in much request in this country, unless it be at the tables of the aristocracy, for which they are prepared by efficient cooks.'[19] This same colour plate also shows another dish equally challenging for a domestic cook, 'Chartreuse of Partridges'.[20] Yet there are no corresponding recipes in the text for either the timbale or the chartreuse. 'Chartreuse of Vegetables' is described by Charles Elmé Francatelli in his *Cook's Guide* as, 'A mixed preparation of vegetables symmetrically and tastefully arranged in a plain mould, the interior of which is garnished with game, quails, pigeons, larks, fillets, scollops, or tendons, &c.,&c.' 'Chartreuse à la Parisienne, &c.' was an ornamental entrée made of *quenelle* forcemeat filled with ragoûts or scallops or similar ingredients.[21]

To recognize what these elaborate dishes were like was useful for visits to the pastry shop, for negotiating with outside-caterers, or when invited to a new experience such as a grand dinner or ball supper. Books by the great chefs also offered knowledge of exclusive *haute cuisine*. Serving a similar function were etiquette manuals offering '*Hello*-ish' glimpses of élite eating that helped 'Bran new people'[22] to know the etiquette that accompanied *haute cuisine*.

A taste for elaborate cuisine was not a universal aspiration. Both middle- and upper-class men during the nineteenth-century repeatedly defended traditional English cookery. Thomas Walker was a frequently-quoted arbiter of Victorian upper-middle-class male taste. He was born in Manchester in 1784, and was called to the Bar at the Inner Temple by 1812. In 1835 he both founded and closed a weekly journal, *The Original*. Twenty-nine issues were published, to be followed by *Aristology, or the Art of Dining* compiled from *The Original* in the same year.[23] He writes: 'Gentlemen keep more in view the real ends, whereas ladies think principally of display and ornament, of form and ceremony – not all, for some have excellent notions of taste and comfort.'[24]

Walker was forced to give up issuing the journal because a consequential increase in dinner invitations no longer permitted him time to write. His health was weak, which may partially explain his taste for simpler dinners. He died a bachelor, in Brussels, on 20 January 1836.[25]

Quotations were popular ammunition against the feminization of the table which, like *haute cuisine*, was set in opposition to an eighteenth-century patriotic and classically-derived simplicity. Throughout the century, Walker's *Aristology* was constantly quoted in other male-oriented dining-books. The values and attitudes that he there promulgated, and that were so often repeated, were principally concerned with a 'masculine' simplicity of taste enforced with firm authority. Though it was written ten years after *Physiologie du goût* (1826) by the great French gastronome, Brillat-Savarin (1755–1826),[26] there is no evidence that it was imitative.

Walker's *Aristology* was reissued with additional editorial notes by Felix Summerly (Henry Cole's *nom de plume*) in 1881. Cole considered that Walker's 'first principles' should govern all dinners and, therefore, 'seem well worthy of reproduction at this time.'[27] Cole valued rules, and Walker's rules covered most aspects of dining. Cole also quoted extensively from *Physiologie du goût*. Brillat-Savarin's 'Aphorisms' offered several Victorian favourites such as, 'Animals feed: man eats: only the man of intellect knows how to eat.'[28] Cole includes all twenty aphorisms in an appendix to his 1881 edition of Walker.[29] But Cole, the energetic organizer of the Great Exhibition of 1851, was a man unencumbered by doubts. Nor did Beeton let such an anecdote-rich resource go un-plundered.[30]

Charles Cooper, in a 1929 review of Hayward's *Art of Dining* (published in 1852, and which took Walker's sub-title), comments on his (Hayward's) liking for élite society.[31] Though Cooper was born in 1844, and though both were barristers, Cooper does not seem to have known Hayward but could well have known those who did. In *The Art of Dining*,[32] Hayward admired more elaborate cuisine than Walker and he also quotes both Walker and Brillat-Savarin. Hayward, like Walker, went to a late edition in 1883 but without any new editorial comments. These, however, can be found in an 1899 edition by Charles Sayle.[33] Another lawyer, A. V. Kirwan, in *Host and Guest* (1864), also quotes Walker.[34]

William Blanchard Jerrold, '*Fin-Bec*' (1826–1884), was an admirer of the simplicity of French bourgeois cookery and, he noted in 1871, that, 'the present generation knows little of Walker'.[35] He later quotes him in *The Dinner Bell* (1878), recommending Walker's ideal dinner with 'everything on the table'[36] which made spontaneous informality easier, and avoided too much dependence on footmen. Another favourite of Victorian traditionalists, William Kitchiner, earlier explained a similar preference in slightly eccentric detail. In *The Cook's Oracle*, first published in 1817, he suggested issuing diners with a single set of cutlery for the entire dinner. In 1874, Jerrold

Beyond Beeton

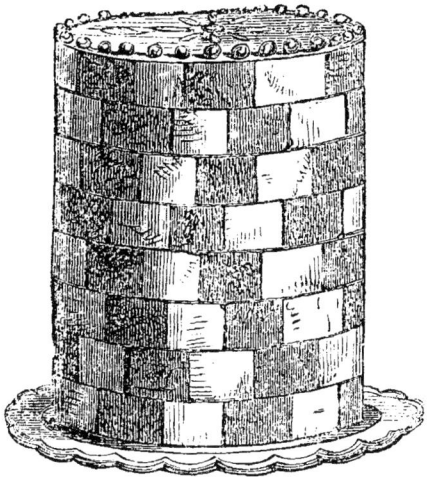

CHARTREUSE OF PARTRIDGES.

Figure 69. C.E. Francatelli's Chartreuse of Partridges from The Housekeeper's and Butler's Assistant *is a typical example of fashionably intricate French* haute cuisine.

wrote a short biography of Thomas Walker.[37] Others who also quote him include John Timbs in *Hints for the Table* (1838, with further editions to *circa* 1860).

This continuing taste for simplicity, although promoted by men, does not necessarily mean that some women did not share the same taste and it would be mistaken to suggest that traditional style was simply a male preference. There were metropolitan men whose taste was for French *haute cuisine*. In many of their critical works they asserted their reactionary preferences in a continuing opposition to the growing fashion for a feminized cuisine.

All sorts of cookery: the new diversity in print

In addition to these two themes, reaction and innovation based on the traditions of French and English cuisine, there was also new diversity in culinary topics. There were many works for 'niche markets'. These included some traditional subjects, such as cookery for invalids. Lady Cust's *The Invalid's Own Cookery Book: a collection of recipes from various books and various countries*[38] has as its organizing principle a single invalid being cared for in several countries, with local repertoires being collected and reproduced.

There are several books for vegetarians, including *Vegetarian Cookery* (1852)[39] by Mrs Brotherton, wife of a founder of the Vegetarian Society, published five years after the society was established in 1847. Janet Ross's 1899 *Leaves from our Tuscan Kitchen or how to cook vegetables*,[40] although not entirely vegetarian, offers Italian recipes using local vegetables.

A selection of Jewish cookery books for domestic use was published giving Jewish housewives current recipes within the dietary laws. There were also books for schools such as Miss M.A.S. Tattersall's *Jewish Cookery Book: compiled for use in the Cookery Centres under the School Board for London* (1895).[41]

Foreign tastes would have been well known to those who increasingly travelled for work and leisure, but travel was still beyond the experience of many middle-class English people. Trade beyond Europe and within the Empire, however, offered some exotic possibilities, which were eagerly adopted by authors like Lady Cust. But, for many colonialists, a perception of themselves as superior beings made it more important to reject rather than to adopt native cuisines. In India, English-style meals were considered appropriate, especially for entertaining. Recipes were concocted from a combination of imported tinned foods and local produce. Colonel Arthur Robert Kenny-Herbert recorded an Anglo-Indian cuisine in cookery books such as *Culinary Jottings for Madras* under the pseudonym 'Wyvern'. In the fifth edition of 1885, he remarked that 'the best curry in the world would never be permitted to appear at a *petite dîner* composed by a good disciple of the new regime.'[42] *Dainty Dishes for Indian Tables* (1879)[43] included European dishes alone in its first edition, though adding two chapters on Indian curries and pilaus [sic] to the second edition of 1881. A typical menu included Spinach Purée with Cream, Grilled Mushrooms, Charlotte of Apples and Orange and Cream Jelly.[44]

In England there was a limited but recurring range of imported Anglo-Indian recipes which included mulligatawny soup, curries, kedgeree and chutneys.[45] Some recipes were closer to their Indian originals than others, and several dishes given by travellers and expatriates appear in the 1855 edition of Acton's *Modern Cookery* in the section, 'Foreign and Jewish Cookery'.[46] Among them are kedgeree, as an 'Indian breakfast dish', 'curries' and a 'Real Indian Pilaw [sic]'.[47] Two mulligatawny soups are separated from these exotica and are incorporated into the chapter on soups.

Beeton also has some colonial recipes, typically West-Indian Pudding,[48] Indian Chetney sauce and Indian Trifle.[49] This last is a lemon-flavoured rice-flour blancmange covered with custard then decorated. Beeton's recipe for

Indian curry powder is based on Dr Kitchiner's instructions.[50] Curry is often suggested by Victorian writers as a useful disguise for leftovers, to be eaten at family meals. The most frequent leftover, cold mutton, is found in *What to do with Cold Mutton* (1863, reissued in 1887). Predictably, it includes a recipe for curried mutton.[51]

An example of an 'exotic' cookery was Turabi Efendi's *Turkish Cookery Book*,[52] published in London in 1862, six years after the Crimean war. It has recipes for a cuisine praised by Alexis Soyer in a letter to *The Times* in September 1856: '[the Turks] have many dishes which are indeed worthy of the table of the greatest epicure' which should 'be adopted and Frenchified and Anglicized.'[53]

Joseph Bregon and Anne Miller's *The Practical Cook, English and Foreign* (1845)[54] was a cosmopolitan offering with 'original receipts in English, French, German, Russian, Spanish, Polish, Dutch, American, Swiss, and Indian Cookery.' Bregon had been cook to two Russian princes and the Russian Ambassador in Paris. Like Soyer, he had seen the need to 'Frenchify' some of the recipes to make them acceptable to his employers. Miller had been cook to 'several English families of distinction'.

Readers' choice was further expanded with Cassell's *A Dictionary of Cookery* (1875/6), which claimed to contain 'over nine thousand recipes'.[55] Thirty years earlier, James Jennings, in *Family Cookery*,[56] had offered a mere two thousand five hundred. While in theory cooks might choose to experiment with the cookery of any nation, practical considerations may have inhibited them. However, by 1875 the rail network was well established and imported ingredients were correspondingly more available. But books like Cassell's and those on more distant cuisines would have been invaluable sources of esoteric knowledge for genteel housewives rather than collections of recipes from which to cook. Informed conversation had more virtue for the genteel than did hands-on cookery.

Simple instruction and superfluous 'facts'

Beeton includes some excellent recipes but these frequently offer more by way of irrelevant information than practical advice on cookery. She is offering information for genteel women who wished to accumulate 'facts' as knowledge and, in doing so, to acquire the 'symbolic capital'[57] necessary to a new aspiring middle class. To give an example, she offers the barest cooking instructions in some fifty words for a simple boiled barley soup. But she gives three times as many words in accompanying information on barley in antiquity, its nutritional properties and, albeit more usefully, on its suitability for invalids.[58] It was such knowledge that allowed middle-class ladies to distance themselves from the 'lower' world of cooks and kitchens. While Beeton was careful not to address too specific a constituency, this alternative was embraced by John Walsh in his *Manual of Domestic Economy, Suited to Families Spending from £100–£1000 a Year*. This was first published in 1856, three years before Beeton was issued in instalments. Inflation took hold of his title, which was adjusted for the 1879 edition to incomes ranging from £150–£1,500.[59] Walsh was 'Assisted In Various Departments by A Committee of Ladies.' He was primarily a sports-writer and was editor of *The Field* but, like several Victorian male writers, had opinions on improving household arrangements. Similarly, but in a much slimmer volume, Charles Selby, an actor (and female impersonator, as 'Tabitha Tickletooth'),[60] offered advice on household management and recipes. Another male writer was Thomas Webster FGS (1773–1844), a geologist and architect. His *Encyclopaedia of Domestic Economy* was published in 1844 with the assistance of Mrs [William]Parkes. Frances Byerley Parkes was also author of *Domestic Duties; or, instructions to young married ladies on the management of their households.*[61] Webster and Walsh's works were far wider-ranging than Beeton's *Household Management*.

The flight to gentility is one of the most notable characteristics of Victorian domestic middle-class cookery, but like so much that was Victorian it was by no means universal. Whether the ladies who assisted Walsh were familiar with their own kitchens or how much involvement they had with the finished work is so far unknown. In 1844, Thomas Webster and/or Mrs Parkes remarked on 'the instruction of young cooks':

> Young servants have not in the present day so much practical instruction from their mistresses, as was the case in former times, when ladies, except those of the highest rank, superintended and assisted in the preparation for well served tables.[62]

Acton, like Rundell, belonged to the earlier tradition, whereas Beeton's appeal was partly to these 'new mistresses'.

Importing French 'haute' and 'bourgeois' cuisines

The eighteenth-century habit of English writers borrowing and plagiarizing

French recipes continued. As there had been previously, there were also nineteenth-century English books that were truly French, being translations from the originals. Among these was *French Domestic Cookery* (1846),[63] from the great French middle-class *La Cuisinière de la campagne et de la ville*,[64] which the translator describes as 'the French Rundell'. Other works were in varying degrees French and English or, to be more precise, French recipes and techniques incorporated into an English repertoire. Eliza Acton is a good example of such Anglo-French cookery, typified by her advice on making good everyday soup like the French.[65] Knowledge of French bourgeois cookery would also have been useful for those readers who took up residence in France for financial, social or health reasons.

When the Victorians referred to French cookery, they were not usually thinking of the bourgeois style that might have been more in accord with middle-class resources but rather were dreaming of elaborate *haute cuisine*. The three best-known practitioners of this style – who both cooked in England and wrote cookery books for their milieu – were Louis Eustace Ude,[66] Charles Elmé Francatelli,[67] and Alexis Soyer.[68] There were others, such as the great Antonin Carême (1784–1833)[69] and Felix Urbain Dubois (1818–1901),[70] whose books were translated for English chefs, although they were themselves not based in England. Another was Jules Gouffé, whose *Royal Cookery* was translated and adapted for English use by his brother Alphonse.[71] Nineteenth-century *haute cuisine* culminated with the internationally acclaimed Auguste Escoffier (1846–1935) who re-organized and codified the French repertoire.[72]

This group of books – especially Carême, Gouffé and Dubois – had fine engravings to illustrate the most elaborate dishes. Gouffé's first translated edition of 1868 is beautifully illustrated in colour. Colour is not only used to show finished dishes, but also to show texture and differences in the colour of fat and lean meat.

Diners could use books written for professional cooks when ordering a dinner from outside-caterers that required some gourmet knowledge. Soyer in *The Gastronomic Regenerator* not only offered advice for cooks but his notes could be useful in providing standards for the inexperienced. His list 'How everything should be in cookery',[73] has the comment: 'All clear soup must not be too strong of meat, and must be of a light brown, sherry, or straw colour.'[74] Felix Urbain Dubois similarly addresses the amphytrion, as a gastronomically-aware host who selects a dinner.[75]

BEYOND BEETON

L'Extravagance Culinaire à l'Alderman, or the One Hundred Guinea Dish.—The opportunity of producing some gastronomic phenomenon for the royal table on such an occasion as the York Banquet was irresistible; accordingly, the following *choice morsels* were carefully selected from all the birds mentioned in the general bill of fare, to form a dish of delicacies worthy of his Royal Highness and the noble guests around him.

The extravagance of this dish, valued at one hundred guineas, is accounted for, by supposing, that if an epicure were to order a similar one for a small party, he would be obliged to provide the undermentioned articles, viz.:

		At the cost of		
		£	s.	d.
5	Turtle heads, part of fins, and green fat	34	0	0
24	Capons, the two small *noix* (nuts) from each side of the middle of the back only used, being the most delicate part of every bird	8	8	0
18	Turkeys, the same	8	12	0
18	Fatted pullets, the same	5	17	0
16	Fowls, the same	2	8	0
10	Grouse	2	5	0
20	Pheasants, *noix* only	3	0	0
45	Partridges, the same	3	7	0
6	Plovers, whole	0	9	0
100	Snipes, *noix* only	5	0	0
3	Dozen Quails, whole	3	0	0
40	Woodcocks, *noix* only	8	0	0
3	Dozen Pigeons, the same	0	14	0
6	Dozen Larks, stuffed	0	15	0
	Ortolans from Belgium	5	0	0
	The *garniture*, consisting of cockscombs, truffles, mushrooms, crawfish, olives, American asparagus, *croustades* (paste crust), sweetbreads, *quenelles de volaille* (strips or slices of fowl), green mangoes, and a new sauce	14	10	0
		£105	5	0

Figure 70. Alexis Soyer's Hundred Guinea Dish was produced for the royal table at the York Banquet on 25 October 1850. He gives this as an example of the superiority of his cuisine over that of the previous ages in The Pantropheon, the History of Food and its Preparation in Ancient Times *(1853).*

Chefs who published were discussed in newspapers and in books on dining. Hayward praised Francatelli's dinners at Chesterfield House as 'the admiration of the gastronomic world of London'. Soyer, he admits, is 'a very clever man, of inventive genius and inexhaustible resource; but his execution is hardly on a par with his conception.'[76] Soyer had designed the kitchens and was head chef at the Reform Club from 1837 to 1850.

Soyer had much in common with some of today's TV chefs. His culinary exploits provided wonderful journalist copy. *The Morning Post* describes and praises a Soyer dinner at the Reform to honour Egypt's ruler, Ibrahim Pasha on 3 July 1846, and singles out his Crême d'Egypte à l'Ibrahim Pasha,[77] a spectacular confection which incorporated the portrait of the honoured Egyptian guest's father on a pyramid of meringue. Reviewers, too, loved Soyer's entrepreneurial exploits. The taste of the cuisine had no place in their descriptions – there were no gastronomic reference points for readers, for few had a repertoire of gastronomic knowledge. But Soyer's *haute cuisine* and showmanship offered Victorian readers images of an élite lifestyle and a vision of plenty, as in his 'Hundred Guinea Dish'.[78]

Equally opulent was a costly Soyer dinner prepared for Osborne Sampayo which demonstrated the wonders of a new industrial age. Live salmon were rushed to London, by train, to be served a few hours after leaving the River Severn. Soyer's eventful life was recorded a year after his death in 1859 by his secretaries F. Volant and J.R. Warren in *Memoirs of Alexis Soyer*.[79]

Cookery for all classes

Francatelli[80] and Soyer[81] also wrote for the middle classes and the poor. Their books, with clearly classified titles for the appropriate rank and class, offered definition in a changing social world. Readers were served by an increasing range of books directed at specific social constituencies, and had titles like Soyer's *Modern Housewife* – directed at middle-class readers. The 'modern houscwife' writes from her house in St John's Wood to her friend in a country cottage with a mixture of recipes and didactic anecdotes.

Francatelli's *Cook's Guide*[82] simply offered less elaborate dishes than appear in his book *The Modern Cook*,[83] which is directed at those with larger kitchens and the necessarily highly skilled cooks.

At the base of the hierarchy of cookery books were improving books for the working classes and the poor. Mary Jewry edited and compiled *Warne's Model Cookery and Housekeeping Book*, which was produced in a 'People's

Figure 71. Soyer's front plate for The Modern Housewife *shows the fashionably crinolined housewife offering her advice, wreathed by traditional festoons of fruit, vegetables and game.*

Edition'.⁸⁴ The publishers note they have 'been careful that such receipts should be selected as would best suit the requirements of housekeepers of small incomes. At the same time a few dishes have been added for home entertainments, &c., of a rather more expensive kind.'⁸⁵

Writing cookery books for the poor was a contribution to the great Victorian pursuit of charitable work and reform. Soyer's and Francatelli's small books for the poor offered both recipes and advice, as well as recipes for those doing charitable work. Francatelli offers three economical and substantial soups for distribution to the poor.⁸⁶ This reforming tendency was also formalized with the introduction of school cookery classes. An example from 1849 is *The Finchley Manuals of Industry. No. I., Cooking; or, Practical and economical training for those who are to be servants, wives and mothers*. Such cookery teaching involved learning by rote. Here is a fragment from an account of how to broil mutton chops:

> Q. And then?
> A. I broil them over a clear fire as I would steaks.
> Q. How do you serve them?
> A. Generally with potatoes, or pickles, or both; and if approved, with a little ketchup.[87]

Farmhouses where farm servants no longer lived-in, removed girls from learning larger-scale cookery. Also town employers, who did not visit their own kitchens, frequently left inexperienced young countrywomen to do the cooking. Victorian enthusiasm for educating cooks culminated in the National Training School for Cookery, an enterprise 'driven' by Henry Cole, who was Charles Dickens' model for Gradgrind, the MP who has a passion for education as memorizing facts.[88] The School's cookery book, compiled by Cole's daughter, Rose, gives recipes in numbered stages: 'Savoury hash' from 'Australian Mutton' begins: '1. We will put *one ounce of butter* on the fire to melt. 2. We take *half an onion*, peel it, and cut it in slices. 3. We put the *onion* into the *butter*.'[89] There are sixteen of these directions to follow for the complete recipe.

During the last quarter of the century entrepreneurial women writers like Anne de Salis were encouraging ladies once again to return to cookery. Mrs A.B. Marshall[90] and Mrs Hannah Young[91] both gave classes and demonstrations. Anne de Salis and Mrs Young promoted gas stoves for genteel ladies' cookery. They were much cleaner and easier to use than the coal-fired kitcheners to which their cooks were accustomed. The recherché cookery Marshall and de Salis encouraged was the apogee of feminized decorative food for home entertaining. Recherché was a favourite adjective, described as 'Exquisite; dainty', in Herman Senn's *Dictionary of Foods and Culinary Encyclopædia*.[92] This cuisine did not require the ongoing resources of authentic French *haute cuisine*, but was an eclectic style that focussed on decorative dishes. Short cuts were offered. Mrs Marshall gives recipes for consommé but she also sold tinned consommé. The National School and Mrs Marshall's School gave lessons for ladies and their cooks. Both Marshall and Young also offered ranges of kitchen equipment to make these elaborate dishes.[93]

There are plenty of similar examples of nineteenth-century middle-class food that was polarized as either extremely plain or as an over-elaborate cuisine with more décor than flavour. Anne de Salis remarks in the preface to *A la Mode Cookery*, the collected recipes from her *à la mode* books from the previous decade:

> I hope the feature of the illustrations will render the book of special service to many housewives; especially in the present century, when everything is so decorative, and cookery has become a fine art, it is quite necessary to have plates for cookery fashions as for dress, furniture, &c.[94]

This direct approach opposes the traditional values of William Kitchiner. In 1824. he had scorned diners who 'ate with their eyes and not their mouths'.[95]

NINETEENTH-CENTURY TASTES IN THE TWENTIETH CENTURY

As there was a 'long' eighteenth century, there is similarly considered to have been a long nineteenth century closing in the devastation of 1914. That may be a useful construct for many purposes, but there is plenty of evidence within our own lifetimes that the culinary nineteenth century certainly survived to the end of the twentieth. As our lives have become longer, so tastes that had been formed before 1914 have lived on. Plain cookery and elaborate decorative dishes are two well-known extremes of Victorian cookery. My grandparents married in 1899 and employed a plain cook who used *The Official Handbook for the National Training School for Cookery*. Their daughter's taste, for what in the late twentieth century would be described as overcooked meat and vegetables, was her parents' ideal plain cooked food.[96]

Some late twentieth-century decorative food owes much to late Victorian elaboration. A few years ago the Army Catering Corps was still producing this style of presentation while works like *Leaves from our Tuscan Kitchen* give recipes that are in accord with many twenty-first century tastes. A taste revived in the mid twentieth-century by Elizabeth David was more in tune with Acton than Beeton, a reminder that some of the nineteenth-century recipes are not so inaccessible.

This paper's theme of the tensions between plain and elaborate cuisine during a time of growing diversity in Victorian taste is reflected in the greater range of cookery books that became available. The Leeds Special Collections have many more nineteenth-century works than I have been able to include. I have therefore, touched on only a few aspects of this wide range of material. There are related works to explore on etiquette, servants, kitchen equipment, food sciences, foreign language recipes, special ingredients and techniques, food history and anecdote offering a rich and accessible field for nineteenth-century culinary and social research.

Notes

1. Isabella Beeton, *The Book of Household Management* (London: S.O. Beeton, 1861).
2. The instalments were printed as monthly supplements to S.O. Beeton's *The Englishwoman's Domestic Magazine*, 1859–1861.
3. Richard D. Altick, *The English Common Reader* (Chicago and London: Phoenix Books, University of Chicago Press, 1963), p. 389, quoting Hyde on Mr and Mrs Beeton, pp. 89, 109; *Publishers Circular*, 31st Dec. 1898, p. 769.
4. Beeton 1861, op. cit., preface.
5. Thomas Webster FGS (1773–1844), geologist and architect, Professor of Geology at University College London 1842. Webster was assisted by the late Mrs Parkes, author of *Domestic Duties, an Encyclopedia of Domestic Economy*, Longman, Green and Longmans, London 1844, final edition 1861.
6. Eliza Acton, *Modern Cookery for Private Families* (London: Brown, Green and Longman, 1845 and 1855).
7. Eliza Acton, op. cit., 1855, pp. 6, 53, 96, 171.
8. Persil was first produced in 1918 as a soap powder. Later, to remain competitive; it was changed to a detergent. An ex-Unilever Chairman gave the secret of brand success as continual innovation.
9. Anon. ('By the wife of a Homeopathic physician'), *A Manual of Homeopathic Cookery, designed chiefly for such persons as are under homeopathic treatment*, (London: G. Bowron, 1846).
10. H.L. Sidney Lear, *Maigre Cookery* (London: Rivingtons, 1884); this later book is an expanded version of *A Lenten Cookery Book* (London: A.R. Mowbray & Co, 1876).
11. From 1875, the number of cookery books, as with other categories of book production, expanded. See Elizabeth Driver, *A Bibliography of Cookery Books published in Britain, 1875–1914* (London: Prospect Books, 1989), p. 13.
12. Hannah Glasse, *The Art of Cookery made plain and easy*, London 1747.
13. Elizabeth Raffald, *The Experienced English Housekeeper*, Manchester, 1769.
15. A Lady, (Maria Eliza Rundell), *A New System of Domestic Cookery. Formed upon Principles of Economy And Adapted To The Use Of Private Families* (London: John Murray, 1806).
16. E. Rundell, *The English Cookery Book Comprising Mrs Rundell's Domestic Cookery revised with several modern dishes added thereto, carefully selected and simplified*, revised by Frederick W. Davis (London: Darton and Co, 1856), p. vi.
17. *Mrs Rundell's Cookery: Meats,* ed. The Rev. H.R. Haweis, MA (London: Routledge's World Library, 1886).
18. Roy Porter, *London, A Social History* (London: Penguin Books, 1996), p.194.
19. Eliza Acton, 1855, op.cit. p. 390.
20. Beeton, 1880s, Plate IX.
21. Charles Elmé Francatelli, *The Cook's Guide and Housekeeper's and Butler's Assistant* (London: Richard Bentley & Son, first published 1848, this edition 1884), pp. 497–8.
22. 'Bran new people', the Veneerings, are satirized in Charles Dickens, *Our Mutual Friend*, 1864/65.
23. Thomas Walker, 'The Art of Dining', *The Original*, No. XVI, 2nd September 1835; followed by *Aristology, or the Art of Dining* (London: Henry Renshaw, 1835, 1838).
24. Thomas Walker, *The Original*, edited by Felix Summerly (pseudonym of Sir Henry Cole) (London: George Bell and Sons, 1881), p. 18.
25. Thomas Walker, op.cit. 1881, pp. v–vi.
26. Jean-Anthelme Brillat-Savarin, *Physiologie du goût*. This edition, translated as *The Philosopher in the Kitchen*, by Anne Drayton (Harmondsworth: Penguin Books, 1970).

27. Thomas Walker, 1881, op cit. p. v.
28. *Physiologie du goût*, Penguin translation, *ut supra*, p. 13.
29. Thomas Walker, op.cit. 1881, Appendix B.
30. Beeton 1861, p. 905 quoting *Physiologie du goût*.
31. Charles Cooper, *The English Table in History and Literature* (London: S. Low, Marston & Co., 1929), p. 186.
32. Abraham Hayward QC (1801–84), *The Art of Dining, or Gastronomy and Gastronomers* (London: John Murray, first published 1852, subsequent edition, 1883).
33. Abraham Hayward QC, *The Art of Dining*, with annotations and additions added by Charles Sayle (London: John Murray, 1899).
34. A.V. Kirwan, *Host and Guest, A Book about Dinners, Wines, and Desserts* (London: Bell and Daldy, 1864), p. 80.
35. *Knife and Fork*, edited by 'Fin-Bec' (W. Blanchard Jerrold, 1826–84), November 1871, p. 56.
36. 'Fin-Bec'(W. Blanchard Jerrold), *The Dinner Bell* (London: William Muller & Son, 1878), pp. 84–5.
37. Thomas Walker, *The Original*, edited by 'Fin-Bec' (W. Blanchard Jerrold) (London: Grant & Co., 1874).
38. The Hon. Lady Cust, *The Invalid's Own Book: a collection of recipes from various books and various countries*, second edition (London: Longman, Brown and Green, 1856).
39. *Vegetarian Cookery With an Introductory Explanatory Of The Principles Of Vegetarianism*, by a Lady (Mrs Brotherton), (London: Fred. Pitman, 1852).
40. Janet Anne Ross (1842–1927), *Leaves from our Tuscan Kitchen or how to cook vegetables* (London: J. Dent and Co., 1899).
41. Miss M.A.S. Tattersall, *Jewish Cookery Book: compiled for use in the Cookery Centres under the School Board for London* (London: Wertheimer Lea and Co., 1895).
42. 'Wyvern', pseudonym of Colonel Arthur Robert Kenny-Herbert, *Culinary Jottings for Madras*, a facsimile of the fifth edition of 1885 with a new introduction by Leslie Forbes (Blackawton: Prospect Books, 1994), p. 286.
43. *Dainty Dishes for Indian Tables*, (Madras: W. Newman, 1879), 1881.
44. Ibid., p. 423.
45. 'Kitchri', 'muligatawny', 'pilaw' and 'chutney' were all both cooked and spelled with many variations.
46. Eliza Acton, 1855, pp. 605–22.
47. Eliza Acton, 1855, pp. 613–4.
48. Beeton, 1861, p. 693.
49. Beeton, 1861, p. 722.
50. Beeton, 1861, p. 215.
51. *What to do with Cold Mutton, A Book of Réchauffés* (London: Richard Bradley and Son, 1863 & 1887), pp. 22–3.
52. Turabi Efendi, *Turkish Cookery Book*, anonymously translated and published, London 1862.
53. Alexis Soyer, *A Culinary Campaign*, 1857, pp. 305–306, includes letter to *The Times* from Hotel d'Angleterre, Pera, Constantinople, Sept. 8, 1856.
54. Joseph Bregon and Anne Miller, *The Practical Cook, English and Foreign*, 1845.
55. *Cassell's Dictionary of Cookery, Containing about Nine Thousand Recipes* (London: Cassell, Petter, Galpin & Co., *ca.* 1877). New editions published until 1914.
56. James Jennings, *Two Thousand and Five Hundred Practical Recipes in Family Cookery* (London: Sherwood, Gilbert and Piper, 1825, 1837).
57. Pierre Bourdieu, *Distinction, A social Critique of the Judgement of Taste*, translated by Richard Nice (London: Routledge & Kegan Paul, 1986).
58. Beeton, 1861, p. 61.
59. Dr John Henry Walsh, FRCS, and a Committee of Ladies, *A Manual of Domestic Economy*

Suited to Families Spending from £100 to £1000 a Year (London: G. Routledge & Co.), first published 1856, then 1857, 1874; revised in 1879, as *...For Families Spending £150 to £1500 a Year*. Last issued in 1890.

60. Charles Selby, 'Tabitha Tickletooth', *The Dinner Question: or How to Dine Well & Economically, Combining the Rudiments of Cookery with Useful Hints on Dinner Giving and Serving* (London: Routledge, Warne and Routledge, 1860; repr. Blackawton: Prospect Books, 1999).
61. Webster, Thomas, FGS, assisted by the late Mrs Parkes, (author of *Domestic Duties, an Encyclopedia of Domestic Economy*) *An Encyclopedia of Domestic Economy* (London: Longman, Green and Longmans, 1844).
62. Thomas Webster, 1844, p. 876.
63. *French Domestic Cookery, combining elegance with economy* (London: David Boyne, 1846). Adapted and translated from, Louis-Eustache Audot, *La Cuisinière de la campagne et de la ville, ou la nouvelle cuisine économique* (Paris: Audot, first published 1818).
64. Louis-Eustache Audot, *La Cuisinière de la campagne et de la ville* (Paris: Audot, 1868). This had been published by the author (a publisher by profession) from 1818. Audot died in 1870, but the book continued to be issued reaching a 100th edition in 1928.
65. Eliza Acton, 1855, op. cit.. pp.1–5.
66. Louis Eustache Ude, *The French Cook; a System of Fashionable, Practical, and Economical Cookery, adapted to the use of English Families* (London: Ebers & Co., 14th edition, 1841).
67. Charles Elmé Francatelli, *The Modern Cook: a practical guide to the culinary art in all its branches* (London: Richard Bentley, first published 1845/1846).
68. Alexis Soyer, *The Gastronomic Regenerator* (London: Simpkin, Marshall, & Co., first edition, 1846).
69. Antonin Carême, *The Royal Parisian Pastrycook and Confectioner*, translated from the original of M. A. Carême of Paris, edited by John Porter, London 1834.
70. Felix Urbain Dubois, *Artistic Cookery* (London: Longmans, Green & Co., 1870).
71. Jules Gouffé, *The Royal Cookery Book*, translated and adapted by Alphonse Gouffé (London: Sampson Low, 1868).
72. Georges Auguste Escoffier, *A Guide to Modern Cookery* (London: Wm. Heinemann Ltd, first published 1907, fifth impression, 1968).
73. Alexis Soyer, *The Gastronomic Regenerator*, 4th edition, 1847, pp. xxviii–xxix.
74. Alexis Soyer, 1847, p. xxxviii.
75. Amphytrion is defined simply as a 'Host' by C. Herman Senn, in his *Dictionary of Foods and Culinary Encyclopedia* (London: Ward, Lock & Co. Ltd, 1919), p. 8. Dubois gives it extra meaning by suggesting it also implies 'gourmet' in his *Cosmopolitan Cookery*. Amphytrion, a dinner-giving host from Greek mythology and also in a play by Molière.
76. Abraham Hayward, 1883, pp. 75–77.
77. *The Morning Post*, London, 3rd July, 1846.
78. Alexis Soyer [and Albert Duhart-Fauvet ?], *The Pantropheon: the History of Food and its Preparation in Ancient Times* (London: Simpkin Marshall, 1853), p. 406 and opp. p. 406.
79. F. Volant and J.R. Warren, *Memoirs of Alexis Soyer* (London: W. Kent & Co., 1859); facsimile reprint Rottingdean, 1985.
80. Charles Elmé Francatelli, *A Plain Cookery Book for the Working Classes* (London: Routledge, Warne, and Routledge, new edition, 1852).
81. Alexis Soyer, *Charitable Cookery, or the Poor Man's Regenerator* (London: Simpkin, Marshall, & Co., 1846); Alexis Soyer, *A Shilling Cookery for the People* (London: G. Routledge & Co., 1854).
82. Charles Elmé Francatelli, *The Cook's Guide and Housekeeper's and Butler's Assistant* (London: Richard Bentley & Son, 1848).
83. *The Modern Cook*.

84. *Warne's Model Cookery and Housekeeping Book*, edited and compiled by Mary Jewry (London: Frederick Warne and Co., [?1868], this edition [?1899]).
85. Ibid., preface.
86. Charles Elmé Francatelli, 1852, pp. 99–101.
87. *The Finchley Manuals of Industry. No. I. Cooking; or, Practical and economical training for those who are to be servants, wives and mothers* (London: John Masters, 1849), p.30.
88. Thos Gradgrind MP and Unitarian, in Charles Dickens, *Hard Times*, 1854.
89. *The Official Handbook for the National Training School for Cookery*, compiled by R.O.C. [Rose Owen Cole] (London: Chapman and Hall Ltd., 1899), p.49.
90. Agnes B. Marshall, *Mrs Marshall's Larger Cookery Book* (London: Marshall's School of Cookery, *ca.* 1899).
91. Hannah M. Young, *Choice Cookery* (Manchester and London: H. M. Young, John Heywood, 1889).
92. C. Herman Senn (1864–1934), *Dictionary of Foods and Culinary Encyclopedia* (London: Ward, Lock & Co. Ltd, 1898, fifth edition, 1930).
93. Young, Hannah M., *Domestic Cookery With Special Reference to Cooking by Gas* (Manchester: H. M. Young, 1888).
94. A. de Salis, *A La Mode Cookery* (London: Longmans Green and Co., 1902), preface.
95. Dr William Kitchiner, *The Housekeeper's Oracle* (London: Whittaker Teacher and Co., 1824).
96. My grandparents, Arthur (1867–1955) and Grace (1875–1955) Stern, having grown up as Victorians, survived into the mid-twentieth century. Their daughter Babette (1911–1998) lived with her parents until her father's death.

INDEX

A la Mode Cookery, 191, 192
A.W., 22, 73
Abbot, Robert, 151
The Accomplisht Cook, 75, 83, 119, 128, 131, 135; figs. 12, 13, 41
The Accomplisht Ladies Delight, 137, 138; fig. 46
Acetaria, 24
Acton, Eliza, 128, 175, 181, 184, 187; fig. 67
Adam's Luxury and Eve's Cookery, 24
Amman, Jost, 99
Anne, Queen, 109
Arcana Fairfaxiana Manuscripta, 76, 83, 91
Argyll Rooms, London, 159
Aristology, or the Art of Dining, 181, 182
The Art of Cookery made plain and easy, 22, 25, 177
The Art of Dining, 182

Bailey, Nathan, fig. 22
banquets, 101, 103, 105-107; figs. 23-25
Beert, Osias, 105, 131; fig. 42
Beeton, Isabella, 128, 175-177, 180-182, 184-186; fig. 66
Beeton, Samuel, 175
Bell, Joseph, 144, 145; figs. 57, 59
Bethnal Green, Bishop's Hall, 64
Boke of Kervynge, 123
Boke of Nurture, 123
Bolton, Duchess of, 145
A Book of Fruits and Flowers, 23; fig. 21
The Book of Household Management, 175-177, 180, 181; fig. 66
A Booke of Cookry, 22, 73
Borella, ——, 151
Bradley, Richard, 140; figs. 17, 54, 55
Brears, Peter, 21
Bregon, James, 185

Brillat-Savarin, Jean-Anthelme, 182
Brookes, Nathaniel, 128
Brotherton Library, 19ff.
Brotherton, Mrs, 184
Browne, John, 105
butchery, 139ff.
Butler, Charles, 23; fig. 3

Camden, London Borough of, 22, 23
Le Cannameliste français, 143
Carême, Antonin, 154, 187
Carter, Charles, 111, 112, 117; fig. 32
Cartwright, C., 24
carving, 101ff.
Cassell's Dictionary of Cookery, 185
Cervio, Vicenzo, 100
Chambers, Edmund, 158
Charles II, coronation of, 107
chartreuses, 181
Chaucer, Geoffrey, 39
cheese, 65
Chesterfield, 4th Earl of, 113, 115; fig. 29
Chesterfield House, London, 189
Chiswick, 159
A Closet for Ladies and Gentlewomen, 74, 103
The Closet of the Eminently Learned Sir Kenelme Digby, Kt., Opened, 74
Cobbett, Anne, 25
Cole, Henry, 182, 191
Cole, Rose, 191
Collingwood & Woollams, 128; fig. 40
Colorno, Italy, 155, 159
The Compleat City and Country Cook, 117; fig. 32
The Compleat Cook, 74, 77-79, 81, 86, 87, 90, 94; fig. 14
The Compleat Housewife, 22, 24
The Compleat Practical Cook, 111

Index

The Complete Confectioner, 105, 144, 151; fig. 58
Confect buch und Hausz Apoteck, 99; fig. 21
The Confectioner's Oracle, 151, 162
confectionery, 143ff.
Cook's Guide, 181, 189
The Cook's Oracle, 183
cookery techniques, 90ff.
Cooper, Charles, 182
coronation feasts, 107ff.
Countrey Contentments, 74
The Country Housewife and Lady's Director, 140; figs. 17, 54, 55
The Country Housewives Garden, 24
The Country Magazine, 27
The Court and Country Confectioner, 151
The Court and Country Cook, 109; fig. 26
The Court & Kitchin of Elizabeth, Commonly called Joan Cromwel, 79, 84, 85, 125; fig. 16
Crespin, Paul, 113
Cromwell, Elizabeth, 84, 85; fig. 16
Cromwell, Oliver, 92
Crosley, ——, apothecary, 62
Culinary Jottings for Madras, 184
Curye on Inglysch, 29
Le Cuisinier François, 23, 133
Le cuisinier roïal et bourgeois, 109
La Cuisinière de la campagne et de la ville, 187
Cust, Lady, 183, 184

A Daily Exercise for Ladies and Gentlewomen, 74, 105
Dainty Dishes for Indian Tables, 184
Davis, Frederick W., 179
Dawson, Thomas, 73
De honesta voluptate, 20
De l'Usage du Caphé, du Thé et du Chocolat, 23
de Lamerie, Paul, 113; fig. 29
de Salis, Mrs Anne, 191, 192
Delightes for Ladies, 22, 55ff., 74, 75, 79, 103; fig. 8
A Delightfull Daily Exercise for Ladies and Gentlewomen, 103, 105; fig. 24

Dictionarium Domesticum, fig. 22
Dictionary of Foods and Culinary Encyclopaedia, 191
The Dietetic Reformer, 27
Digby, Sir Kenelm, 78, 87, 92
The Dinner Bell, 182
Diuersa Cibaria, 29, 35
Domestic Duties, 186
Dormer, Lady, 83
Du Four, Philippe-Sylvestre, 23
Dubois, Felix Urbain, 187, 189

L'ecole du jardin potager, 24
Efendi, Turabi, 185
Encyclopaedia of Domestic Economy, 186
England's Newest Way, 111; fig. 47
Englefield, Lady, 83
The English Cookery Book Comprising Mrs Rundell's Domestic Cookery, 179
The English Housekeeper, 25
The English House-wife, 68, 69, 73-74, 77, 79, 87, 89, 93, 101; fig. 12
The English Husbandman, 74
The Englishwoman's Domestic Magazine, 27, 175
The Epicure's Almanack, 157
Escoffier, Auguste, 187
L'escole parfait des officiers de bouche, 106, 111, 125
Evelyn, John, 24
The Experienced English Housekeeper, 151, 177

Fairfax, Rev. Henry, 76
Fairfax, Mary, 76
Family Cookery, 185
Farrance's, confectioner, 157
The Feminin' Monarchi', 23; fig. 3
field kitchen, fig. 6
'Fin-Bec', 182
The Finchley Manuals of Industry. No. I, 190, 191
'The Fine Art of Eighteenth Century Table Layouts', 111
Finemore, William, 158
Five Hundreth Pointes of Good Husbandrie, 24

Index

Floreas Paradise, 59, 61, 67, 69
Food and Drink in Britain, 21
The Forme of Cury, 19, 29, 33, 43ff.
Fourment, Nicholas, 109
Frambotto, Paolo, 101
Francatelli, Charles Elmé, 181, 187, 189, 190
Frazer, Mrs, 143; fig. 54
Freemasons' Tavern, London, 179
The French Cook, 23; fig. 20
French Domestic Cookery, 187
French words in English recipes, 29ff.

The Gardeners Dictionary, 24
Gascoine, Thomas, 63
The Gastronomic Regenerator, 187
Gelleroy, William, 117
The Genteel House-Keepers Pastime, 125
Gerard, John, 23, 91, 92
Germain, François-Thomas, 113
Germain, Thomas, 113; fig. 29
Giegher, Matthias, 101, 103, 106, 111, 123, 125, 127; figs. 23, 25, 27, 36, 37, 38
Gilliers, Joseph, 143, 145
Glasse, Hannah, 22, 25, 105, 177
The good huswifes Iewell, 73, 90
Gouffé, Alphonse, 187
Gouffé, Jules, 187
Gunter, James, 153
Gunter, Robert, 153
Gunter, William, 151, 162
Gunter's, 145

Hagger, Conrad, 131, 135, 137-139; figs. 43, 45, 49, 52
Hall, T., 137; fig. 48
Hasard, Mrs, schoolmistress, 161
Hatfield House, 118, 119; figs. 33, 34
Haweis, Hugh Reginald, 179
Hayward, Abraham, 182, 189
Helme, widow, 105
Henderson, William Augustus, 128; fig. 40
Henrietta Maria, Queen, 19, 73, 81, 84; fig. 15
Herball, 23, 91, 92
Herebert, William, 29, 53-54
Hill, Auditor, 63

Hill, John, 23
Hints for the Table, 183
The History of the Coronation of James II, fig. 26
Hollinsworth, Arthur,
The Honours of the Table, 128; fig. 39
Horticultural Society, 159
Host and Guest, 182
The Housekeeper's Instructor, 128; fig. 40
The Housekeeper's Valuable Companion, 151
How to be a Domestic Goddess, 29
Howard, Henry, 111, 137; fig. 47
Hunter, Lynette, 21

Ibrahim Pasha, 189
ice-creams, 151ff.
'Ideal Meals and their Menus', 111
illustrations in cookery books, 99ff.
The Invalid's Own Cookery Book, 183
The Italian Confectioner, 145, 151ff.; figs. 60, 63

James II, coronation of, 107, 112; fig. 26
Jarrin, William (Guglielmo) Alexis, 145, 151ff.; figs. 60-63, 65
Jarrin's Patent Water Cooler, fig. 64
Jeanes, William, 151, 162
Jennings, James, 185
Jerrold, William Blanchard, 182, 183
The Jewel House of Art and Nature, 60, 61, 64, 74; fig. 10
Jewish Cookery Book, 184
Jewry, Mary, 190
Jonson, Ben, 132

Kemmish, Maister, 62
Kenny-Herbert, Col. Arthur Robert, 184
Kidder, Edward, 132, 135, 137, 138, 139; fig. 43, 50
King's Theatre, London, 161
Kirwan, A.V., 182
kitchen equipment, 89-91
Kitchiner, William, 182, 185, 192
Kuchemeysterey, 99

La Chapelle, Vincent, 113, 115, 117; fig. 29

INDEX

La Varenne, François Pierre de, 23, 133, 134; fig. 20
The Ladies Companion, 138
The Ladies Delight, fig. 20
The Ladies Directory, fig. 20
The Lady's Assistant, 105
The Lady's Best Companion, 24
Lamb, Patrick, 107, 109, 111, 112; figs. 27, 28
language in recipes, 28ff.
Lawson, Nigella, 29
Lawson, William, 24
Lear, Sydney, 177
Leaves from our Tuscan Kitchen, 184, 192
Leeds Symposium on Food History, 22
Leigh, Blanche, 20
Leigh, John, 107
Leigh, John, 109
Lémery, Louis, 23
Library Association Record, 22
Lister, Dame Mary, 75, 82
Lister, Sir William, 75
London, Argyll Rooms, 159
    Chesterfield House, 189
    Cromer Street, 158
    King's Theatre, 161
    New Bond Street, 155ff.
    Reform Club, 189
    Regent Street Quadrant, 161
    Tichbourne Street, 161
The London and Country Cook, 117
The London and Country Cook, fig. 22
The London Cook, 117
Lucraft, Fiona, 111
Luncheon, Nuncheon and Other Meals, 25

Madam Johnson's Present, 25
Maigre Cookery, 177
Maison Rustique, or, The countrey farme, 74
The Manner of Making of Coffee, Tea and Chocolate, 23
A Manual for Homeopathic Cookery, 176
Manual of Domestic Economy, 186
marchpanes, 101
Markham, Gervase, 24, 68, 69, 73, 74, 75, 77, 87, 89, 93, 101, 103, 112, 133; fig. 12
Marnette, ——, 134

Marshall, Mrs Agnes B., 139, 191
Mason, Charlotte, 105
Massialot, François, 109; fig. 26
'A Master of the Household', 106
May, Robert, 75, 77, 79, 83, 86, 119, 124, 125, 128, 129, 131-135, 139; figs. 12, 13, 41, 43, 44, 52
Memoirs of Alexis Soyer, 189
Menon, ——, 143
Meynstnor, Nathaniel, 137; fig. 52
Middle English Dictionary, 36
Miller, Anne, 185, 24
The Modern Confectioner, 151
The Modern Cook, 113, 115, 189; fig. 29
Modern Cookery for Private Families, 175, 184; fig. 67
The Modern Housewife, 189; fig. 190
The Modern Method of Regulating and Forming a Table, 144
Moore, S., fig. 26
Moritz, Landgrave of Hesse, 67
Murrell, John, 74, 77, 79, 103, 105, 122-125; fig. 24
Murrels Two Bookes of Cookerie and Carving, 75, 105; fig. 13

Naples, 64
National Training School for Cookery, 191
Negri, Domenico, 151
Nepper, ——, 63
Neues Saltzburgisches Koch-Buch, 131
New Booke of Carving and Sewing, 123
A New Book of Cookerie, 74, 77, 105
Ein new Kochbuch, 99
A New System of Domestic Cookery, 25, 179; fig. 68
A New System of Practical Domestic Economy, 25
Newcastle-upon-Tyne, 144
Nott, John, 124
Nutt, Frederick, 144, 151; fig. 58

The Official Handbook for the National Training School of Cookery, 192
oglia putrida, fig. 27
olio, 81, 93-94, 111-112, 115; figs. 14, 28-30

INDEX

olla potrida, 111
The Original, 181

The Pantropheon, fig. 70
Paracelsus, 62
Paradisus terrestris, 23; fig. 4
Parkes, Frances Byerley, 186
Parkinson, John, 23; fig. 4
Parry, James, 132-134
Parsons, ——, apothecary, 63
Partridge, John, 19, 22
pasta, fig. 5
pastry and pie designs, 128ff.
Le Pâtissier françois, 134
The Pearl of Practise, 74
Peeters, Clara, 105
The Perfect Cook, 134
A Perfect School of Instructions for the Officers of the Mouth, 106; fig. 25
Physiologie du goût, 182
Plat, Sir Hugh, 22, 55ff., 74, 75, 79, 103, 105; fig. 9
Platina, 20
The Practical Cook, English and Foreign, 185
The Practice of Cookery, Pastry, Pickling, Preserving, &c., 143; fig. 54
Preston, John F., 20-21
A Proper newe Booke of Cokerye, 73
Public Record Office, 155f.

The Queen-like Closet, 75, 77, 81; fig. 11
The Queens Closet Opened, 19, 73, 74, 81, 83-84, 128; fig. 15
A Queens Delight, 74, 79, 90
The Queen's Royal Cookery, 131-132; fig. 48

Rabisha, William, 75, 77, 79, 91, 124
Raffald, Elizabeth, 151, 177
Receipts in Pastry and Cookery, 132, 135; fig. 50
Reform Club, London, 189
Retailing in England during the Industrial Revolution, 155
Rich, Master, 63
Romero, Sr, 63-64
Rose, Giles, 106-107, 111, 125, 127; figs. 25, 27, 36, 38
Ross, Janet, 184
Routledge's World Library, 179
Royal Cookery, 111, 187, fig. 27
Rumpolt, Marx, 99, 112
Rundell, Maria Eliza, 25, 179; fig. 68
Russell, John, 123, 125
Ryff, Walther Hermann, 99; fig. 21

Salisbury, 4th Earl of, 118, 119
Sampayo, Osborne, 189
Sandford, Francis, 107; fig. 26
Sandys, William, 161
Sayle, Charles, 182
Lo scalco, 101
Scappi, Bartolomeo, 61, 100, 112, 123; figs. 5-7, 35
Scarborough, 144
La Science de maître d'hôtel, confiseur, 143
The Second Book of Cookerie, 75
The Secrets of Maister Alexis of Piedmont, fig. 18
Selby, Charles, 186
Senn, Charles Herman, 191
Simpkins, W., fig. 56
Sinclair Rohde, Eleanour, 61
Smith, Eliza, 22, 24
Society for Bettering the Conditions of the Poor, 25
Solis, Virgil, 100
Soyer, Alexis, 25, 185, 187, 189, 190; figs. 70, 71
Soyer's Military Campaign, 25
The Staple of News, 132
Stead, Jennifer, 21
Summerly, Felix, 182
Surflet, Richard, 74
surtouts de table, 115; fig. 58

T.P., 137; fig. 46
T.T., 59, 60, 79; fig. 9
table layouts, 101ff.
Taillevent, 31
Tattersall, Miss M.A.S., 184
Taylor, Randal, 84
Thacker, John, 131, 135, 139; fig. 43

Index

Thornton-in-Craven, 82
Thurland, Thomas, 60
Tickletooth, Tabitha, 186
Timbs, John, 183
Times Bookshop, 20
Towneley plays, 39ff.
Traité des Aliments, 23
Li tre trattati, 101, 111; figs. 23, 27
A Treatise of Confectionery, 144; fig. 57
A Treatise of Foods in General, 23
Il trinciante (1581), 100
Il trinciante (1621), 101
Trusler, John, 128; fig. 39
trussing, 139ff.
Turkish Cookery, 185
Tusser, Thomas, 24
Two Fifteenth-Century Cookery Books, 28, 29
Tymme, Thomas, 60

Ude, Louis Eustace, 187
The Universal Cook, 128; fig. 40

Vegetarian Cookery, 184
The Vegetarian Messenger, 27
victualling, military, 66
The Virtues of Honey…, 23

Volant, F., 189

W.M., 19, 74, 83
W.W., 75, 83
Wakefield pageants, 39ff.
Walker, Thomas, 181-183
Walsh, John, 186
Warne's Model Cookery and Housekeeping Book, 190
Warren, J.R., 189
The Way to get Wealth, 24
Webber, ——, cook, 63
Webster, Thomas, 186
Weekly Miscellany, 140
Weiditz, Hans, 100
What to do with Cold Mutton, 185
The Whole Body of Cookery Dissected, 75, 79, 91
The Whole Duty of a Woman, 138; fig. 53
The Widowes Treasure, 19, 22, 59, 73
Wilson, C. Anne, 111
Wolley, Hannah, 75, 77, 79, 81, 92, 128; figs. 11, fig. 20
Worde, Wynkyn de, 75, 123
'Wyvern', 184

Young, Mrs Hannah M., 191